CW01657953

MILLENNIAL PEOPLE, BOOMER PRIEST

Millennial People, Boomer Priest

MY YEAR ELDERING A YOUNG CONGREGATION

Stephen Noll

ANGLICAN HOUSE

Copyright © 2024 by Stephen Noll

Published by Anglican House, an imprint of Anglican House Publishers®, the registered trade name of Anglican House Media Ministry, Inc., Newport Beach, California. Anglican House is a Ministry Affiliate of the Anglican Church in North America.

anglicanhousepublishers.org

Cover design by Ben Jefferies
Cover image by cottonbro studio
Text design by Becky Pruitt MacKenney

This work is protected under the copyright laws of the United States, Canada, the U.K., and some 90 other countries. No part of this work may be reproduced or transmitted in any form or by any means, including photocopying and recording, or by any information storage and retrieval system, without written permission from the publisher. Any translation of this work into another language for distribution requires the written permission of the copyright owner, and any such authorized translation is a derivative work in which the copyright owner owns the copyright.

Unless otherwise noted, all Scripture quotations are from The Holy Bible, English Standard Version® (ESV®), copyright © 2001 by Crossway, a publishing ministry of Good News Publishers. Used with permission. All rights reserved.

Unless otherwise noted, all quotations from the Book of Common Prayer are from The Book of Common Prayer (2019), copyright © 2019 by the Anglican Church in North America and published by Anglican Liturgy Press, an imprint of Anglican House Publishers.

ISBN 979-8-9878026-3-2

For
Seth Zimmerman
Martyn Minns
Wicks Stephens
Karen Getz
coworkers in the ministry at Redeemer Anglican Church

Contents

Incarnational Sermon Cycle

Evangelical Sermon Cycle

Selected Pastor's Podcasts

Preface

A BOOMER'S BOAST

Like St. Paul, the Hebrew of Hebrews, let me boast if I must of my Boomer credentials: conceived two weeks after VJ Day; raised in the DC suburbs with Howdy Doody and Alfred E. Neuman; folded mailings for JFK's campaign; attended the March on Washington wearing a UU (Unitarian Universalist) armband; studied under Allan Bloom (author of *The Closing of the American Mind*) at Cornell, Massey Shepherd (an editor of the 1979 Episcopal Book of Common Prayer) in Berkeley, and F.F. Bruce (Rylands Professor of Biblical Criticism and Exegesis) in Manchester, UK. Reader, if none of these credentials rings a bell with you, count yourself a Millennial.

Midway through college I joined the Jesus Revolution; was converted, baptized, and confirmed in the Episcopal Church; and married my high school sweetheart, a cradle Episcopalian. Midway through seminary in Berkeley, California, I was baptized in the Spirit with speaking in tongues. Ordained deacon and priest by age twenty-six, I served five years in a large charismatic Episcopal congregation in Northern Virginia. After getting my Ph.D. in England, I joined the faculty of a startup seminary near Pittsburgh named Trinity Episcopal School for Ministry (now Trinity Anglican Seminary).* We aimed to revolutionize the Episcopal Church.

Have I boasted enough? Oh, and I am a digital dinosaur, perhaps from the Jurassic period. I traded in my IBM Selectric (thank God for the Greek and Hebrew balls!) for a laptop, which sits in place on my desk. Alongside it sits my iPhone 6, so if I don't pick up, try my home phone. Caving to the need to reach my Millennial parishioners, I learned to text with the help of the voice input mic, which is a good thing since it seems no one answers voice messages—or even answers the phone at all! I am

*I refer to Trinity School for Ministry (Trinity Anglican Seminary as of June 2024) as simply Trinity Seminary throughout the book.

fundamentally app-horrent. I stopped attending Pittsburgh Pirates games when they ceased issuing paper tickets and required an app to get through the gate! I do follow the Google map lady to a strange address, while keeping paper maps in my glove compartment in reserve and on occasion lowering my car window and hailing a passerby with "Help! I'm lost!"

But…whatever generational gain I have had—or generational shame ("Hey, Boomer!")—I count it as loss because of the surpassing worth of knowing Christ. In Christ, there is neither Jew nor Greek, slave nor free, neither male nor female, Boomer nor Buster, Global South nor Global North, for, to quote the hymn, "all Christly souls are one in him throughout the whole wide earth."

MY CREDENTIAL FOR ELDERING

I do possess a less ephemeral credential: my calling as priest or presbyter (Greek *presbyteros*, "elder") to preach the unchanging Word and to administer the Sacraments commanded by Jesus Christ, who is the same yesterday, today, and forever (Matt 28:18; Heb 13:8). I have been a young elder and an old elder. Over the past half century, I have had a variety of ministries—seminary teacher and administrator, missionary and founding president ("vice chancellor") of a university in Uganda, and now several gigs in retirement ("getting a new set of tires," I call them).

As part of my calling, I have served five "interim" assignments, four of them as interim pastor in churches in transition.* My fifth and latest interimship has been in publishing—Anglican House Publishers, to be precise! In each case, my interim role has been to equip the institution for a transition in leadership.

*Millennial People, Boomer Priest*** is the account of my year as interim pastor of a congregation of young Christians in Bellevue, Pennsylvania, an inner suburb of Pittsburgh. I describe this ministry in terms of "eldering" not only because of the age gap involved but because it drew from my experience in *shepherding* (leading), *teaching* (preaching and catechizing), and *exhorting* (via podcasts) in order to build up the Body

* I chose "interim pastor" as the more generic and biblical name for this role (1 Pet 5:1–4). North American Anglican churches often designate this role as "interim rector" or "priest-in-charge."

** The book's title is my feeble attempt at a meme, aimed to attract readers of all ages. In all honesty, I did not begin each sermon or podcast with the question: "How do I reach Millennials?"

of Christ "until we all attain to the unity of the faith and of the knowledge of the Son of God, to mature manhood, to the measure of the stature of the fullness of Christ" (Eph 4:13).

SO WHO IS THIS BOOK FOR?

This is a book for priests and pastors—and also for lay leaders of congregations. A surprising number of churches spend considerable periods between full-time pastors, and a surprising number of clergy serve as interims—some of them young and beginning their ministry, others retired but sensing that ordained ministry does not stop with the gold watch.

This is a book for pastoral theologians. I readily admit that this is an unbalanced guide to pastoral leadership: it is long on doctrine and short on practice. I am not ashamed of this imbalance. It is a common mistake to see theologians as dwelling in clouds of theory, while pastors are down and dirty with real life. My aim is to equip pastors for their calling as "public theologians," especially in our skeptical age. At the same time, I have included as bookends some "pastoral steps" I took in guiding the young congregation and some selected "table talks" I sent out to members in weekly podcasts.

This is a book for "mere Christians." The so-named catechetical, incarnational, and evangelical sermon cycles and the Easter "doxology" refer simply to biblical basics: to the commandments and Apostles' Creed, to the Person of Jesus, to the Apostle Paul and his gospel, and to the testimonies to the resurrection. Mere Christians, I hope, will find this subject matter faithful to Scripture and of interest and importance to their lives. As for the suitability of the sermon format, see my plea in the introduction to that section.

This is a book for "mere Anglicans." Many in my congregation had come from Evangelical homes and colleges and were new to Anglicanism, but they wanted to find out more about the tradition. Many of those who had worshiped in an Anglican church had never touched a Book of Common Prayer, services having been printed or projected. In the sermons and especially in the podcasts, I sought to explain why Anglicans worship the way we do. My own background is Evangelical and charismatic, but I am strongly committed to the catholicity of the Church, high, low, and muddling-middle. Having served as a missionary in Africa, I have observed the remarkable ways Anglican Christianity is lived out in the global communion of churches.

This is a book for "my" congregation, my little flock for a year. I continue to pray for you under your new pastor and trust God will bless your increase.

This is a book for myself. As one winds down one's life and vocation, one often wishes to leave a testament of sorts. Some of what I write here is, I hope, the ripe fruit of years of teaching the Bible and contending for the faith in a time when the Christian Church has been under attack from without and from within.

So there you have it, reader. Is this for you? Why don't you taste and see!

Stephen Noll
Easter 2024

Introduction

What is the specific calling of pastors? St. Paul speaks of the ministries of God's Church this way: "And he gave the apostles, the prophets, the evangelists, the pastors and teachers, to equip the saints for the work of ministry" (Eph 4:11–12). In this image of the Church, the role of apostles, prophets, and evangelists is both foundational and occasional. They plant churches and speak to these congregations authoritatively. In the case of Paul, Peter, Matthew, John, James, and Jude, that testimony has been enshrined in the New Testament Scripture.

The secondary and regular ministry of the Church falls to "pastors and teachers," which is the dual vocation of the clergy. This is an "Apollos" ministry, according to Paul's dictum: "I planted, Apollos watered, but God gave the growth" (1 Cor 3:6). It has become common now to connect this role with "equipping the saints," that is, the laypeople, "for the work of ministry," for the life of mature discipleship. To fulfill this task, pastors are called to be theological educators as well as skilled artisans, building up the Body of Christ on the foundation that has been laid by the apostles and prophets in Scripture.

Clergy in the early Church were usually residential "elders" (*presbyters*) well-known and respected in the community. The practice of long-term clergy residencies has been characteristic of Anglican parishes in England and North America. While such tenure can be lackluster (as with "The Vicar of Bray"), it is often the case that the most fruitful churches have had long-term rectors. The calling of the interim rector is to prepare the way for a transition in leadership.

Each situation is of course different. In my first parish, the rector's departure was tumultuous. I realized that I could best help the transition by not being a candidate to succeed him but rather by building on the confidence I had earned in my previous years as an assistant. As I used to say, I hoped to keep the bus running so that the new leader could step on board and drive away. Fortunately, the vestry of that church was mature and competent, and after eighteen months it called an excellent priest who led the church into a powerful new period of fruitfulness.

That was nearly fifty years ago. I was not looking for a repeat performance, but, it seems, God had something in mind for an encore.

I happened into the role as interim pastor at Redeemer Anglican Church. Redeemer had been a church plant of St. Stephen's in Sewickley, one of the cardinal parishes and my family's home church in the Anglican Diocese of Pittsburgh. After a year of preparation, Redeemer began regular worship in 2016 on Sunday afternoons.

The principal church planter was a young clergyman, Seth Zimmerman, who had served as youth minister at St. Stephen's. He had attended a local non-denominational Christian college and attracted a number of its graduates to join him in getting the new congregration off the ground. He was an effervescent "sandals and guitar" Christian, and over five years he built up the congregation to about fifty members. He invited me to join him as a clergy associate, and I agreed to do so in June 2020. While continuing to worship at St. Stephen's, my wife Peggy and I began attending services at Redeemer on Sunday afternoons, and I would preach from time to time.

This arrangement changed early in 2021. The new rector at St. Stephen's offered Seth a job on staff, and Seth accepted, saying that he felt his gifting was as a planter, not a builder. At the same time, St. Stephen's posed a choice to the congregation: either return to worship in Sewickley or become an independent congregation within our diocese. Having set aside the season of Lent to pray about this choice, Redeemer's executive team polled the congregation and chose to become independent.

As adjunct clergy, I happened to be on hand and sat in on these meetings. I advised the membership that while there were signs of vitality, especially their youthful enthusiasm, the church was not currently viable, financially or institutionally. There were not any children's or youth programs, for instance. Becoming independent, I said, was a real risk. I also asked them if they were sure they wanted to be an Anglican congregation. Many of them came from non-Anglican backgrounds, and there was already another lively Evangelical congregation in Bellevue.

Just before Easter, the executive team voted unanimously to become independent. At that point, the executive team became the proto-vestry and appointed me as interim pastor as of May 1, 2021.

This book follows my one-year course as interim pastor of Redeemer Anglican Church. I begin with an overview of the different pastoral steps I took in forming and organizing the church, such as visiting the members and advising on the search process for a permanent rector.

The bulk of the book has to do with my teaching and preaching ministry, presented in three cycles of sermons during the year. Each of these cycles has a different focus, the first on catechesis—basic Christian doctrine based on the biblical commandments and the Apostles' Creed. The second cycle I call "incarnational," as we first meet Jesus in the gospels. The third cycle is "evangelical," focusing on Paul's gospel, as concisely presented in the letter to the Galatians. I conclude the sermon cycles with a "doxology" of three Easter sermons.

Finally, I have included some selected pastor's podcasts that I sent out weekly to the congregation in written and oral form. These short miscellaneous messages are a kind of "table talk" with the congregation.

These materials will give the reader some sense of the scope of the ministry of the pastor-teacher in the Anglican tradition. Clearly my work as interim is peculiar to me and to the situation of this particular church, but I hope readers, clerical and lay, can find in it some nuggets of treasure for their own life in the Body of Christ.

Pastoral Steps

CONSTITUTING THE CONGREGATION

Having made the decision to separate from its planting church, Redeemer faced a number of official steps ahead to become an independent Anglican congregation. These steps took place over the first six months of my tenure there. As interim pastor, I had little official role in these matters, but as advisor to the leadership team, I was intimately involved in this stage of the church's growth.

The first steps had to do with constituting the congregation in secular and church law. These are mundane matters, but then the Lord Jesus himself was an astute observer of mundane affairs, as when he said:

> Hear another parable. There was a master of a house who planted a vineyard and put a fence around it and dug a winepress in it and built a tower and leased it to tenants, and went into another country. (Matt 21:33)

Every planting needs a fence and some internal structures and rules. Every property, every business, is established in law before it can begin to operate. Each church is recognized within the laws of the state externally, and internally it has its own polity, or church order.

The Church of England was "established" as a state church in the sixteenth century, in which the Sovereign and Parliament had important roles to play. When the Episcopal Church broke away from the mother church in 1787, its founders adopted a constitution and canons modeled in many ways on the U.S. Constitution, and when the Anglican Church in North America broke away from the Episcopal Church in 2008, it adopted its own "C&C." The constitution sets out the basic principles, structure, and leadership of the church. The canons accompany the constitution and spell out in more detail matters of church organization, discipline, and worship.

The polity of the province of the Anglican Church in North America (which includes both the United States and Canada) is a "mixed regime" with distributed authority at all levels, provincial, diocesan, and congregational. Each diocese has its own subsidiary constitution and canons, and each congregation has a set of by-laws. Being an episcopally ordered church, bishops exercise spiritual authority in dioceses and share spiritual oversight of congregations with rectors (the technical title for the chief pastor). Rectors in turn share governance of local churches with the vestry, a body of elders elected by the congregation.

What complicated matters somewhat in 2021 was the fact that our diocese, the Anglican Diocese of Pittsburgh, was in an interim situation between bishops. The bishop's authority was temporarily held by the standing committee of nine clergy and lay leaders, and an interim bishop had been appointed to carry out particular sacramental and spiritual functions, such as confirmations and ordinations. The good news for Redeemer was that our link person on the standing committee, Wicks Stephens, and Martyn Minns, the interim bishop, were long-time friends whom I could go to easily when questions arose. This was one of the perks of seniority in an organization.

The final meeting of the executive team laid out a plan to become a vestry. At the next meeting, the by-laws were adopted and six vestry members were elected. Three were men and three women; three continued from the executive team and three were new. The new vestry then elected officers: a senior and junior warden, a secretary, and a treasurer. (The senior warden presides at meetings during the interim period, whereas the interim rector attends and advises.) I thank God for the choice of these men and women. For the entire year that I served, they offered excellent guidance to the church. At the same meeting, the new vestry selected a search committee to look for a new rector. It was headed by the junior warden and included one other vestry member and six members of the congregation.

There were two further steps in getting Redeemer established. The first was negotiating the separation from St. Stephen's, the founding church. The second was applying for legal recognition in Pennsylvania. With hard work from the senior warden and our advisor from the diocese, Redeemer was officially recognized as an independent congregation on July 1, 2021. At that point, it got its own PO Box and account books. Our treasurer did a remarkable job of researching available software packages.

So much giving and paying out is done online today, so much so that we did not have an offertory in the Sunday services.

The next step was receiving recognition from the Anglican Diocese of Pittsburgh. While informally recognized as a "congregation-in-formation," Redeemer needed to apply to the annual convention for formal recognition as a "mission fellowship," which is the first step toward becoming a full congregation.* This required among other things a projected budget and a strategic plan. This was done, and Redeemer was unanimously and joyfully accepted in November 2021.

PASTORAL CARE AND CHALLENGES

The Good Shepherd says: "My sheep hear my voice, and I know them, and they follow me" (John 10:27). It has always seemed to me that pastoral visitation is an essential step of the clerical vocation. The job description in my first curacy included the expectation, among other duties, that I should make thirty-five parish calls a week! Need I say that the rector of that church had driven numerous assistants to distraction and early departure.

At Redeemer I inherited a spreadsheet with about thirty singles or family units. In addition, there were another dozen families who had attended Redeemer formerly or left recently due to the transition. I attempted to get in touch with all of these.

I found, however, that the old method of making cold calls on suburban households was out of the question. Most of the women worked, and in any case, for a pastor to show up unannounced was no longer acceptable. I even found that trying to set up visits via email often fell flat. I overcame my resistance to texting and gradually began to make "visits." Often these were scheduled at one or more local coffee houses.

I experienced one problem which had not plagued me as a twenty-five-year-old: remembering names and linking them to faces. For this reason, I pleaded with my part-time administrator to create a photo directory. Again, somewhat to my surprise, I encountered reluctance of people to publish their names and contact information known even to their fellow parishioners. After eight months, the directory did appear—print only—just in time to be bequeathed to the rector-elect.

* In the ACNA, local churches are called congregations. Unlike English parishes, they are non-geographical.

Finally, there was the challenge of responding to the waves of national discord that emerged in 2020 due to the racially charged atmosphere following the murder of George Floyd, coinciding with the coronavirus pandemic. Those waves had already crested when I became interim pastor. I did preach a sermon on July 4, 2021 (included among the selected podcasts) on the topic of "critical lovers" and "loving critics" of our national life. Although Redeemer was largely a white, college-educated congregation in a racially and economically mixed inner suburb, it has benefited from the involvement of international students from Trinity Seminary and the presence of mission leaders in the congregation—and now a new pastor with cross-cultural experience.

Redeemer also avoided the worst impact from Covid restrictions. Because it was a small body meeting in a spacious sanctuary and outdoors in summer in a local park pavilion, in-person services were shut down only once during my time (services were available throughout on the Facebook page). We had begun to relax the mask requirement indoors in mid-2021 when the Omicron variant struck. The vestry and I concluded that we should return to voluntary masking following CDC guidance (see my August 5 message in the podcast section). During this time, I introduced two relevant practices I had learned in Uganda: exchanging the Peace "virtually" by hand-waving all around while singing the chorus "Peace, peace, wonderful peace of God"; and by the priest dipping and distributing the Communion elements into the congregants' hands.

This litany of challenges should not obscure the fact that I truly did enjoy getting to know members of the congregation, even if it was for a short while. One of the endearing farewell gifts they gave me was the photo directory, with personal comments from each of them.

AN ANGLICAN CONGREGATION IS BORN

During the discernment process in Lent, I had asked: "Do you really want to become an Anglican church?" Many of the young people had come from Evangelical Protestant families and attended conservative Christian colleges. Quite a few had participated in a one-year fellows program at St. Stephen's, which was their first real introduction to an Anglican church. And the founding pastor, while an Anglican, barely toed (remember the sandals) the line when it came to traditional Anglican worship and piety. "So are you sure," I asked, "that you would not be happier to attend the local Evangelical church?" Some indeed did decide to leave, but most said, "No, we want to become Anglicans."

So I felt authorized to prepare Redeemer formally to join the Anglican Diocese of Pittsburgh and to nudge it toward a more standard Anglican way of worship and practice. In particular, I was able to distribute Books of Common Prayer to each member. They were free of charge from the publisher because of defective bindings but were otherwise brand new. While we did not use these books in the worship service, I began to commend particular elements of Prayer Book worship through my weekly podcasts.

At the first vestry meeting, I was not really surprised to find out that three of the six members were not confirmed. Technically, this would have disqualified them to serve, but I asked if they were willing to work toward that end. That led me to a larger idea that I could prepare the entire congregation for a kind of corporate confirmation and renewal of faith in the context of the bishop's visit in mid-September.

The Lenten discernment period had featured a sermon series on the petitions of the Lord's Prayer. So as we headed into the Easter and Pentecost seasons, I proposed that we have two further series on the Ten Commandments and the Apostles' Creed, which would complete the standard expectation for confirmation.

The week before the bishop's visit, I baptized one child by immersion in an inflatable swimming pool in the park. The next Sunday, the bishop baptized one adult, confirmed ten members, and received six others. He then asked others who wished to reaffirm their baptismal vows to stand, and most of the remaining worshipers did so. Hence I announced, "a congregation is born."

The names of God's elect are written in the Lamb's Book of Life, which is ethereal, but I think it is important for us here on earth to write names down, as in Scripture (cf. Exod 1:1–5). So each of the new members received an inscribed certificate from the diocese, and I purchased a parish register and recruited a member to ink in the new names.

WORSHIP AT REDEEMER

Before his departure, Seth had found a lovely and well-kempt old Presbyterian church on the main road of Bellevue which we used for worship. The small resident congregation that worshiped on Sunday morning was very cooperative, and we shared an Ash Wednesday service together—including the imposition of ashes!

From the beginning worship at Redeemer had been informal by most Anglican standards. Seth had introduced a hybrid Holy Communion service with elements from the ACNA Prayer Book and elements from the Kenyan liturgy. One striking feature of the service is at the end when the congregation, gesturing to the Cross, says:

> All our problems, *we send to the Cross of Christ*;
> All our difficulties, *we send to the Cross of Christ*;
> All the devil's works, *we send to the Cross of Christ*;
> And all our hopes, *we set on the risen Lord!*

The most noticeable difference in the worship from my point of view was the music. I cherish traditional hymnody but have also been involved with charismatic prayer-and-praise from the 1970s and '80s; nevertheless most of the songs at Redeemer were outside my repertory. "You need to listen to WORD FM," someone told me. Knowing how sensitive congregations can be to musical changes, even more than to bad preaching, I left the choice of music to others. However, I did think to preach a sermon series on "psalms and hymns and spiritual songs" to suggest the breadth of Christian music.

SEARCH FOR A NEW RECTOR

The search committee, chaired by the junior warden, got off to a quick start and worked long and hard. The junior warden's day job was corporate recruitment, and I think that at the beginning he thought they could find someone in a couple months. In fact, they did issue a call within eight months, which is near record time in most Anglican churches.

The Diocese of Pittsburgh had a set of guidelines that helped the search committee move forward. In Anglican polity, calling a rector involves an interplay of the bishop (in our case, the standing committee); the vestry, which makes the final call; and the search committee, which does the legwork. The congregation does not formally elect its pastor but is informed generally on the progress of the search.

I raised a delicate issue with the vestry at the beginning of the process: whether they would consider a female candidate. In the Anglican Church in North America, there are differing views on women's ordination. As it turned out, there were diverse views among vestry members, but after two honest discussions, the vestry adopted this statement:

> After careful deliberation, considering our experience and backgrounds and with the knowledge that we are not of one mind about biblical, theological, and cultural issues surrounding women as presbyters, we have decided to seek a male candidate for this position. We believe this will serve the unity and mission of Redeemer at this time.

This decision was stressful at the start but cleared the way as the process went forward. I was prepared to support the vestry whichever direction they took, but I did feel strongly that it would be unfair and unkind to consider a female candidate if they were not prepared to call her.

Next the search committee prepared an attractive parish and rector profile, and on November 1, 2021, we went public. At that time, the diocese told us there were no available candidates in its files, so we were on our own. After posting the profile on the ACNA message board, we received one immediate application, followed by several more. The search committee diligently contacted candidates, reviewed their resumes and requested materials, gave a welcome meeting to each by Zoom, and then recommended candidates for the vestry to consider and send on to the diocese. Four candidates were approved by the diocese and were interviewed, with their wives, by the search committee and vestry via Zoom.

The Rev. Ethan Carlson, a young priest who was serving as a missionary in Rwanda, became the clear frontrunner in the search. He and his wife were invited to come—across seven time zones—for a visit and further interviews. The visit convinced both the vestry and the candidate himself that he was the right choice for Redeemer. So after eight months the call was made, approved by the diocese, and confirmed by the candidate. However, due to his commitments in Rwanda, he asked to delay his employment five months until July 1, 2022.

THE HANDOVER

From my time in Africa, I learned the significance of the word "handover," which is what happens when one leaves an office to another. African handovers often have a ceremonial element of literally handing over keys, files, and office furnishings.

It is usually easier for an interim to hand over his work to a new person than it is for an incumbent. Although I had developed personal affection for and some knowledge of church members, I and they had understood that my role was transitional. Nevertheless, I decided to step away from the church on May 1, 2022, at the end of my one-year contract. This left two months between my departure and the new rector's arrival. I did, however, offer to arrange for the services and find "supply clergy" to fill in for intervening weeks. As it turned out, my friend the interim bishop, who was also leaving the diocese, was able to come to a service on May 22. The church put on a lovely reception for my wife and me that Sunday after the service. My time was up.

On the Sermon Cycles

> [Rev. Mr. Collins] protested that he never read novels. Kitty stared at him, and Lydia exclaimed. Other books were produced, and after some deliberation he chose Fordyce's Sermons. Lydia gaped as he opened the volume, and before he had, with very monotonous solemnity, read three pages, she interrupted him with, "Do you know, mamma, that my uncle Philips talks of turning away Richard? and if he does, Colonel Forster will hire him."
>
> Jane Austen, *Pride and Prejudice*

It is thus with Lydia's and Aunt Jane's skeptical hilarity ringing in my ears that I take up the task of presenting several cycles of sermons I preached at Redeemer Anglican Church during my tenure there as interim pastor.

In the course of my ministry, I have spoken in a variety of venues and employed a variety of styles. At Redeemer, I saw the opportunity to lay a biblical and theological foundation for a young community through an ordered series of Sunday sermons. As noted earlier, I discovered that half the congregation and half the new vestry had not been confirmed as Anglicans! It happened that the departing pastor had begun a sermon series on the Lord's Prayer for Lent. After his departure, I suggested that we continue with a "catechetical season" on the commandments and the Apostles' Creed, to conclude in late September with the visit of Bishop Minns for baptism, confirmation, reception, and renewal of vows.

After five months of catechetical preaching, I concluded it might be best to continue a series of sermon cycles devoted to pastoral themes. So in October and November I preached two more series on worship and stewardship, not included in this book, titled "Psalms and Hymns and Spiritual Songs" and "Managing God's Economy."

In these first cycles, I chose readings ("lections") from the Old and New Testaments appropriate to the topic of the day, rather than follow those in the Book of Common Prayer.* There is much to be said for lectionary preaching, but there is also benefit, I believe, in using the open half of the Church Year from Trinity Sunday until Advent for topical sermons or for whole-book expositions of Scripture.

I returned to the Church Year and to the seasonal texts for the Advent, Christmas, and Epiphany seasons. I wished the congregation to behold "the True Light Coming into the World" during Advent; to consider Jesus' early years during the Christmas season, and to follow Jesus in his early ministry, from his baptism by John to his first sign at Cana in Galilee. The sermons also highlight particular feast days of these seasons.

In writing this "incarnational cycle" of sermons, I was particularly influenced by two books—*The Jesus We Missed: The Surprising Truth about the Humanity of Christ* (2012) by Patrick Henry Reardon, my former colleague at Trinity Seminary, and *Jesus Becoming Jesus: A Theological Interpretation of the Synoptic Gospels* (2018) by Thomas Weinandy, a Roman Catholic theologian. Finally, my wife and I had been belatedly watching *The Chosen* television series, which presents the life of Jesus through his various apostles. We followed up my sermon on the Wedding at Cana with a showing of the corresponding episode in the parish hall.

In Lent, I turned to the Apostle Paul and offered a six-week "evangelical cycle," expounding the letter to the Galatians. I have taught Galatians over the years as a short course on "What is the Gospel?," a question that occupied Martin Luther and that was at the heart of the Protestant Reformation. This seemed an appropriate Lenten preparation for Holy Week, as Paul concludes the letter: "Far be it from me to boast except in the cross of our Lord Jesus Christ, by which the world has been crucified to me, and I to the world" (Gal 6:14). I published a study booklet with the text for members to follow along chapter by chapter and week by week.

Finally, I have attached a "doxology" of three Easter sermons, titled "Risen Indeed! Testimonies of the Resurrection." These three sermons are based on three witnesses to the risen Lord—the empty tomb, the apostles, and the Lord's Supper—and they may, in a sense, round out the Advent testimony of the prophets and John the Baptist to Immanuel.

By then a year had passed. I had preached forty-seven sermons—frankly, more than I had preached in the ten previous years—and Fordyce's time was up.

*It would be helpful to read these lessons along with the sermons, as I do not include particular references to these texts. See the lections index for a full list.

Catechetical Sermon Cycle

LOVING GOD,
KEEPING HIS COMMANDMENTS

The Ten Commandments: Channeling God's Love

EXODUS 20:1–17; PSALM 119:1–8; JOHN 14:8–17

Blessed Lord, who has caused all Holy Scriptures to be written for our learning: Grant that we may so hear them, read, mark, learn, and inwardly digest them, that by patience and comfort of your Holy Word, we may embrace and ever hold fast the blessed hope of everlasting life, which you hast given us in our Savior Jesus Christ. Amen.

This is the first of a series of sermons seeking to understand more fully what it means to love God and keep his commandments.

Jesus said: "If you love me, keep my commandments." (John 14:15)

This saying comes from some of the last words Jesus spoke before his death. It was at the Last Supper, the night before he was betrayed, tried, and crucified. They are, in a sense, Jesus' last will and testament.

"If you love me, keep my commandments." I must confess, I have been wrestling with these words, because I am not sure what they mean. I'm not sure what they mean for me, a follower of Jesus, or for us, the church of Jesus Christ here in Bellevue. So please follow along with me over the next few weeks, as we search the Scriptures.

"If you love me, keep my commandments." What are we to make of this statement? What does Jesus mean by "love," and what does he mean by "keeping my commandments"? Specifically, what does Jesus mean as a first-century Jew—whose Bible was the Old Testament, who from his earliest years knew the Scriptures better than his elders, who each Sabbath attended synagogue, where the Torah scroll was taken from its box, its tabernacle, and read, the divinely revealed words of Almighty God to Moses?

I think we can get a good sense of how Jesus the Jew understood what "Torah" meant because we can hear him praying Psalm 119, as we did today:

> Blessed are those whose way is blameless,
> and walk in the law (*torah*) of the Lord.
> Blessed are those who keep his testimonies
> and seek him with their whole heart,
> Even those who do no wickedness
> and perfectly walk in his ways.
> You have commanded your precepts
> that we should diligently keep them.
> O that my ways were set firm
> that I might keep your statutes!

Now the word *torah* here refers specifically to the first five books of the Bible (the Pentateuch), which contain the Law of Moses. Rabbis later calculated that precisely 613 "statutes" were contained in the Torah. It was clear to first-century Jews, as it is to Orthodox Jews today, that Torah, which means "instruction," was not only a *head-matter*—"reading and memorizing"—nor only a *heart-matter*—seeking to live a godly life—but it was also a *"foot-matter"*—"walking in the way," that is, practicing the Law in everyday life. To be a faithful Jew was to be a "keeper of Torah" in body, mind, and spirit. Jews of the first century and down to today described the Law as a *yoke*, as in a yoke of oxen. Taking up the yoke of the Law was for them an honor, a privilege, and a necessity. Here is an explanation from a website about Jewish life and faith:

> Because the Jews constitute a covenant-community rather than a faith-community, the decision to convert is a decision not only to believe in the Jewish idea of God, but to act on that belief. When one "enters into the covenant"...one accepts the divine mandate requiring distinctive behavior. This is called "acceptance of the yoke of the commandments."...The rabbis rule that the candidate for conversion may not willfully reject even one of these [613 commandments].

The Torah was a law code, in fact the only law code for the people of

Israel, but it was more than that. It was embedded in a story, a narrative. The story stretched back to Creation, to the Fall of man into sin, to the promises to the patriarchs, and preeminently to the Exodus, the salvation of the Hebrew people from Egypt. One could find an analogy in American history, from the founding of the thirteen colonies to the revolution against England in 1776, with the Declaration of Independence and Constitution serving as fundamental "torah." In this case, there would be one crucial difference. The Torah of Israel was commanded by a God who spoke to Moses saying, "I am the Lord your God, who brought you out of the land of Egypt, out of the house of bondage"; and it was inscribed in stone by the finger of God, not by the quill of Thomas Jefferson.

Now I have called the commandments "channels for the love of God." Let me illustrate. After high school, I attended a very strange two-year college—Deep Springs College—one of the smallest liberal arts colleges in the USA, twenty students! And free, to boot. (You can Google it if you wish.) Anyway, Deep Springs is located in an isolated valley in the high desert east of the Sierra Nevada in California. The campus is on a cattle ranch, and students work twenty hours a week on the ranch in addition to their studies. One of the primary work assignments in my day was mucking out the irrigation ditches. You see, the valley floor is arid, with only a couple inches of rainfall per year. The ranch depends on run-off from the surrounding high mountains. So water is precious, and our job was to keep the channels clear to be sure we had a steady flow to the alfalfa fields, which in turn fed the cattle in winter. The ranch looked like a green oasis in the midst of a drab desert floor.

As I see it, the Ten Commandments are making channels through which the love of God may flow. I am not going to preach ten sermons on the Ten Commandments but will give a broad overview of what they say about the kind of love—the yoke, if you will—which the people of Israel accepted when they entered the covenant on Mount Sinai.

First thing to notice: there are two Tables of the Law—duties to God, duties to neighbor. Unlike the American founding, there is no mention of rights. These duties are summarized in the first and the tenth commandments: "you shall have no other gods before me" and "you shall not covet." These bookend commandments cover two basic sins of the human heart: *idolatry*, putting self before God, and *iniquities*, putting self before others.

Second thing to notice: the Commandments are framed negatively. *Don't* worship idols, *don't* blaspheme God, *don't* murder, commit adultery, steal, or lie. All except two: "*Keep* the Sabbath," and "*honor* your father and mother." Even these two come with a warning label against Sabbath-breaking and dishonoring parents, both of which are severely punished in the covenant Law.

Third thing to notice: the commandments refer to concrete actions, not inner attitudes. As in our day, the law at its most basic is about outward order, not inner virtue. Of course, there is a formative and educative component by which the Law will help develop a character of godliness and just-dealing (see Psalm 119). But much of this character development will take place at home and be assisted by local wisdom (proverbs) and worship (psalms).

Fourth thing to notice: the commandments span the major areas of life under God.

Religious and family life (piety, reverence)

- Honoring the one God
- Keeping the Sabbath—work, rest, and worship
- Respecting father and mother—God's creation order

Moral life (probity, i.e. personal integrity)

- Hatred
- Sexuality
- Greed
- Lying

Final thing to notice: the commandments are aimed not only at individuals but at a whole society of families and tribes which are God-honoring and righteous-dealing.

Let me now return to my image of the water system at Deep Springs College. The primary goal of our human endeavors was to channel the natural flow of melt-water to the fields where it could soak into the soil and grow the crop. This, I am arguing, is the main purpose of the Ten Commandments: to make channels for God's love to flow. But the commandments are not love itself, and that is where we come to Jesus' own commandment, which we shall be considering in later weeks.

Let me end with a request to you, that you make a self-inventory. Go through the commandments and ask yourself: would I qualify to be a good Hebrew according to the commandments? Take each commandment externally according to your conduct, not according to your inner feelings. For instance,

- Have you literally been part of a cult, worshipping a false god?
- Have you intentionally stayed away from worship for months or years on end?
- Have you disavowed your relationship to your father or mother?
- Have you murdered someone, or—and I say this advisedly for men and women—have you knowingly caused an abortion?
- Have you committed adultery or forced a divorce on your spouse?
- Have you defrauded a person of property or money?
- Have you lied publicly in a legal matter or pretended to be someone you are not?

I am not asking you to take any action about these matters. If you have broken a commandment of this sort, I hope you have repented and made appropriate reparation.

Now let me suggest one more step. Ask yourself: do I know someone—it could be a family member, a fellow worker, or a church member—who has violated God's commandments in this way? Again, I am not asking you to do anything about this observation but simply to note that ordinary people break the law, whether or not they are ever called to account for it.

This exercise is like digging the channel in the field so that the love of Jesus may flow into it. Do this, if you would, and may God bless you.

Next week I'll move on to talk about the "love of God" and the two commandments of Jesus.

THE FIFTH SUNDAY OF EASTER — MAY 2, 2021

The Two Great Commandments: Jesus' Transforming Love

PSALM 26; PHILIPPIANS 3:3–9; MARK 12:28–34

Jesus said: "If you love me, keep my commandments." (John 14:15)

This is the second sermon in a series seeking to understand more fully what it means to love God and keep his commandments.

I began this series last week by confessing that I am somewhat mystified by this saying of Jesus. What does he mean by "love"? What does he mean by "commandment"?

I think the easiest way to investigate this mystery is to go back to the Ten Commandments, which Jesus knew from childhood as God's Law etched on two tablets of stone. We noticed several things about the Ten Commandments.

There weren't just ten commandments; there were 613 commandments which every Jew was to gladly shoulder as the "yoke" of the Law. It was by keeping the whole Law, not just the Ten Commandments, that a young man found his way in the world, as we saw last week in Psalm 119.

That said, I suggested that the Ten Commandments lay out the channel, the parameters of the Law, like the forms of a pipeline or an irrigation ditch taking water across the desert and channeling it into fields of alfalfa.

The commandments are wide-ranging, covering major areas of life grouped in two clusters: *piety*—fearing God and honoring parents, and *probity*—conducting an upright life.

The commandments are also rigid and framed negatively. They are "don't-filled": don't worship idols, don't speak God's name casually or rashly, don't break the Sabbath, don't dishonor one's parents; don't murder, don't commit adultery, don't steal, don't make false witness.

What a marvel the Ten Commandments are! They are in many ways the foundation of Judeo-Christian and Western society. And we should take them so. After all, they come from our God!

But—and now I come back to my quandary about Jesus. What does he mean when he says, "If you love me, keep *my* commandments?"

I want to look at three of Jesus' sayings that give us clues as to how he *upheld*, *critiqued* and *transformed* the Jewish Law.

Jesus' first saying is well-known. In fact, we hear it every week at the beginning of the Communion service. In today's gospel lesson, a Jewish "scribe," an expert in the Jewish law, asks Jesus: "Which commandment is the most important of all?" Jesus answers him:

> The most important is, "Hear, O Israel: The Lord our God, the Lord is one. And you shall love the Lord your God with all your heart and with all your soul and with all your mind and with all your strength." The second is this: "You shall love your neighbor as yourself." There is no other commandment greater than these.

Jesus' summary divides the commandments into two groups—God and neighbor. It's a brilliant insight, and in some ways a no-brainer. Many Jews of his day down to today would concede: "Rabbi, you have spoken well." The real bombshell in his reply isn't identifying God and neighbor, but his use of the word *love*. You shall *love the Lord your God* with all your heart, soul, mind, and strength and *love your neighbor* in the same way. Love God and your neighbor with the same passion that you love the Stillers.*

So maybe Jesus was just giving a pep talk to the Jewish audience. "Put your heart into keeping the whole Law and you will do well. Keep those water-pipes clean, muck out the reservoir, dig those weeds out of the trenches, and you will do well. You can keep those 613 commandments, if you put your neck in the yoke and puff and pull the plow."

But is that what *love* means—"Try harder"? I don't think so. In fact, Jesus knew the heart of the man who asked him the question. He knew it was hardened, hardened by *keeping* the Law. You can hear this man's voice in today's psalm:

* For the uninitiated, "Stillers" is the local pronunciation of the iconic Pittsburgh Steelers football team.

> *Vindicate me*, O LORD, for I have walked in my integrity, and I have trusted in the LORD without wavering. *Prove me*, O LORD, and *try me*; *test my heart and my mind*. For your steadfast love is before my eyes, and I walk in your faithfulness. *I do not sit* with men of falsehood, *nor do I consort* with hypocrites. *I hate* the assembly of evildoers, and *I will not sit* with the wicked. *I wash my hands in innocence* and go around your altar, O LORD, proclaiming thanksgiving *aloud*, and telling all your wondrous deeds.

I have no doubt that what is portrayed in this psalm is a God-fearing and upright man. But is this *love*? I'd say more likely, this man has the form of godliness without the power of love. He has dug the channel of righteousness, but there is no water coming down into it.

This brings me to a *second* saying of Jesus:

> Come to me, all who labor and are heavy laden, and I will give you rest. Take my yoke upon you, and learn from me, for I am gentle and lowly in heart, and you will find rest for your souls. For my yoke is easy, and my burden is light. (Matt 11:28–30)

In the Book of Common Prayer, this is called a "comfortable word," which means "comforting word," for so it is! But it might not be comforting to those rigorists toiling with the yoke of 613 commandments. Think of yourself as the Prodigal's elder brother working away day by day in the fields. You're sweaty, you're tired, maybe you are feeling vindicated before God and man. And then this profligate son of your father shows up! Like the Prodigal's father, Jesus is saying to the elder brothers in Judaism, "Come this way, friend. I have a different, kinder, gentler yoke for you. It will refresh your soul, not just your body. It is the yoke of love, my love."

Who wouldn't take that offer? Sounds good, but it comes with one condition: "Come to me." You cannot enjoy the law of love unless you put on the yoke of the Great Lover, Jesus. This comfortable word reminds me of the old gospel hymn:

> Come, ye sinners, poor and needy
> Weak and wounded, sick and sore
> Jesus ready, stands to save you
> Full of pity, love and power.

I will arise and go to Jesus
He will embrace me in his arms
In the arms of my dear Savior
Oh, there are ten thousand charms.

Who wouldn't arise and go to Jesus? Well, the elder brother perhaps. The man who wants to be vindicated, who boasts in his righteousness under the Law. Such a man was Saul of Tarsus. Here, from our epistle today, is how he described his mindset before he came to Jesus:

> If anyone else thinks he has reason for confidence in the flesh, I have more: circumcised on the eighth day, of the people of Israel, of the tribe of Benjamin, a Hebrew of Hebrews; as to the law, a Pharisee; as to zeal, a persecutor of the church; as to righteousness under the law, blameless.

But then this man came to Jesus—or rather, Jesus came to him on the road to Damascus. And this is what Paul the *Apostle* went on to say:

> But whatever gain I had, I counted as loss for the sake of Christ. Indeed, I count everything as loss because of the surpassing worth of knowing Christ Jesus my Lord. For his sake I have suffered the loss of all things and count them as rubbish, in order that I may gain Christ and be found in him, not having a righteousness of my own that comes from the law, but that which comes through faith in Christ, the righteousness from God that depends on faith.

Paul knew and said clearly what it meant to be a keeper of the Law, down to the last statute: *blameless*! He also knew how worthless that righteousness was when compared to the righteousness that comes from faith in the risen Jesus. Paul put off the yoke of what he came to call bondage and put on the yoke of liberty in the service of Christ (Gal 5:1).

Now I come to the third saying of Jesus with regard to the commandments of the Law. It comes from the Sermon on the Mount:

> Do not think that I have come to abolish the Law or the Prophets; I have not come to abolish them but to fulfill them. For truly, I say to you, until heaven and earth pass away, not an iota, not a dot, will

> pass from the Law until all is accomplished. Therefore whoever relaxes one of *the least of these commandments* and teaches others to do the same will be called least in the kingdom of heaven, but whoever does them and teaches them will be called great in the kingdom of heaven. For I tell you, unless your righteousness exceeds that of the scribes and Pharisees, you will never enter the kingdom of heaven." (Matt 5:17–20)

Let me confess again, I find this a difficult statement to get my mind around. Jesus seems to claim the complete adequacy of the Commandments of Moses, but goes on to challenge his disciples to go beyond them. What does that mean? Are Christians to add on commandments 614 and 615? Of course not! Jesus, I think, is saying, if you love God with all your heart and love your neighbor as yourself, you have in fact fulfilled all 613, and then some, because love has a different calculus.

So does this let us off the hook? Is Jesus saying, "love mankind" and "pursue world peace" and all will be well? (Ok, I'm alluding to the *Peanuts* character Linus—"I love mankind…it's people I can't stand!"—and to actress Sandra Bullock, as a beauty contestant in the film *Miss Congeniality*, answering the emcee's question about "the one most important thing our society needs." "Harsher punishment for parole violators," she replies, "…and world peace.")

No, it's not that kind of "easy" yoke. Jesus goes on in the rest of the Sermon of the Mount to describe the kind of commandment he has in mind. Don't just abstain from killing, abstain from *hating*; don't just abstain from fornicating, abstain from *lusting*; don't just deal fairly by letting the punishment fit the crime, but *give your accuser whatever he demands*; don't just love your brother, but love your *enemy*.

In speaking of love, Jesus revolutionizes the means of keeping commandments. He drives a wedge between love of God and love of neighbor. We don't love our neighbor because God is just and we are just. We love our neighbor because we are fundamentally *unjust*—fallen into sin—and God has taken our injustice upon himself on the Cross. So when we look at our neighbor, we see not a vindicated man but rather an outcast, a prodigal, a prostitute, a Roman tax-collector, a thief on the cross, a Roman centurion below the Cross. Because that is who we are!

At the end of my sermon last week, I encouraged you to take a personal inventory. In what ways have you kept or broken the Ten Commandments? I asked you to be rather concrete about this: have I bowed down before a wooden idol, have I cursed and disowned my parents, have I murdered or maimed someone, have I committed adultery or spent the night in a brothel, have I defrauded someone or committed perjury in a lawsuit? Few of you, I suspect, are guilty of these gross offenses. But then I asked a second question: do you know anyone who is guilty of breaking these commandments?

What I think Jesus is saying in his law of love is this: these are the very people that you should be reaching out to, rubbing shoulders with, bringing good news to. *These are our neighbors*. And they are no different from ourselves in the eyes of the pure Lamb of God, who takes away the sins of the world.

As Redeemer moves to becoming an independent church, I think that our willingness to reach out to these unfortunates—the least, the last, and the lost—will be the fulcrum on which our success will rest.

As we come forward today and extend our hands to receive the Holy Communion, let us come to Jesus, as we truly are—weak and wounded, sick and sore. In taking the Body and Blood of Christ, may we be embraced in the arms of our dear Savior, lost in wonder, love, and praise.

If You Love Me, Love My Church

PSALM 45; ROMANS 14:1–23; JOHN 19:25–27

Jesus said: "If you love me, keep my commandments." (John 14:15)

This is the third sermon in a series seeking to understand more fully what it means to love God and keep his commandments.

At Christmas I received a gift from Redeemer Church: a lovely little book of meditations titled *Gentle and Lowly: The Heart of Christ for Sinners and Sufferers,* by Dane Ortlund. I have read it through twice. The title is drawn from the "comfortable word" of Jesus that I mentioned last week:

> Come to me, all who labor and are heavy laden, and I will give you rest. Take my yoke upon you, and learn from me, for I am gentle and lowly in heart, and you will find rest for your souls. For my yoke is easy, and my burden is light. (Matt 11:28–30)

Ortlund says this about the passage:

> In only one place—perhaps the most wonderful words ever uttered by human lips—do we hear Jesus himself open up to us his very heart…In the one place in the Bible where the Son of God pulls back the veil and lets us peer into the core of who he is, we are not told he is "exalted and dignified in heart." We are not told he is "joyful and generous of heart." Letting Jesus set the terms, his surprising claim is that he is "gentle and lowly in heart."

Love according to this image comes from below, bubbling up from the fathomless love of the Father and Son and breaking out over the channels of righteousness according to the Law. Another image we might draw on to display the heart of Jesus is a maternal one, the love he first drew from his mother's breast that first Christmas night.

Today is Mother's Day, as I am sure you are all aware. It is a strange fact that in our screwed-up world of broken families and broken identities Mother's Day is still seen as something to celebrate. So let's do it: Happy Mother's Day to the mothers among us. And to all of us who have mothers—and I think that's pretty much everybody!—don't neglect to remember your mother with gratitude in memory if she is dead and, if she is alive, let her know you love her. I am not saying that honoring one's mother is always an easy thing to do, given that fallen human nature infects every relationship, but "honor your father and mother" is one of those forms God has given us to live within.

I suppose one reason Mother's Day is widely loved is because motherhood is so *natural*. In a just-published book *Mom Genes*, Abigail Tucker amusingly describes the role of various hormones, male and female, zipping around in the body of a newly pregnant woman. Then there is the social side of motherhood: from the ecstasy of sex to the labor and pain of childbirth, to the joy of discovering "It's a boy!" or "It's a girl!" (OK, we did it the old-fashioned way, but it's a joy whenever it happens—unless you happen to be Henry VIII, in which case only "it's a boy" works—Peggy and I have been watching *Wolf Hall*.) So when a mother offers her breast to her newborn infant, it is the first act of opening her heart: "Welcome to the world, child! Come to me and I will give you refreshment." That sounds something like Jesus' "comfortable word" of love—"Come to me and I will refresh you"—which he learned at his mother's breast.

So with this in mind, I want to propose this: *Jesus loves the Church his bride and mother, and so should you.* To paraphrase our sermon theme: "If you love me, love my Church."

Let's continue to think about Jesus and his earthly mother, the Virgin Mary. One strange thing about Jesus of Nazareth is that from childhood on, he displayed a rather formal relationship with his mother, some might even say cool and aloof. In his first sign at the Wedding at Cana, his mother urged him to help out with the wine shortage, and he replied: "Woman, what is that to me? My time has not yet come" (John 2:4). Later, when his mother and brothers sought an audience with him, he turned them down, saying, "'Who is my mother, and who are my brothers?' And stretching out his hand toward his disciples, he said, 'Here are my mother and my brothers!'" (Matt 12:48–49) In another incident, a woman called out to

Jesus (in the earthy words of the King James Version): "'Blessed is the womb that bare thee, and the paps which thou hast sucked.' But he said, 'Yea rather, blessed are they that hear the word of God, and keep it'" (Luke 11:27–28). These responses, one might say, are a strange way to honor one's mother, not to mention that she's the Virgin Mary! I doubt that Jesus ever sent her a bouquet of roses and a Hallmark card on Mother's Day!

Jesus explained this attitude early on when as a twelve-year-old he said to his parents, "I must be about my Father's business." But he did open his heart of love for her at the end, when her heart was breaking, in one of his last words from the Cross (from our gospel today):

> When Jesus saw his mother and the disciple whom he loved standing nearby, he said to his mother, "Woman, behold, your son!" Then he said to the disciple, "Behold, your mother!" And from that hour the disciple took her to his own home.

In the midst of his agony, Jesus entrusts his mother to the Beloved Disciple John, the author of the gospel. In John's gospel, one constantly finds levels of meaning below the surface of the text. In this case, Jesus continues to speak to her as "woman." She is not only Mary of Nazareth but the new Eve, the mother of a new family, the Church. Likewise, John is not just Jesus' best friend, he is the apostle and evangelist extraordinaire, and his home is not a private residence but the dwelling-place of a new community of the Spirit, the Church, the family of those born "not of blood nor of the will of the flesh nor of the will of man, but of God."

Let me try to summarize this simple, but not so simple, word from the Cross. Jesus loved his mother Mary, and Jesus loved his own people, those who would receive him and be born again through faith. He not only loved them one by one, sheep by sheep, fish by fish, but he loved them as his own Body, the Body of Christ, the one, holy, catholic, and apostolic Church.

There is a biblical basis for speaking of the church as our mother, and it goes hand in hand with another image: the Church as the bride of Christ. Our psalm today portrays a royal betrothal, which is addressed to the Messiah, the Son of God:

> Your throne, O God, is forever and ever. The scepter of your kingdom is a scepter of uprightness; you have loved righteousness and

> hated wickedness. Therefore God, your God, has anointed you with the oil of gladness beyond your companions.

The psalm then turns to the royal bride, the queen-in-waiting:

> Hear, O daughter, and consider, and incline your ear: forget your people and your father's house, and the king will desire your beauty. Since he is your lord, bow to him.

The young queen is portrayed not only as a lover and spouse but also as a royal mother of generations and nations to come. It continues:

> In place of your fathers shall be your sons; you will make them princes in all the earth. I will cause your name to be remembered in all generations; therefore nations will praise you forever and ever.

In the most striking passage about marriage in the New Testament, St. Paul picks up on this Old Testament imagery, reflecting on the deep meaning of the first couple in the garden. He says:

> "Therefore a man shall leave his father and mother and hold fast to his wife, and the two shall become one flesh." This is a profound mystery, and I am saying that it refers to Christ and the church. (Eph 5:31–32)

The context of this saying is Paul's call for mutual submission of husband and wife, in which the wife submits to her husband as the Church submits to Christ, and the husband loves his wife, as Christ loved the Church. Some people today object to Paul's call to the wife to submit to her husband, but what they miss is that in the deepest sense, Paul is saying that *we are all together Christ's beloved bride*, and he is the great Lover who has loved the Church and given himself up for *her* so that he might sanctify her. In another place Paul speaks of the Church as a city, "the Jerusalem above, which is our mother" (Gal 4:26).

So let's return now to Jesus' statement: "If you love me, keep my commandments." I am suggesting that Jesus is taking love in its most basic and powerful sense—the love of husband and wife and the love of mother and child—to characterize the way we are to keep his commandments. These are "household" loves because they are experienced and practiced first in the family and later in the Church. The New Testament refers frequently to the Church as "the household of God," and Paul urges love among Christians in this way: "as we have opportunity, let us do good to everyone, and especially to those who are of the household of faith" (Gal 6:10).

Paul calls this virtue *philadelphia*—"love of the brethren"—which of course included "sistern." It was a preferential option of love among Christians. I mentioned last week Linus, from the comic strip, crying out, "I love mankind…it's people I can't stand!" Love that is as broad as Linus's tends also to be as shallow, like a flash flood quickly soaked up in the desert.

Twice at the Last Supper, Jesus commanded brotherly love when he said, "This is my commandment, that you love one another as I have loved you" (John 15:12; 13:34). In the dramatic parable of the Sheep and the Goats, Jesus shows exactly what that love looks like. The scene is Judgment Day, when the Son of Man returns in glory. The judge divides the sheep and goats according to what they had done for him or not done for him when he was hungry, thirsty, naked, a stranger, and in prison. Both groups, the sheep and the goats, are amazed, saying, "When did we see you hungry, thirsty, naked, lonely, and in prison?" To the sheep, the King answers, "Truly, I say to you, as you did it to one of the least of these my brethren, you did it to me." And likewise to the goats, he says, "As you did *not* do it to one of the least of these, you did *not* do it to me."

We miss the meaning of this commandment if we imagine this brotherly love as a kind of back-slapping camaraderie of the well-off in life. This gets the matter exactly wrong. Next week I'll come back to the subject when I talk about "who is my neighbor?" Jesus' focus in this parable is on the *family of God under persecution.* I think a more specific application today would be to think of the persecuted church throughout the world. The recent ACNA Prayer Book, I am pleased to say, has now included in its Prayers of the People a specific petition "for our brothers and sisters in Christ who are persecuted for their faith."

Jesus' love of the Church is radical because he sees the Church constantly reproducing and its love extending to others. He calls the Church the salt of the earth and the light of the world, so that outsiders "may see your good works and give glory to your Father who is in heaven" (Matt

5:16). That can happen only as we "do good to everyone," especially the poor and needy, the widows and orphans, the prisoners and refugees. Paul is not saying we "do good" to fellow Christians first and then throw any scraps to the pagan dogs. What he is saying is that we cannot effectively show forth Christ's love if we are disunited and biting at each other's ankles.

For this reason the love of the Church must include the passion for *peace* among us. In the reading from Romans today, we see Paul giving guidance on an issue that divided his first converts: whether to buy and eat meat from the marketplace that may have been part of a pagan sacrifice. Paul describes two views on this matter: that of the strong and of the weak. He himself holds the strong view, which is that "nothing is unclean in itself," but he also recognizes the reality of the weak conscience, saying "it is unclean for anyone who thinks it unclean." So what is the church to do? Paul's reply to the strong is: Don't eat, because it puts a stumbling block in front of the weak. The higher principle of pursuing peace and mutual upbuilding trumps freedom of conscience, even if you are right.

This brings me to a specific application of this teaching this Mother's Day. I am appealing to you at Redeemer Anglican Church to *love this church*—just as Jesus loved the Church, his bride and mother. This past week we received word from the Diocese of Pittsburgh and from St. Stephen's Church that they have accepted our petition to become an independent congregation of the diocese. Let us thank God and be grateful for those who have brought us to this point, including of course our own Seth Zimmerman.

At the same time, let's recognize the burden this puts on us all to come together to realize this vision. As a body we prayed for discernment and we trusted our leadership to seek God's will for this church. Now is the time for us to be working together for the goal of becoming an outpost of the church here in the North Boroughs.

I know there are some who feel like this decision is a kind of burden, more work for fewer hands. This is probably true. But with what spirit do we approach this—like the elder brother with grumbling about our share or like the younger son overjoyed at the excitement of a new life?

Let me now speak about the "Anglican" part of our name—Redeemer Anglican. I know that many of you were not raised as Anglicans and may not even consider yourselves Anglicans now. That's OK. Anglicans are not some walled-off sect but merely Christians who honor a certain tradition. I would like to encourage you to take this moment to deepen your knowledge and grow your love for this tradition.

Brothers and sisters, today is Mother's Day. Let's take the opportunity not only of renewing our gratitude and love for our earthly mothers but of responding to Jesus, who says in effect, "If you love me, love my Church."

Let me conclude with this well-known prayer for the Church (Book of Common Prayer, page 646):

> Gracious Father, we pray to you for your holy Catholic Church. Fill it with all truth, in all truth with all peace. Where it is corrupt, purify it; where it is in error, direct it; where in anything it is amiss, reform it. Where it is right, strengthen it; where it is in want, provide for it; where it is divided, reunite it; for the sake of Jesus Christ your Son our Savior. Amen.

The Great Commandment and the Great Question

LEVITICUS 19:11–19; LUKE 10:25–37

Jesus said: "If you love me, keep my commandments." (John 14:15)

This is the fourth sermon in a series seeking to understand more fully what it means to love God and keep his commandments.

In this series I surveyed the Ten Commandments, noting that they can be divided into two "tablets," one focusing on *piety* and one on *probity*: fear of God and uprightness in human relationships. Both tablets are rather formal and framed in negative terms: shunning godlessness and shunning immorality. I noted that while Jesus rightly observed the division of these two tablets, he defined it in terms of *love*: loving God and loving one's neighbor. In the Sermon on the Mount we see that this kind of love far exceeds the standard legal interpretation by the Jewish authorities, because it delves into the motivations of the heart. Love, Jesus teaches, goes beyond outward performance to surprising acts like turning the other cheek and loving one's enemies.

Last week, I suggested that Jesus directed this love in particular to the "household of faith," to "these my brethren," to the Church. Jesus loves the Church, I concluded, and so should we.

But that is not the end of the matter, for Jesus also commands his disciples to love a wider circle of "neighbors." He puts it this way: "If you greet only your brothers, what more are you doing than others? Do not even the Gentiles do the same?" (Matt 5:47).

Our gospel lesson today tells the story of the Good Samaritan. It begins with a series of questions about the commandments of the law. A lawyer approaches Jesus and asks: "Teacher, what shall I do to inherit eternal life?" Do any of you remember learning the difference between an "information question" and a "quiz question"? In the case of the information question, someone actually wants to know something they do not know; in the case of the quiz question, the person already knows the answer and is testing you to find out whether you know it too. This lawyer is asking a quiz question. Jesus sees through this man, so he turns the question back on him: "What is written in the Law? How do you read it?" To paraphrase Jesus: "You already know the answer. You tell me."

The man answers in words quite close to Jesus' own teaching: "You shall love the Lord your God with all your heart and with all your soul and with all your strength and with all your mind, and your neighbor as yourself." Jesus replies: "You have answered correctly. Do this and you will live." Give that man an A-plus on his exam paper and a gold star on his forehead! *But*—and now Jesus turns the quiz question into an action item: *Do this!* It isn't what you know, but what you do that counts as love, Jesus is saying.

The man attempts to switch the subject back from doing to knowing, from hands to head. "But who is my neighbor?" he asks. Maybe he gets a glimpse that there is something to learn from the Teacher, or maybe he is just talking his way out of what has become an uncomfortable situation.

Jesus answers the lawyer's question with the parable of the Good Samaritan. You probably know the basics of the story: a man was waylaid by thieves along the road from Jericho to Jerusalem, which is a very desolate area. (I can attest to that! Some years ago Peggy and I were driving a rental car down the Jericho road from Jerusalem. She had eaten some bad food the night before and was suffering from all that that entails. Let me assure you, there were no rest stops on that road in Jesus' day nor today. So we were praying for continence all the way!) Anyway, two religious figures, a priest and a Levite, pass by on the other side, and a third figure, a Samaritan, whose people "have no dealings with Jews," stops for the man, binds up his wounds, and takes him to an inn, promising to come back later and cover all his expenses.

What I want to observe is the way Jesus frames the question at the end: "Which of these three," Jesus asks, "became a neighbor, which one of these *neighbored* the man who fell among the robbers?" Do you see how Jesus inverted the question? Jesus looks at "who is my neighbor?" not as a quiz question nor as an information question, but as an *action item*! You become the neighbor, Jesus says, when you show mercy in action like the Samaritan. So, he concludes, "go and do likewise."

When I moved to Uganda twenty years ago, I found that Africans had a rather formal way of creating agendas for meetings, in contrast with the rather loosey-goosey way we conducted business at Trinity Seminary. Sometimes, these agendas were a bit fussy, but I did come to appreciate the idea that "action items" were attached at the end of every meeting. Don't just talk. Do something!

Love, I think Jesus is saying, is not primarily a piece of head-knowledge or a warm fuzzy feeling, but something you do. Maybe we can put it this way: love emerges out of an unexpected encounter which may cut across the agenda you had in mind. No doubt the priest and Levite passed by for fear of being contaminated by the wounded man; they probably had a busy schedule in mind, like getting to the temple on time, and they suspected that helping this man out would complicate their schedules and get them in trouble with their colleagues in Jerusalem.

Perhaps at this point, I should simply end the sermon, dismiss you, and say, "Go and do likewise." Find the first person you meet and "neighbor" him or her. But I won't do this: that's when preaching becomes meddling, you know.

In fact, it is not so easy to obey the commandment to love your neighbor. There is an "art" to it. I want to recommend a little book called *The Art of Neighboring*—and a website linked to it. It has a lot of practical ideas on how to take steps toward being a better neighbor. With the help of this book, I want to suggest several guidelines to the art of neighboring.

The first guideline is to say that neighboring involves a kind of proactive seeing. One way you can prepare yourself for the occasion of neighboring is by thinking of occasions when you yourself would like help or fellowship. This, by the way, is what Jesus means by "loving your neighbor *as yourself*" and his citing of the "golden rule": "Whatever you wish that others would do to you, do also to them, for this is the Law and the Prophets" (Matt 7:12). If your car breaks down on a lonely road with no cell phone service, how would you wish for someone to stop and help?

Here is one little example of proactive seeing. The more I flew around the world on long-haul flights, the lighter I packed my carry-on luggage. I'd check my main bags in Pittsburgh and hope to see them twenty-four hours later on the carousel in Uganda. But I found that many older, vertically challenged people would come onboard bringing huge carry-on bags. So rather than buckling myself in as soon as I got to my aisle seat,

I would watch the other passengers stopping near my row and would try to pop up and help them get their bags into the overhead compartment.

Then there is a second guideline: be ready to hear God's prompting. In a recent sermon at St. Stephen's, Todd Murden told of jogging past a woman who was smoking a cigarette, when he heard the Spirit say, "Tell her to stop smoking." He had passed her by but then turned around in some trepidation and jogged back and said, "I think I'm supposed to tell you to stop smoking." To his surprise, the woman did not ream him out, but said: "I have been trying to stop smoking for months, and this is the first cigarette I have had. Thanks for reminding me!"

The third guideline has to do with making time. To be available to your neighbor, you have to have time, to build it into your pattern of living. Another thing we learned in Africa is that Africans put relationships over time. This can be pretty frustrating when people come in late or stay late. But on the whole, we Westerners err in the other direction, with our packed schedules and our idea that listening to someone go on is a waste of time.

I think the freeing up of time is inherent in the commandment to "keep holy the Sabbath day." Many years ago, I became acquainted with an Israeli scholar, who visited us at our home in Sewickley. When Saturday came, he would not go anywhere in a vehicle, so we took a long walk up to the cemetery and later sat out on our porch and talked. It was a wonderful time. The following summer, I was in Jerusalem, and he invited me to his home for Shabbat (the Sabbath). Around five on Friday afternoon, the buses stop running in Jerusalem and the streets become empty. Families start coming out of their homes, walking and pushing prams and greeting each other with "*Shabbat shalom*!"—"Happy Sabbath!" The men go to synagogue while the women prepare the Sabbath supper. Sunday used to be something like this in the US and is still a little bit that way. Keeping a Sunday sabbath could be an opportunity to take time to meet and greet your neighbors. Some years past, our neighbors planned a block party on Sunday afternoons in the fall, complete with refreshments—and of course TV cable connection to the Steelers game.

One final guideline has to do with motivation, if I can frame it this way: *care*, *share*, and *prayer*. Jesus addresses the "cares" of our hearts. We tend to be anxious about reaching out to others; Jesus says: "Don't be anxious. Trust your heavenly Father. Step out in faith." And caring is reciprocal. We don't just care for our neighbors, we share with them. Sometimes we are not the Good Samaritan; sometimes *we* are the hurting man on the roadside, and *they* are the ones who come to our aid. Neighborliness is ultimately the building of a give-and-take relationship that expands out to others even beyond the neighbor. Finally, there is prayer, because ultimately love comes from God and is returned to him. I have found in visiting strangers in hospital and at other stressful times, very few people object to your asking, "May I pray for you?" Also, when you pray, "Lord, direct my steps this day," it's surprising how often you encounter a potential neighbor.

So while there is no absolute method of loving one's neighbors, we can prepare our hearts, make time in our schedules, and purify our motivations through caring, sharing, and praying so that we can begin to be better at the art of neighboring.

Now let me conclude with a specific application to our church and society at this moment. I'm sure that you have by now heard that the Centers for Disease Control has revised its advice to say that vaccinated people may associate indoors and outdoors without wearing masks, and things seem to be opening up rapidly. I'd like to make a few comments about this, especially in light of Jesus' teaching.

First, let's be thankful to God for his resources in creation and to all who have worked to produce and distribute the current vaccines. This is not a political statement, nor personal advice. It is a simple fact that due to the vaccines, infections and deaths are going down in our country, and we should be grateful for that.

Secondly, I think we are going to see a transition to a "new normal" emerge in a month or two having to do with how we relate to others at work and play and worship. The new normal may not be exactly the same as the old normal: like the pandemic itself, there is much we cannot see at this point.

This brings me to a third point for the church. Let's be patient and tolerant with each other as this transition happens. Last week I mentioned the way St. Paul addressed the matter of the "strong" and the "weak" consciences in the church when it came to eating food sacrificed to idols. Paul urged the strong not to force the weak to violate their conscience in this matter. I'll add this corollary, the weak should not use their conscience as an excuse to avoid learning. The overriding principle, Paul says, is that "each of us please his neighbor for his good, to build him up" (Rom 15:2).

At present, there may be differences of opinion as to what is the strong opinion on vaccines and what is the weak. The majority view now—and

I share this—is that people should get vaccinated, that vaccines are effective and will restore confidence in relating to others. However, I recognize there are those who have reservations—and from all sides of the political spectrum. Also, I think the speed with which the transition happens is not clear. It seems to me we at Redeemer have the great advantage of meeting outside this summer, and we have established a pattern of worship which we do not need to change abruptly. So my advice is that we take our time, and when we make changes, the executive team/vestry can advise us after polling the congregation.

The Great Question asked by the lawyer is: Who is my neighbor? In our age of telecommunications and global awareness, I could pose another question: "How near—and how far—is my neighbor?" We'll come to that question next week when we talk about the Great Commission.

Let us pray, in the well-loved words of Richard of Chichester:

> Thanks be to thee, my Lord Jesus Christ,
> for all the benefits thou hast given me,
> for all the pains and insults thou hast borne for me.
> O most merciful redeemer, friend and brother,
> may I know thee more clearly,
> love thee more dearly,
> and follow thee more nearly, day by day. Amen.

PENTECOST — MAY 23, 2021

The Great Commandment and the Great Commission

ACTS 2:1–11; MATTHEW 28:16–20

Jesus said: "If you love me, keep my commandments." (John 14:15)

This is the fifth sermon in a series seeking to understand more fully what it means to love God and keep his commandments.

The last two weeks I have preached on Jesus' second Great Commandment—"love your neighbor as yourself"—in terms of his loving the Church, "these my brethren" as he calls them, and his redirecting love for the neighbor toward "the other," the stranger, a love that emerges out of a surprise encounter which may cut across one's personal acquaintances and agenda. It has made me rethink those two little words "as yourself."

What does it mean to love someone "as yourself"? Some people take those two words in a narcissistic sense—remember Narcissus, the beautiful youth who fell in love with his own image reflected in a pool? To be sure, it is difficult for a person with too high—or too low—a self-image to love others. In any case, Jesus is not saying "fall in love with yourself" in this sense.

In the past, I have understood this "as yourself" to suggest a normal, "healthy" self-image. Of course you love yourself. That's what people do. So, I have thought, Jesus is directing us to have the same regard for others that we have for ourselves. It's a two-fer!

But I am being challenged in this view by this saying in the Sermon on the Mount, where Jesus says:

> For if you love those who love you, what reward do you have? Do not even the tax collectors do the same? And if you greet only

> your brothers, what more are you doing than others? Do not even the Gentiles do the same? (Matt 5:46–47)

So here is my new interpretation of "as yourself." It refers to your family, your tribe or network, your social class, your peers in age or education. In the ancient world, people did not think so much about individual identity as about social identity. This is even true today. Some people's identity today is dependent on how many "likes" they get on Facebook or Twitter, which college they attended—Harvard or Grove City—which political party they voted for, which borough they reside in—Brighton Heights or Ben Avon Heights.*

Here is where the Good Samaritan comes in. The lawyer asks Jesus a conventional question: how wide is my neighborhood? Jesus comes back with a parable about a man, a religious outsider, who has compassion on another outsider, a bloody pulp of a victimized traveler. *This is how you neighbor*, Jesus says. Go and do likewise. How wide is my neighborhood? As wide as God's world.

This brings us to the Day of Pentecost, which we celebrate today. The Day of Pentecost fulfils the prophecy in the Old Testament that God would pour out his Spirit *on all flesh*. The Day of Pentecost fulfils the risen Jesus' Great Commandment, making everyone a neighbor. It's also the fulfillment of Jesus' Great Commission—to his Church:

> All authority in heaven and on earth has been given to me. Go therefore and make disciples of all nations, baptizing them in the name of the Father and of the Son and of the Holy Spirit, teaching them to observe all that I have commanded you.

The Day of Pentecost reveals the *all-encompassing extent* of Jesus' commandment and the *all-sufficient enablement* to fulfil it that comes through the Holy Spirit. I am going to concentrate on the first of these elements—the extent of the Spirit's work—this week, and the second—the Spirit's enabling us to love—next week.

The Day of Pentecost is rightly called the birthday of the Church. Jesus had promised his disciples that he would not leave them orphaned after he ascended to the Father. His final prayer before Calvary was for the

* Brighton Heights and Ben Avon Heights are the opposite socio-economic poles of the North Boroughs.

Church, and his first act on Easter night was constituting the Church by "breathing on the disciples" and saying: "Receive the Holy Spirit. If you forgive the sins of any, they are forgiven them; if you withhold forgiveness from any, it is withheld" (John 20:22–23). But who are the "any" they are to reach out to, and how many are the any?

The extent of the Great Commission is the extent of Jesus' authority, which is a matter of "heaven and earth." But having commissioned them, he also tells them not to rush out handing out tracts, but to "wait for the promise of the Father," when "you will be baptized with the Holy Spirit not many days from now" (Acts 1:4-5).

Ten days later, that promise was fulfilled on the Day of Pentecost, when the Holy Spirit descended on a crowd from

> every nation under heaven from Parthians and Medes and Elamites and residents of Mesopotamia, Judea and Cappadocia, Pontus and Asia, Phrygia and Pamphylia, Egypt and the parts of Libya belonging to Cyrene, and visitors from Rome, both Jews and proselytes, Cretans and Arabians.

And the Day of Pentecost was just the beginning. The book of Acts goes on to show how this same Spirit fell later on the Samaritans—yes, the despised Samaritans—and then finally on the pagan Gentiles throughout the Mediterranean world, and even as far as sub-Saharan Africa, with the conversion of the Ethiopian eunuch.

Pentecost reveals the all-encompassing extent of Jesus' vision for the Church. This Church was not to be a holy huddle but an amazingly diverse community of disciples. And the vehicle by which the Church was extended was no power of nature nor scheme of man but a Person, the Person of the Holy Spirit. Here is the difference between Jesus, the Second Person of the Trinity, and the Holy Spirit. As truly man, with a body—a glorified body to be sure—the risen Lord could be only spatially in one place, even after the resurrection. Seated at the right hand of the Father, he dwells in one location until he returns in glory.

But the Spirit of God is by his very nature divisible like the tongues of fire. And just as the Spirit of God swept across the whole creation at the beginning, so now the Spirit can penetrate every nook and cranny of the world. And because the Spirit is the Spirit of the Father and the Son, it is very much the case that Jesus comes to dwell in our hearts in Word and

Sacrament while remaining at the right hand of the Father in heaven. For this reason, as he said to his disciples: "I tell you the truth: it is to your advantage that I go away, for if I do not go away, the Helper will not come to you. But if I go, I will send him to you" (John 16:7). It may sound strange to us, but Jesus actually promises that for this reason, "whoever believes in me will also do the works that I do; and greater works than these will he do, because I am going to the Father" (John 14:12).

The all-encompassing extent of Jesus' Commission is worldwide, but it is also *local*, "beginning in Jerusalem." The neighbors we are called to serve are near and far, and any church obeying this commission needs to have a local and a global vision. Today I am going to ask Stewart Wicker* to speak about the worldwide work of SAMS—Society of Anglican Missionaries and Senders. In a couple weeks we shall be hearing from Greg Miller and Herb Bailey about the local ministry of Church Army USA and what it might mean in the North Boroughs.

Twenty-some years ago Peggy and I were caught up by the Spirit—much to our amazement—in the Great Commission overseas. We are now back home retired, but I must confess I am not a little amazed how we ended up here in Bellevue. But while I have a lesser role to play, I no way belittle the work God is calling me—is calling us—to do here at Redeemer. Jesus' love and his commandment and his Spirit are the same yesterday, today, and forever, and on every continent, among every race or tribe, or degree of wealth or status.

Next week I want to return to the source of the love of God which comes to us through the Spirit. That source is God the Father. But for us this day, the Day of Pentecost, let us rejoice that the Spirit has come down and is here abiding with us, and may we as a church let it show in how we live our lives.

Before I turn it over to Stewart, I thought I'd share a little jazzy chorus I learned fifty years ago. It's so old I can't even find it with Google, but here goes:

> When the Day of Pentecost came 'round,
> The disciples were just sittin' down
> When they heard a mighty rushin' sound

* Stewart Wicker is head of SAMS and is a member of the congregation and served later on the Redeemer vestry. On this day he spoke of the global mission of the Church.

It was the Holy Spirit comin' down

Well, it's the Spirit that makes us one,
It's through the Spirit God's work is done,
You've got to feel that Spirit deep inside
To let it show in how we live our lives.

Loving in the Triune God

I JOHN 5:1–4; JOHN 14:19–30, 15:1–11

Jesus said: "If you love me, keep my commandments." (John 14:15)

This is the sixth and final sermon in a series seeking to understand more fully what it means to love God and keep his commandments.

The last two weeks I have preached on Jesus' second Great Commandment—"love your neighbor as yourself." These sermons made me rethink those two little words: to love your neighbor *as yourself*. I don't think Jesus means "as yourself" in the sense of the "self-care" of contemporary pop culture, nor in the sense of "self-esteem" which is part of normal ego formation. Rather, "as yourself" refers to a person's world of human relationships, which usually begins with family and then extends to loyalties to village, clan and cult. By cult, here I mean a particular "denomination" or religious tradition like those of the Jews and Samaritans, or Catholics and Protestants.

Loving your neighbor as yourself as Jesus teaches requires us to love the *Church*, not for its buildings or its worship style or even its warm sense of belonging, but because it is the Body of Christ, of which we are all members, "brethren for whom Christ died." Loving your neighbor also requires us to think of the Church not just as it is today but as it might become when the Spirit expands it to reach every tribe and language and people and nation. Through his Spirit Jesus is redirecting love for the neighbor toward "the other," the stranger, the persecuted, the unconverted throughout the world. At this point the Great Commandment has become the Great Commission. We heard from Stewart Wicker last week of the worldwide extent of the Spirit's work by one Anglican mission agency, the Society of Anglican Missionaries and Senders.

Today in the Church Year is Trinity Sunday. While most Christians pay lip service to the doctrine of the Trinity, many privately think of the doctrine the way the writer Dorothy Sayers put it: "God the Father Incomprehensible, God the Son Incomprehensible, the Whole Thing Incomprehensible." Sometimes clergy illustrate the doctrine with a diagram like a wheel with a hub—God—and three spokes—Father, Son and Spirit—a kind of divine space station or fidget spinner. That doesn't help. Some Evangelical churches tend to focus on Jesus only; some Pentecostal churches on the Spirit only; liberal churches used to preach the Fatherhood of God and brotherhood of man, until those terms became politically incorrect. This won't do either.

I'll come back to the Trinity, but let me turn to another question: why did Jesus say so much about loving the neighbor and so little about loving God? As I think about all his parables, the only example of loving God I come up with is the Pharisee and the Publican, the unclean tax collector. The Pharisee thanks God he is not like other men, especially the unclean ones; the Publican "standing far off, would not even lift up his eyes to heaven, but beat his breast, saying, 'God, be merciful to me, a sinner!'" (Luke 18:13). It seems to me there is a noticeable disproportion in Jesus' public teaching between the two Great Commandments. I wonder why? So let me take a stab at answering this question.

First, *Jesus was a Jew speaking to Jews.* If the Jewish people had learned anything from their desert wandering under Moses and their exile in Babylon, it was that the Lord God meant business when he said, "You shall worship me alone." Jews were and are militantly monotheistic. Jews therefore could commend Jesus for teaching "love the Lord your God" as the first Great Commandment. But what they overlooked was that such a monotheistic attitude could breed spiritual pride in oneself and blindness to others. The Pharisee could talk the talk about loving God, but he could not see the Publican as his neighbor. The Publican alone knew his need for God's mercy. Jesus' brother James defined loving God in this same way when he said: "Religion that is pure and undefiled before God the Father is this: to visit orphans and widows in their affliction, and to keep oneself unstained from the world" (James 1:27). Love for others comes first, then spiritual purity will follow.

Secondly, *Jesus led by example.* No one who followed him could doubt that here was a man totally committed to God and God to him: in his unique knowledge of the Scriptures; in his commanding demons to depart; in his retreat to the mountain to pray, and in his words and cries from the Cross. To love God is to imitate Jesus. The disciples followed his example, preaching the Gospel of the Kingdom, empowered at Pentecost by the Holy Spirit.

Thirdly, *Jesus called God Father*. I cannot emphasize enough how foreign this language of God as Father was to Judaism. None of the Old Testament figures—not Moses or David or the prophets—addressed God as Father. The same absence is largely true of pagan religions and is specifically condemned in Islam. But Jesus, when he prayed, began simply "Abba, Father." He taught his disciples to pray likewise to "Our Father" in the Lord's Prayer. Jesus was teaching his disciples to pray the way he prayed, not that they understood the significance of this language at first.

Now I return to the Holy Trinity. I titled this sermon "Loving *in* the Triune God," because we love God by participating in the divine nature (2 Pet 1:4). At the Last Supper, Jesus begins to explain what we theologians call the trinitarian relations. There is the relation of the Father and the Son. Jesus says: "Do you not believe that I am in the Father and the Father is in me? The words that I say to you I do not speak on my own authority, but the Father who dwells in me does his works" (John 14:10). And there is the relation of the Spirit, sometimes called the Paraclete or Advocate, to the Father and the Son. Jesus continues: "When the Paraclete comes, whom I will send to you from the Father, the Spirit of truth, who proceeds from the Father, he will bear witness about me" (John 15:26).

The relations within the triune God do not end there. They include *us*, the believers, the sheep of Jesus' flock who hear his voice and follow. Jesus speaks of the coming Day when he has departed and then "you will know that I am in my Father, and you in me, and I in you" (John 14:20). The bringer of this knowledge, this assurance is the Spirit: "You know him, for he dwells with you and will be in you" (John 14:17).

Theologians speak of these relations as *ontological*, that is, they express *who God is*, and *who we are* as a new creation in him. The New Testament makes crystal clear that we have a new identity, a new nature, we are "in Christ" through repentance and faith. As St. Paul says: "I am crucified with Christ; nevertheless I live; yet not I, but Christ lives in me: and the life which I now live in the flesh I live by the faith of the Son of God, who loved me, and gave himself for me" (Gal 2:19–20).

These relations are also *moral*; they are relations of love, which fulfill the commandments, and they flow naturally, as it were, from our new identity. St. John uses two striking analogies to make clear the connection between being and doing. The first analogy is *familial*, being born of God. In our epistle reading today John says:

> Everyone who believes that Jesus is the Christ has been born of God, and everyone who loves the Father loves whoever has been born of him. By this we know that we love the children of God, when we love God and obey his commandments. For this is the love of God, that we keep his commandments. And his commandments are not burdensome. For everyone who has been born of God overcomes the world. And this is the victory that has overcome the world—our faith. (1 John 5:1–4)

John connects faith and love. Being born again or born from above, we have a new spiritual DNA, and this DNA is recognizable by our response to God in faith and love. By faith we overcome the power of the world, the flesh, and the devil. By our love we are enabled to fulfill the commandments by loving God and loving "the children of God"—and as I have been interpreting Jesus, these children include both our brothers and sisters in the Church and also those "neighbors" whom God is bringing in through her mission to the last, the least and the lost—and for that matter the lapsed.

The second analogy of our new life is *organic*, having to do with trees and fruit. In our gospel today, Jesus likens our life to that of a fruit-bearing tree.

> I am the true vine, and my Father is the vinedresser. Every branch in me that does not bear fruit he takes away, and every branch that does bear fruit he prunes, that it may bear more fruit. Already you are clean because of the word that I have spoken to you. Abide in me, and I in you. As the branch cannot bear fruit by itself, unless it abides in the vine, neither can you, unless you abide in me. I am the vine; you are the branches. Whoever abides in me and I in him, he it is that bears much fruit, for apart from me you can do nothing.

The key word in this analogy is *abide*. What a comforting word this is! We are not out there digging our own stony field. Jesus tells us we are already grafted into the vine, "made clean" by his love. To be sure, we may be tempted and sin, and he will prune us back, but he will never simply break off and toss a true vine away. Jesus goes on then to describe our grafting into God's nature and bearing fruit as fulfilling the commandments.

> By this my Father is glorified, that you bear much fruit and so prove to be my disciples. As the Father has loved me, so have I loved you. Abide in my love. If you keep my commandments, you will abide in my love, just as I have kept my Father's commandments and abide in his love.

From the time of the sixteenth-century Reformation down to the present, there has been an argument about whether our relationship with God—our justification—is a matter of faith alone or a package deal with God to do our part. In this image of the vine, Jesus makes clear that our moral life, our works, flow naturally from our incorporation into God. That does not mean we simply lie back, floating as it were on a raft in God's swimming pool, sipping a margarita. But it does speak of our trusting God to work through us by his Spirit to fulfill his holy will.

Let me now sum up this sermon series on "loving God, keeping his commandments." I suggested that the Ten Commandments on Mount Sinai construct a channel for God's to flow through. This channel sets the external boundaries of morality but not the inner flow of love. Jesus makes clear that there are two main sources of this flow: the love of God and the love of one's neighbor. Jesus' unique teaching about the second of these commandments—"Who is my neighbor?"—begins with and then overflows the common Jewish interpretation by suggesting that potentially every one of his "brethren" made in the image of God is a neighbor for whom Christ died. The reality of this vision of neighbor love breaks into history on the Day of Pentecost in the Person and power of the Holy Spirit. From this day on, the Great Commandment to love the neighbor is also the Great Commission to take the Gospel to the nations. And finally, on Trinity Sunday, we come to understand that the First Commandment to love God with all our hearts is not something we strain to do but is a revelation of the love within the Godhead himself, the love of the Father and the Son and the Holy Spirit, a love which is born into and planted in our hearts and shown forth in our lives: "You've got to feel that Spirit deep inside to let it show in how we live our lives."

Finally, keeping Jesus' commandments is a matter of *joy*. "These things I have spoken to you," he says, "that my joy may be in you, and that your joy may be full. This is my commandment, that you love one another as I have loved you." When all is said and done, keeping God's commandments is enjoyable. For this reason, as Paul says and we sing: "Rejoice in the Lord always, and again I say rejoice."

Brothers and sisters at Redeemer, on this Trinity Sunday let us rejoice and praise God for his inestimable grace and love! Loving and keeping his commandments is not burdensome. If we come to him, he will give us "abiding" peace and rest. This is why the Anglican liturgy, echoing Scripture, ends with this trinitarian blessing:

> The peace of God, which passes all understanding, keep your hearts and minds in the knowledge and love of God, and of his Son Jesus Christ our Lord; and the blessing of God Almighty, the Father, the Son, and the Holy Ghost, be amongst you, and remain with you always. Amen.

BASIC BELIEVING:
THE APOSTLES' CREED

Creeds in the Bible

DEUTERONOMY 26:1–11; 1 CORINTHIANS 15:1–11

May the words of my mouth and the meditations of our hearts be always acceptable in your sight, O Lord, our Rock and our Redeemer.

I am beginning a series of sermons today on the Apostles' Creed with the title "Basic Believing," because that is the meaning of the word creed or *credo*—"I believe."

I am going to begin by addressing two negatives, two bad raps on the Creeds. The first objection to the Creeds is that they are about "beliefs," dead, wooden "doctrines" about God in contrast with the pure spiritual realities of "trusting the Father God," "walking with Jesus," "feeling the Spirit moving in your heart."

Many years ago, I heard a song by the Cameron Family titled "The Holy Ghost Will Set Your Feet a Dancing." One stanza went like this:

> Now many saints are cold and bound by unbelief today,
> They want the blessings of the Lord but worry what men say,
> O, let the Lord have full control, from dead traditions part,
> And he will set you free within, you'll have a dancing heart.

There is an element of truth in this accusation against creeds. Knowing the Creeds as a set of answers to quiz questions about God is somewhat like knowing about the Ten Commandments and then going out and breaking every one of them. Similarly, a confirmand can stand before the bishop and recite the Creed with crossed fingers, only to walk out of the building a committed atheist. That's called hypocrisy, and it is not limited to creeds. I had an employee in Uganda, a member of the Miracle Church, who could pray up a storm at our staff meetings, even as he stole money out of the till. He had a dancing heart all right, along with itchy fingers.

The Creeds are somewhat like the Ten Commandments. They set the boundaries that channel genuine faith and piety, just as the commandments channel genuine acts of love. They came into existence as various heretics challenged or distorted the biblical Gospel. And most of the ancient heresies are hardy perennials. They may pop up again with different names, but the satanic deception is always the same: not believing that Jesus Christ is the Son of God and that salvation and eternal life are found in his name alone (1 John 5:12).

Years ago, a student wag at Trinity Seminary referred to the candles on the Lord's Table as the landing lights on the Holy Spirit's runway. The articles of the Creed are something like that. So to those like the Cameron Family who disparage the Creeds, I say, take them for what they are: landing lights which liberate our spirits to take off in worship of the true God and to land safely back in reality.

The second objection to the Creeds is that they are not found in the Bible. This objection goes back to the Protestant Reformation and continues today in many free churches. The Reformers discovered the truth and power of the Word in Scripture, and they tossed out many of the traditions of the Roman Catholic Church. Some radicals among them argued that Scripture was not only sufficient for salvation but sufficient for everything. You had to find a text to brush your teeth in the morning (okay, I exaggerate—when did toothbrushes come in?). This mindset led these biblicists to argue that since you could not find the word "Trinity" in the Bible, then the doctrine of the Trinity was to be rejected as some kind of false flag meant to lead believers astray. "Nothing but the Bible," they said.

The Anglican Reformers phrased the question of Bible and doctrine more carefully. They said: "Holy Scripture contains all things necessary for salvation so that whatsoever is not read therein nor may be proved thereby is not to be required of anyone as an article of the Faith" (Article 6). First of all, they saw the main purpose of the Bible as proclaiming salvation through the death and resurrection of Jesus Christ. Other matters, like the best economic system or end of life issues might combine elements of divine revelation and practical reason. Secondly, they spoke of reading and proving a particular article of faith. From this premise, they believed that the doctrine of the Trinity could be demonstrated from various texts of the Bible, even if the word "Trinity" did not appear. In this regard, the Reformers were in agreement with the early church. The Church Fathers who authored the Creeds never doubted that their doctrine could be proved from the Bible.

It is true that the Bible has a power that the Creeds do not. Men and women have been converted reading the Bible alone. The new Anglican archbishop of Sydney, Australia, Kanishka Raffel, grew up a Buddhist from Sri Lanka who came to faith by simply picking up the Gospel of John and reading it. The Creeds usually come after conversion to clarify and form the faith of new converts. And this is absolutely necessary. The New Testament and church history are full of converts who have gone astray and led others astray by half-believing the truth and cherry-picking verses of Scripture.

There is an even deeper fallacy in posing the Bible against the Creeds: the Bible *itself* contains creeds! The simplest creed in the Old Testament is called the "Shema": "Hear, O Israel: The LORD our God, the LORD is one" (Deut 6:4). This creed was Jesus' starting point in teaching about two Great Commandments (Mark 12:29).

The Shema teaches about who God is. He is the Great I AM. There is another creed in the Old Testament that speaks about what he does. This creed is used in a thanksgiving ritual, in the same way we recite the Creed within the service. You'll find it in our first reading today.

> A wandering Aramean was my father. And he went down into Egypt and sojourned there, few in number, and there he became a nation, great, mighty, and populous. And the Egyptians treated us harshly and humiliated us and laid on us hard labor. Then we cried to the LORD, the God of our fathers, and the LORD heard our voice and saw our affliction, our toil, and our oppression. And the LORD brought us out of Egypt with a mighty hand and an outstretched arm, with great deeds of terror, with signs and wonders. And he brought us into this place and gave us this land, a land flowing with milk and honey.

This creed is a summary of the mighty acts of God for his people: calling the patriarchs—Abraham, Isaac, and Jacob—delivering the Israelites from Egypt and bringing them into the Promised Land.

Likewise, the New Testament has short and long creeds concerning Jesus Christ. "Jesus is Lord!" (1 Cor 12:3) is the briefest confession of who he is. Given the fact that "Lord" in Greek (*kyrios*) is the word used in the Hebrew Bible to translate the sacred name YHWH, Christians were in effect saying from early on: "Jesus is God." At the same time, they were not giving up the core monotheistic faith of the Old Testament; rather, they were moving it in a "trinitarian" direction. Here is how St. Paul put it:

> For although there may be so-called gods in heaven or on earth—as indeed there are many "gods" and many "lords"—yet for us there is one God the Father, from whom are all things and for whom we exist, and one Lord Jesus Christ, through whom are all things and through whom we exist. (1 Cor 8:5–6)

Paul is not making this up from whole cloth. The cloth of an early creed is already there. When he says this teaching is *for us*, he means this is the common teaching of all the apostles.

Just as the Old Testament talks about who God is and what he does, the same is true of the apostolic tradition. Here is St. Paul again (our second reading today):

> Now I would remind you, brothers, of the gospel I preached to you, which you received, in which you stand, and by which you are being saved, if you hold fast to the word I preached to you—unless you believed in vain. For I delivered to you as of first importance what I also received: that Christ died for our sins in accordance with the Scriptures, that he was buried, that he was raised on the third day in accordance with the Scriptures, and that he appeared to Cephas, then to the twelve. Then he appeared to more than five hundred brothers at one time, most of whom are still alive, though some have fallen asleep. Then he appeared to James, then to all the apostles. Last of all, as to one untimely born, he appeared also to me…Whether then it was I or they, so we preach and so you believed.

This passage is one of the clearest statements of the Apostles' Creed in the Bible. Let's notice several things about it. First, Paul calls it the *gospel* that he preached to them. This gospel is none other than the Good News of salvation, "in which you are being saved." He goes on to say that the Corinthians "received" it, and receiving is believing, as he makes clear at the end: "so we preach and so you believed." Paul is not talking about some abstract concept for theologians to ponder but the very heart of the Christian faith itself.

Secondly, Paul describes himself as a kind of middle-man in conveying this Gospel. He says that he delivered to them what he himself had received. The word for "receive" here means "handing over," and handing over is what we call tradition. So Gospel and Scripture are not at odds with tradition.

Thirdly, what Paul is handing over is apostolic tradition, i.e., it is eyewitness testimony of those apostles who followed Jesus and witnessed his death and resurrection, many of whom were still alive when Paul writes. Paul of course describes his own encounter with Jesus on the road to Damascus as a special belated resurrection appearance, but the risen Lord did not communicate the content of this Gospel to him; rather, Paul received it through the other apostles.

Finally, the content which Paul gives here matches up pretty closely to the middle part of the Creeds:

> Christ died for our sins in accordance with the Scriptures,
> he was buried, and
> he was raised on the third day in accordance with the Scriptures…

So in this short passage, we learn the content of what Paul preached and taught. We also can see how he continues to teach them by reminding them. One might say that is exactly what we do when we recite the Creed in the church service. We are reminding ourselves of the truth on which we stand and by which we are saved.

The substance of the creed in Corinthians is expanded in other New Testament writings, where it is referred to as the deposit of faith. Here is one example, where Paul briefly summarizes the deposit for Timothy:

> He was manifested in the flesh,
> vindicated by the Spirit,
> seen by angels,
> proclaimed among the nations,
> believed on in the world,
> taken up in glory. (1 Tim 3:16)

Here Paul is passing on a piece of teaching that includes the incarnation and ascension of Christ, the role of the Holy Spirit, and the Great Commission to the nations.

I am about to stop, but I want to make one more observation about the creeds in the Bible. In some churches, people sing the Creed. In fact, if you listen to recordings of the Mass, the *Credo* is a major section. Personally, I don't find the particular language of the Creed easy to sing, but there is a connection between the Bible, hymns, and the Creeds. Let's take "Holy, Holy, Holy" which we sang two weeks ago on Trinity Sunday.

Notice that the hymn begins with the Old Testament vision of Isaiah in the temple of the exalted one Lord of hosts. But the threefold repetition of "holy" suggests that this one Lord is more complicated than the mere number one. This one God is in three Persons, as taught by the Creed.

> Holy, holy, holy!
> Lord God Almighty!
> Early in the morning
> Our song shall rise to thee.
> Holy, holy, holy!
> Merciful and mighty,
> God in three Persons,
> Blessed Trinity!

The Holy Trinity is a great mystery awaiting further revelation, and the hymn then explains one reason: human sin.

> Holy, holy, holy!
> Though the darkness hide thee,
> Though the eye of sinful man
> Thy glory may not see.
> Only thou art holy;
> There is none beside thee,
> Perfect in power, in love and purity.

In contrast with human blindness and weakness, God himself is known by his holiness: "perfect in power, in love and purity." The third verse moves to a cosmic hymn of praise:

Holy, holy, holy!
Lord God Almighty!
All thy works shall praise thy name
In earth and sky and sea.
Holy, holy, holy!
Merciful and mighty,
God in three Persons,
Blessed Trinity!

This final verse recalls the book of Revelation, where the slain Lamb enters into history, revealing the triune nature of God, and the entire creation breaks out in a hymn of praise.

This is the same message as that of the Apostles' Creed, and I shall be coming back to the Trinity next week when I begin with "I believe in God the Father, Maker of heaven and earth."

Brothers and sisters, the Creeds are not dead and wooden, unless our hearts are cold and stony. Creeds are not unbiblical, as they are embedded in the Scripture and summarize the "faith once for all delivered to the saints."

So as we spend the next weeks examining the Apostles' Creed, line by line, let's ingest its truth with a reverent and thankful heart and be prepared to sing with the angels and archangels: "Holy, holy, holy, Lord God of power and might. Hosanna in the highest!"

God the Father and Creator

PSALM 96; EPHESIANS 3:14–21; LUKE 11:1–13

May the words of my mouth and the meditations of our hearts be always acceptable in your sight, O Lord, our Rock and our Redeemer.

Last week I introduced the sermon series on the Apostles' Creed by noting that the Bible itself, Old and New Testaments, contains creeds. In particular, the New Testament contains short creeds that are trinitarian and that recount in brief the saving life, death, and resurrection of Jesus Christ.

If we look at the Apostles' Creed, we shall easily see that it has three sections, devoted to the three Persons of the Trinity. The first is the shortest: "I believe in God the Father Almighty, Creator of heaven and earth." It is short but it is packed with important meaning. I want to unpack two elements of this short section: who is God the Father, and how did he create the heaven and earth?

What about God the Father? Let me begin with an observation. I'll bet you have heard more sermons about being a good parent or a good father—especially on Father's Day—than you have heard about God the Father. Several decades ago, a leader in the charismatic movement wrote a book titled *The Forgotten Father*—a really good book that! The book itself was soon forgotten, although when I was looking through the Trinity Seminary library on this subject *The Forgotten Father* was the only book there! There is a reason for this absence, I think: the doctrine of God the Father, like the Trinity itself, is a *mystery*. John's gospel states this plainly at the end of the prologue. Here is my translation: "No one has ever seen God the Father; the only-begotten Son, who dwells in the bosom of the Father, the Son has made the Father known" (John 1:18). Later in the gospel, Jesus' disciple Philip says to Jesus, "Show us the Father." Jesus answers:

> Have I been with you so long, and you still do not know me, Philip? Whoever has seen me has seen the Father. How can you say, "Show us the Father?" Do you not believe that I am in the Father and the Father is in me? (John 14:9–10a)

Of course, Jesus is not saying he is the Father nor is he saying that the name Father is mumbo-jumbo, unrelated to human fatherhood. But this text should warn us not to project our own experiences and relationships with our fathers—who may have been wonderful or horrible dads—on God. God the Father of Jesus as revealed in the Scriptures is both like and unlike any human father, and believing in him has little to do with helpful tips on fathering.

As I have said before, the biblical doctrine of God the Father is totally strange to the world's religions. Polytheistic religions have father gods, but they tend to be either senile or promiscuous. Worse yet, many father gods have murdered their fathers. Zeus, for instance, overthrew his father Cronos, who himself had castrated his father Uranos. Although Zeus had a wife, Hera, he raped a number of goddesses and women and even a man. Among the Canaanites, El was the senile father God, whereas Baal was the promiscuous god of fertility.

Among monotheistic religions, Islam sees Allah as an impersonal monad, beyond any human analogy, and is quite explicit in stating that he is not a father nor does he have a son. Among the Hebrews, God may on occasions be likened to a father, but he is never called "Father" as Jesus does. In one dispute with Jesus, the Jews allude to Jesus' illegitimacy, arguing: "We were not born of sexual immorality. We have one father, even God." Jesus sees through this ruse and answers: "If God were your Father, you would love me, for I came from God and I am here. I came not of my own accord, but he sent me" (John 8:41–42).

We can only understand the Creed's "I believe in God the Father" in the terms that Jesus set out when he taught his disciples to pray "Our Father in heaven," which was his unique way of praying himself: "Abba, Father." There is no "Father God," no "Fatherhood of God and Brotherhood of Man" apart from "the God and Father of our Lord Jesus Christ," a phrase that occurs in the salutations of most of Paul's letters. There is no heavenly Father who is not the One God of the Old Testament, who identifies himself as "I AM."

The idea of God as essential Being is shared by the Father and the Son in the act of creation. Here is the way Paul describes it in the short creed I mentioned last week:

> For although there may be so-called gods in heaven or on earth—as indeed there are many "gods" and many "lords"—yet for us there is one God the Father, from whom are all things and for whom we exist, and one Lord Jesus Christ, through whom are all things and through whom we exist. (1 Cor 8:5–6)

God the Father is the *source* "of all things," including us; Jesus Christ is the *mediator* "through whom" all things," and we, come into existence.

The Church Fathers went one step further in inferring that the Father as the Source applies not only to the created order but to what is called the "essential Trinity," God in his very Being. From all eternity, the Father has a priority within the Trinity. The Father *begets* the Son and the Spirit *proceeds* from the Father. You can't reverse the order without talking nonsense. Begetting, that's what fathers do. If mothers are "birthing persons," as some today suggest, then fathers are "begetting persons." But to be more precise, God the Father is the only true Begetter: human fathers pro-create those whom God has already ordained for life.

In many cultures, the father is also the bearer of the family name. God the Father is the name-bearer of the Trinity. This is why the vast majority of New Testament references are to "God the Father" or "the God and Father of our Lord Jesus Christ." In our epistle today, Paul prays to "the Father, from whom every household in heaven and earth is named" (Eph 3:14–15). The universe is a divine *patriarchy*. This is not to say that the Father does not gladly share his "*God*hood" with Jesus. Again, Paul describes the Son's emptying himself on the Cross and then being exalted to God's right hand and given the "name that is above every name" (Phil 2:9). Jesus is God, no doubt about it.

God the Father is Almighty. Indeed, our psalm today begins by acclaiming "the Lord reigns!" But the divine King is also the supreme delegator. From eternity he has enthroned his Son as Lord over the whole creation. Jesus is Messiah, anointed King, and this explains the second part of Paul's greetings: "from God the Father and the Lord Jesus Messiah." The risen Jesus shall reign over all history until the day when, having defeated all his enemies including death and Satan, he hands the creation back to the Father, and God will be all in all (1 Cor 15:28).

Now we come to the second aspect of God the Father, according to the Creed: he is creator of heaven and earth. This doctrine takes us back to the first verse of the Bible: "In the beginning, God created the heaven and earth." Again, many ancient religions have myths of the beginnings, but only Judaism, Islam and Christianity claim that God transcends the cosmos, that is, that God existed "before all worlds." The Hebrew word that translates "create," is a special word, distinct from the words to "make" or "shape." God not only shapes the world, the cosmos, but he brings it into existence out of nothing. There was a time when the world was not.

Most heresies in the early church derived from philosophers and theologians who wanted to defend the sole supremacy of God the Father. The famous heretic Arius claimed that the Son was an exalted divine but created being. "There was a time when he was not," he taught. In effect, Arius made Jesus Christ out to be a gigantic angel.

Speaking of angels, while the Apostles' Creed says God the Father is "creator of heaven and earth," the Nicene Creed adds "and of all things visible and invisible." A footnote here: the phrase "all things visible and invisible" was changed in the 1979 Episcopal Prayer Book to "all things seen and unseen." But these are not synonyms: "seen and unseen" suggests that heavenly and earthly things are in the same material order of nature: we just haven't built a telescope or microscope powerful enough to see them, but someday we will. No, "visible and invisible" means that God has created entities that exist in a completely different realm or dimension. Paraphrasing Shakespeare's *Hamlet*, there are more things in heaven and earth than can be discovered by modern science.

This is no minor matter. One of the offenses that certain people take to the Genesis creation account is the fact that God created light on the first day but the sun, moon and stars on the fourth day. The Bible is making an important point here: the fundamental laws of God that underlie all material reality precede it logically, if not temporally. Modern thought and much empirical science works from a philosophy of materialism, that matter is all there is. But truly, this is absurd.

Put philosophically, there has to be a *metaphysics* undergirding the *physics* of everything that is seen. Theologically, there is what Dorothy Sayers called "the mind of the maker." Recently, our family watched a movie titled *The Man Who Knew Infinity*. It is based on the true life story of a mathematician named Srinivasa Ramanujan, an impoverished Indian in Madras, who was a mathematical genius. He gets an opportunity to study at Cambridge University with a leading mathematician, D.L. Hardy. Hardy, a self-proclaimed atheist, recognizes Ramanujan's genius, and under his tutelage Ramanujan devises the "partitions formula," which solved a puzzle which many mathematicians had considered insoluble. At one point, Hardy asks Ramanujan where he gets his insight, and he says: "I get it from my God." "An equation is nothing unless it expresses the mind of God," he says. Hardy replies: "I just can't believe in God, but I believe in you." Hardy, it turns out, is the close-minded fundamentalist of the two.

The Christian doctrine of creation is not opposed to the discoveries of modern science. It simply says that there is a Wisdom, a *Logos*, that informs and indwells these discoveries but is of a different order. The universe may have begun with the Big Bang in the order of time, but the laws of physics and time itself precede the Big Bang logically if not temporally.

Genesis goes on: "God said, 'Let us make man in our image, after our likeness'" (Gen 1:26). This little sentence reveals a lot about God and a lot about us. Put simply, God can "talk to himself" and when he creates our species male and female, he makes us conversationalists too. I had a student at Trinity Seminary once who had converted from Judaism. When I asked her how this had happened, she said it was because of the way this verse portrays God. Nabeel Qureshi, a devout Muslim who converted to Christianity, compares Tahwid, the Islamic doctrine of Allah's oneness, and the triune God of the Creed this way: "Allah is a monad; he is not inherently relational. Yahweh, on the other hand, is three persons; he is inherently relational." Love is therefore the central principle of God's identity. "God is love," as St. John puts it simply (1 John 4:8). It is out of that selfless love that he created this universe.

The love of the Father is hinted at throughout the Old Testament, but it is Jesus who directs us to the depth of his fatherly love. Our preacher this past Lent, talking about the Lord's Prayer, drew our attention to the scandalous behavior of the prodigal father, who hitched up his robes and ran to meet his returning son. In our gospel lesson today, Jesus moves rhetorically from the natural generosity of a father in providing food to his children, to the supernatural generosity of the heavenly Father who gives his Holy Spirit to those who ask him (Luke 11:13). This is the Father "who did not spare his own Son but gave him up for us all," and this being the Father's nature, "how will he not also with him graciously give us all things?" (Rom 8:32).

Fathers, mothers, sons and daughters, brothers and sisters. As we honor our earthly fathers this day, let us above all be sure to "bless the God and Father of our Lord Jesus Christ, who has blessed us in Christ with every spiritual blessing in the heavenly places" (Eph 1:3).

Let us pray:

> O heavenly Father, you have filled the world with beauty: Open our eyes to behold your gracious hand in all your works; that, rejoicing in your whole creation, we may learn to serve you with gladness; for the sake of him through whom all things were made, your Son Jesus Christ our Lord. Amen.

God the Son, True God and True Man

PSALM 8; HEBREWS 2:5–18; MARK 9:1–13

May the words of my mouth and the meditations of our hearts be always acceptable in your sight, O Lord, our Rock and our Redeemer.

As we continue this series of catechetical sermons, let's move forward from the affirmation of God the Father to God the Son. The Prayer Book version of the Apostles' Creed says this:

> I believe in God the Father almighty,
> creator of heaven and earth.
> I believe in Jesus Christ, his only Son, our Lord.

There is a small discrepancy here: there is no second "I believe" in the original text, which says simply: "I believe in God the Father Almighty, Creator of Heaven and Earth, and in Jesus Christ, his only Son, our Lord."

The Prayer Book is emphasizing the distinct trinitarian Persons: the Father, the Son, and the Holy Spirit. The original Creed is focusing on the unique nature of Jesus Christ, who is true God and true man. The early church had to wrestle with two errors concerning the Son of God. One error called Docetism claimed the Son only *seemed* to be human but was really a manifestation of the one God. According to this view, Jesus was a ghost.

The other error was Arianism, which claimed that the Son was a creature of God, a supreme angel. Arius claimed of the Son that "there was a time when he was not." Arius was half-right. It *is* true to say that there was a time when Jesus of Nazareth was not, which is any time BC. Indeed that is exactly what BC and AD mark: the Son of God became the Son of Man, whose DNA came from a young woman of Nazareth. As AD began, the Son of God passed through every phase of human development, from the womb to the manger, from the carpenter's bench to the Cross. Praise Jesus!

What the Creed teaches is that Jesus Christ is one with God the Father and Creator before all time, *and* one with the race of Adam, the day six creature of dust. We can only grasp the marvelous Good News of Jesus Christ when we can grasp his possessing both natures—divine and human—fully, not half-and-half, but all in all. The Person of Jesus Christ is just as great a mystery as the Trinity, and it was just as hotly contested in the Church that produced the Creeds.

So with this creedal truth in mind, let's look at two Old Testament texts. The first (Gen 1:27–28) comes from the beginning: "So God created man in his own image, in the image of God he created him; male and female he created them." God proceeds to bless them and give them dominion over all the creatures in earth and sky and sea, that is, of all things visible. But what about things invisible (to us)? The Bible says there is an invisible heavenly world, the realm of angels. I once wrote a book titled *Angels of Light, Powers of Darkness*. I believe the angels are out there, or up there. Do you? And if so, aren't they exalted above us (and fallen below us) in the hierarchy of heaven?

The book of Genesis does not raise this question, but Psalm 8 does. Here's my translation:

> O Lord, our Lord, how majestic is your name in all the earth,
> you who sit enthroned above the heavens…
> When I look at your heavens, the work of your fingers,
> the moon and the stars, which you have set in place,
> *what is man* that you are mindful of him,
> and the *son of man* that you care for him?
> See, you have made him a little lower than the angels,
> *and yet* you have crowned him with glory and honor
> and have given him dominion over the works of your hands
> and have put all things under his feet. (verses 1, 2–5)

The Psalmist is looking through his telescope at the orderly cosmos, with God enthroned at the top, next the invisible world of the angels, and only then the earth creatures. And what amazes him is that God over-reaches and bypasses the spirit world and the angels to crown mankind. "What is man and the son of man?" he asks. The phrase "son of man" is particularly significant. A "son of man" is by definition "born of woman"; a "son of man" is mortal, he passes away like the flowers of the field (Isa 40:7–8). How can the divine, eternal Father, David asks, share a throne with such a weak and transient creature?

The Old Testament leaves this conundrum unanswered. The New Testament letter to the Hebrews picks up the matter in light of Jesus. The author of Hebrews begins in much the way John's gospel begins with the Word-made-flesh, except in this case it is *the Son-made-flesh*:

> Long ago, [he says], at many times and in many ways, God spoke to our fathers by the prophets, but in these last days he has spoken to us by his Son, whom he appointed the heir of all things, through whom also he created the world. He is the radiance of the glory of God and the exact imprint of his nature, and he upholds the universe by the word of his power. (Heb 1:1–3)

The Father created the world through his Son, and the Son is the *exact imprint* of his glorious nature—the Nicene Creed uses this language "being of one nature—one Being, one Substance—with the Father." St. Paul puts this same doctrine in other words, saying "Christ is the image of the invisible God, the firstborn of all creation" (Col 1:15). God can only beget God, and God's Son is begotten of the Father before all worlds.

But then, how can he also be a mortal "son of man," an AD man? That is the great mystery. That is the glory of the Incarnation. In our epistle today, the author of Hebrews reaches back to Psalm 8:

> It has been testified somewhere, "What is man, that you are mindful of him, or the son of man, that you care for him? You made him *for a little while* lower than the angels; you have crowned him with glory and honor, putting everything in subjection under his feet."

The Father has crowned his Son Lord of everything from all eternity. He is the true image of the invisible God. He is the true Man, prophesied in the psalm. But, Hebrews goes on to note: "At present"—in the "little while" of this age, BC and AD—we do not yet see everything in subjection to him." What do we see then?

> We see him who for a little while was made lower than the angels, namely *Jesus*, crowned with glory and honor because of the suffering of death, so that by the grace of God he might taste death for everyone.

The decisive event of that little while, the hinge of history, happened on Calvary in 30 AD. There, in the unfathomable love of the Father, he crowned his Son. The crown of thorns which Jesus bore was just that, a crown of victory over sin and death. "It was fitting," the author continues—"fitting!"—"that [the Father], for whom and by whom all things exist, should make the founder of their salvation perfect through suffering in bringing many sons to glory."

The Creed gives the answer to the psalmist's question, "what is man?" and "who is the Son of Man?" And this answer is full of Good News, news of comfort and joy because the "fittingness" of the incarnation is also the fittingness of the atonement, planned for all eternity. In his book *Why God Became Man,* St. Anselm argues the connection of incarnation and atonement in this way: the debt of sin is incurred by man alone against God, and God alone can cancel that debt, so only he who is God and man can offer the perfect sacrifice for our redemption. The truth of the Creed needs to be sung, not merely said, as Charles Wesley knew when he wrote: "Amazing Love, how can it be, that Thou my God, shouldst die for me!"

So far I have been describing the divine Sonship of Christ. But of course, the Creed also speaks of Jesus Christ our Lord, and as I say, Jesus was a real man living in Palestine two thousand years ago. So let's turn to the gospels and see what they say about Jesus. In particular, did Jesus know from Christmas morning that he was the divine Son of YHWH, the God of Israel? Reading Christ's mind is speculative, but I think one can say that like any human being, Jesus "increased in wisdom and stature" (Luke 2:52), including awareness of his Sonship. St. Luke gives a particular moment when the young Jesus, at the time of his Bar Mitzvah, separated himself from his parents, telling them: "I must be about my Father's business." Already at this age, Jesus' reference to "my Father" sets him apart from any Jew of that day.

More than a decade later, Jesus presented himself for baptism by John, and the Father's voice sounded from heaven: "You are my Son; this day I have begotten you." This was the public announcement of Jesus' Sonship—not, as some heretics ancient and modern have it, his divine begetting—and the start of his three-year ministry. He was immediately tested by Satan's "if you are the Son of God…" and refused the bait. While he repeatedly demonstrated his Sonship through teaching and miracle, he refused to use the title "Son of God." Instead, he referred to himself as "Son of Man," mortal man, even as he predicted his resurrection. "The Son of Man," he said, "is going to be delivered into the hands of men, and they will kill him. And when he is killed, after three days he will rise" (Mark 9:31).

As his time drew near and he prepared to go to Jerusalem and the Cross, another revelation of his Sonship occurred (our gospel lesson today).

> And after six days Jesus took with him Peter and James and John, and led them up a high mountain by themselves. And he was transfigured before them, and his clothes became radiant, intensely white, as no one on earth could bleach them. And there appeared to them Elijah with Moses, and they were talking with Jesus.

The scene on the mountain recalls Moses the lawgiver on Mount Sinai, asking to see God face to face (he was denied). Then there was Elijah, who was taken into heaven on a chariot and expected back before the Day of the Lord (the second Elijah came girded in camel's hair and was beheaded). Moses and Elijah were seen talking to Jesus: he was transfigured in glory; they were not. Their inspired words in the Old Testament point to Jesus, but it is God the Father himself who speaks the final word: "This is my beloved Son; listen to him."

Flabbergasted, Peter didn't get it: "Rabbi," he says, "it is good that we are here. Let us make three shrines, one for you and one for Moses and one for Elijah." One for the lawgiver, one for the prophet, and one for the rabbi here! Once the vision ceased, of course, it was only the human Jesus who remained with them and told them not to repeat this vision until he had risen from the dead, which was not hard to do, since they did not know what he meant. But the Day of Pentecost soon came when Peter would proclaim:

> This Jesus God raised up, and of that we all are witnesses…Let all the house of Israel therefore know for certain that God has made him both Lord and Christ, this Jesus whom you crucified. (Acts 2:32, 36)

Brothers and sisters, the Creeds say nothing that is not found in the Bible. It is simply expressed in a concise formula. But the early church did not stop with Creeds alone. One of the earliest hymns is called the *Te Deum Laudamus* ("We Praise You, O God")—I did a podcast on this—which is directed to the triune God. Here is the section of praise to God the Son:

> You, Christ, are the king of glory,
> the eternal Son of the Father.
> When you took our flesh to set us free
> you humbly chose the Virgin's womb.
> You overcame the sting of death
> and opened the kingdom of heaven to all believers.
> You are seated at God's right hand in glory.
> We believe that you will come to be our judge.
> Come then, Lord ["Maranatha!"] and help your people,
> bought with the price of your own blood,
> and bring us with your saints
> to glory everlasting.

The Creed is all about love, God's love for us. "For God so loved the world, that he gave his only Son, that whoever believes in him should not perish but have eternal life" (John 3:16). Another hymn attributed to Thomas à Kempis a thousand years after the *Te Deum* sounds the same praise of God the Son. It begins this way:

> O love, how deep, how broad, how high,
> how passing thought and fantasy,
> that God, the Son of God, should take
> our mortal form for mortals' sake!

It concludes with a trinitarian doxology:

> All glory to our Lord and God
> for love so deep, so high, so broad;
> the Trinity whom we adore
> forever and forevermore.

To which we add, Amen!

Jesus Christ, God with Us, Man for Us

ISAIAH 7:1–14; ROMANS 5:9–19; MATTHEW 1:18–25

May the words of my mouth and the meditations of our hearts be always acceptable in your sight, O Lord, our Rock and our Redeemer.

In my sermon two weeks ago, I mentioned that the primary focus of the Apostles' Creed has to do with the triune God: Father, Son, and Holy Spirit. Hence it speaks in one breath of God the Father and his only Son. But when it speaks of "Jesus Christ our Lord," it moves directly into a brief narrative of his earthly life in the first thirty years of the first century: "conceived by the Holy Spirit and born of the Virgin Mary, suffered under Pontius Pilate, died and was buried."

So let's consider the Virgin Birth. I chose for our text the Old Testament prophecy from Isaiah chapter 7. Here is the context of this prophecy. In the year 732 BC, the mighty Assyrian chariots were bearing down on the petty kingdoms of Syria and Israel (the ten tribes of the Northern Kingdom). The kings of Syria and Israel tried desperately to force King Ahaz of Judah into a defensive alliance. Instead Ahaz made his own desperate appeal to the Assyrians for help. This short-term move would bring long-term disaster, as David's kingdom ultimately became a vassal state of the Near Eastern empires.

But the greater problem, according to Isaiah, was spiritual. Ahaz's deal-making revealed his lack of faith in Yahweh, the nation's God and protector. So Isaiah warns: "If you do not stand firm in your faith, you will not stand at all." The prophet then promises the king "a sign as deep as Sheol (the realm of the dead), and as high as heaven" to assure him, but Ahaz, with fake modesty protests: "I will not ask, and I will not put the LORD to the test." All right, God says, I'll give you the sign myself:

"Behold, the virgin shall conceive and bear a son, and they shall call his name Immanuel [God with us]."

Like many prophecies, this one had a short-term fulfillment: Ahaz did father a son Hezekiah, who became king and trusted God, and Judah survived for nearly a century after Syria and Israel were wiped off the map. But there was a much higher and deeper fulfilment of this promise, pointing to the messianic King, as announced by the prophet in this familiar text:

> For to us a child is born, to us a son is given; and the government shall be upon his shoulder, and his name shall be called Wonderful Counselor, Mighty God, Everlasting Father, Prince of Peace. Of the increase of his government and of peace there will be no end, on the throne of David and over his kingdom, to establish it and to uphold it with justice and with righteousness from this time forth and forevermore. The zeal of the LORD of hosts will do this. (Isa 9:6–7)

It was this promise which was fulfilled seven centuries later when the angel Gabriel announced to the Virgin Mary that she would conceive and bear a son named Jesus. Let me draw several connections with the original prophecy. First, the Virgin Birth was *initiated by God*: "The zeal of the Lord of Hosts will do this." Secondly, the Virgin Birth, or more precisely the virginal conception of Jesus, was a *miracle* as high as heaven. Women do not get pregnant without a man naturally, whatever tricks the magicians in our genetic labs are up to. Mary's husband-to-be knew this and needed a dream from on high to prevent him from putting her away.

Finally, Jesus Christ was true man and true God from the moment of his conception. The name Immanuel, God with us, meant something far deeper than God's intervention in the natural process of conception, as was the case with Sarah and Hannah in the Old Testament. While it is beyond any science to determine how God begot Jesus, it is nevertheless true that it was God himself, God the Holy Spirit, who so "overshadowed" Mary. For this reason, the early church revered Mary as *Theotokos,* "the God-bearer."

But the Creed also says he was "made man," and hence it is equally true that the Mother of God was also the "man-bearer." As I mentioned last week, Jesus referred to himself as "Son of Man," which clearly means "mortal man," born of woman and subject to the inexorable downward drag of death. The messianic line from David was a line of mortals, and

Jesus Christ, the man born to be king, was in that line. But Jesus' genealogy, according to Luke, stretches all the way back to Adam (Luke 3:38). Our epistle reading today takes us right back to Eden. St. Paul says:

> Therefore, just as sin came into the world through one man, and death through sin, and so death spread to all men because all sinned—for sin indeed was in the world before the law was given, but sin is not counted where there is no law. Yet death reigned from Adam to Moses, even over those whose sinning was not like the transgression of Adam, who was a type of the one who was to come.

Paul's portrait of Adam is pretty grim. It's not the God-like Adam walking naked around Eden; it's Adam, clothed in shame, fallen into the bondage of sin and death, cursed and cast out of Eden. That Adam, Paul says, is the prophetic figure of the true Son of Man. Adam foreshadows the broken and humiliated corpse of the man hanging on the Cross.

In linking Adam to the Cross, the New Testament writers were not demeaning Christ or God's good creation of mankind in his image. Just the opposite, Jesus is the true man, "one who in every respect has been tempted as we are, yet without sin" (Heb 4:15). The early church father Irenaeus developed a view that Christ "recapitulated," i.e., passed through, every stage of human life in order to redeem every bit of our humanity. A contemporary writer describes the Gospel story as "Jesus becoming Jesus." I might be so bold as to suggest that it was necessary for Jesus to reach the age of mature adulthood in order to bring us to full maturity "in Christ" (Eph 4:13; cf. John 7:6).

There is another dimension to the Immanuel prophecy. Jesus is *God with us*. In another passage, St. Paul says:

> Thus it is written, "The first man Adam became a living being"; the last Adam became a life-giving spirit. But it is not the spiritual that is first but the natural, and then the spiritual. The first man was from the earth, a man of dust; the second man is from heaven. As was the man of dust, so also are those who are of the dust, and as is the man of heaven, so also are those who are of heaven. Just as we have borne the image of the man of dust, we shall also bear the image of the man of heaven. (1 Cor 15:45–49)

True humanity cannot be understood only from below. Jesus cannot be understood only as a creature of dust, "from the earth, earthy," as the King James Version has it. The first Adam, even before the Fall, was incomplete, needing a partner; and even partnered, Adam and Eve were still incomplete, grasping at knowledge to live a good life. The second Adam fulfilled the divine image by being a man of the Spirit, conceived by the Spirit, baptized in the Spirit, his words being Spirit and Truth, and finally giving back his Spirit on the Cross. And he has promised his Spirit to those who believe in him and are born again. Justification by faith in Jesus, which is once for all, is accompanied by sanctification, which takes time, walking in the footsteps of Jesus.

So the Creed teaches us that Jesus Christ is Immanuel, God with us. It also teaches us that he is Man for us, and the Man for others, including our unexpected neighbors who are ready and waiting to hear the Gospel. The Nicene Creed, which supplements the Apostles' Creed, begins the section on Jesus saying "for us men and our salvation he came down from heaven…and became man."

The Creed, I repeat, is all about love, God's love for us: "For God so loved the world, that he gave his only Son, that whoever believes in him should not perish but have eternal life" (John 3:16). The love shared among the divine persons—the Father, the Son, and the Spirit—is all-sufficient, and out of the overflowing abundance of that love, God reached down in Jesus Christ and lived and died for us. Last week I referred to the hymn which begins:

> O love, how deep, how broad, how high,
> how passing thought and fantasy,
> that God, the Son of God, should take
> our mortal form for mortals' sake!

The hymn continues through the mighty acts of Jesus' life for us:

> For us baptized, for us he bore
> his holy fast and hungered sore,
> for us temptation sharp he knew;
> for us the tempter overthrew.
> For us he prayed; for us he taught;
> for us his daily works he wrought;

by words and signs and actions thus
still seeking not himself, but us.

Before I conclude, I want to mention one other way Jesus Christ continues to be present with us and for us—and that is in the Holy Communion. I would go so far as to say that for Anglicans, he is truly present with us in the Communion. Our view is a middle way between two misunderstandings. We do not believe that Christ's presence in the elements of bread and wine can be localized and concretized; that view, called transubstantiation, rationalizes the divine mystery of our union with Christ. On the other hand, his presence is not merely symbolic, a kind of mnemonic device; Anglicans reject that view, called memorialism, which is also rationalistic and shortchanges Jesus' words when he said "This is my Body and my Blood." Anglicans, along with many Lutheran and Reformed Christians, believe in the real and spiritual Presence of Christ in the Sacrament. The risen Christ is seated bodily at the right hand of God, yet by his Spirit and through faith we *participate* in his Body and Blood (1 Cor 10:16).

In the Eucharist, Christ is not merely present, he is present *for us*, as he promised: "Take this…for the forgiveness of sins"; and our proper response to this gracious presence is *thanksgiving*. That is what the word "Eucharist" means: thanksgiving. That is the spirit of our Eucharistic prayer this day:

> We earnestly desire your fatherly goodness mercifully to accept this, our sacrifice of praise and thanksgiving…Take and eat this in remembrance that Christ died for you, and feed on him in your heart by faith, with thanksgiving…Drink this in remembrance that Christ's blood was shed for you, and be thankful.

To sum up, the Creeds teach that Jesus Christ is the promised Immanuel—God with us—conceived by the Holy Spirit and born of the Virgin Mary. He is also the true Man given for us on the Cross and present in the Sacrament of his Body and Blood. In light of this, let us now, in the words of the 1979 Prayer Book, "draw near with faith, and take this Sacrament to [our] comfort."

Jesus Christ: "When I Am Lifted Up"

ISAIAH 52:13–53:12; ROMANS 6:1–11; MARK 10:32–45

May the words of my mouth and the meditations of our hearts be always acceptable in your sight, O Lord, our Rock and our Redeemer.

I grew up as an unbeliever and only became a Christian and was baptized and confirmed when I was half-way through college. So I have this little doubting Thomas voice etched in my conscience that can comprehend the question "Is it true?" "Is God for real?" By contrast, my wife Peggy is a cradle Episcopalian. When she was in college, in response to a class lecture, she tried to think as if God didn't exist; she lasted only a day or two before giving up the experiment. God just had to be there!

The revolution in my thinking was not just about God but about Jesus. In my preteen years, I attended a Unitarian Sunday School. I remember they had us read the earliest Gospel of Mark where Jesus cries, "My God, my God, why have you abandoned me?" and where on Easter morning, the story ends abruptly with the women running away in fear because they had come to the wrong tomb. Then they took us to the latest Gospel of John where the risen Jesus is walking through walls, telling Thomas to stick his hand in the nail and spear holes from the Cross and then levitating out of sight. You see, they said, the early church perverted the kindly moral teacher of Nazareth into the walking and talking God of the Creeds. A decade later, when I went to seminary, I learned a gussied-up name for this view. It's called "the development of Christology."

Back to my conversion. When I began to read the whole Bible for myself, I found a very different portrait of Jesus Christ and came to the conclusion that C.S. Lewis was right when he said Jesus either was mad or he was bad or he was God. The Creeds come down squarely on the

"God" side of this matter: Jesus Christ, the Son of God from all eternity, was conceived by the Holy Spirit, born of the Virgin Mary, raised from the dead, ascended into heaven, and will come again in glory. Equally, as I said last week, the Creed says Jesus was fully human, born of the Virgin Mary and that he suffered and was crucified, dead and buried under Pontius Pilate, the Roman Procurator in Palestine in 30 AD.

Last week I described Jesus' incarnation not just as the moment of his virginal conception (true though it is) but as "Jesus becoming Jesus." With some fear and trembling (for who can know the mind of the Lord?), I am suggesting that Jesus came to discover his own identity, mission, and destiny as he lived out his life, and he conveyed this life to his apostles, who in turn passed it on to us in the New Testament. This apostolic Good News about Jesus, as summarized in the Creeds, is the only reason on this earth that we can hope for eternal life with God.

Surely the most important influence on the boy Jesus was his immersion in the Scriptures of the Old Testament. By the age of twelve, he was already confounding the Jewish teachers of the Law with his mastery of the Bible. He was already a rabbi, a prodigy. But beyond his comprehensive knowledge of Scripture, Jesus brought an inspired insight that was utterly unique. And this insight is at the heart of the gospel and of the Creeds. It is found in our reading today from the prophet Isaiah.

The book of Isaiah has sometimes been called "the Fifth Gospel" because it is filled with prophecies of Christ. Last week we read from early chapters which speak of the Virgin Birth of a Son whose name will be "Wonderful Counselor, Mighty God, Everlasting Father, Prince of Peace" (Isa 7:14; 9:6). This is the classic description of the Messiah, the greater heir of David's line: the government of the universe, not just of Israel, will rest on his shoulders. Jewish interpreters took these titles as hyperbole. The Messiah was god-like, but not God himself. But Jesus understood the prophecy literally: God himself was coming in person, and this is something new, it is indeed Good News. In chapter 40, God instructs the nation to witness God's coming: "Get you up to a high mountain, O Zion, herald of good news…say to the cities of Judah, 'Behold your God!'" (Isa 40:9). The Good News—and I think Jesus read it this way—is that God the Divine King is coming in Person to save his people and indeed the whole world. This insight is revolutionary, and if false, it is blasphemous: the Messiah and the Great I AM are one and the same, or as the Nicene Creed claims, Jesus Christ is "of one substance with the Father."

But Jesus noted something else equally radical in this latter section of Isaiah. Embedded in it are four passages describing a figure called "the Servant of the Lord." Modern scholars call these four texts "Servant Songs." When we first meet the Servant in chapter 42, he is identified with the people of Israel, recalling God's promise to Abraham that in his seed, the nations of the world would be blessed (Gen 12:3). Now the Lord repeats this promise to his Servant: "I will make you as a light for the nations, that my salvation may reach to the end of the earth" (Isa 49:6). Why do I think Jesus knew this passage? We can hear in it an echo of Jesus' Great Commission to go into the world and preach Good News to the nations.

Not just the Great Commission, but the great Commissioner: "All authority in heaven and earth are given to me," Jesus says. Isaiah's vision of the unique Son of God, born of a Virgin, was confirmed when Jesus was baptized and the Voice from heaven said: "You are my Son: this day I have begotten you." For most Jews, the title Son suggested the power and majesty of the coming Messiah, the second King David. But Jesus—and only Jesus—turned the title "Son" into "Son of Man," the second Adam, born under the curse of sin and death, and he alone linked Isaiah's messianic title "Son" with that of "Servant," i.e., slave.

That's not all. Jesus went one step further when he identified the "Servant" with a life of *obscurity and suffering*. We see this theme most clearly in the final Servant Song in Isaiah, chapters 52–53, which is our text today. The song begins with a glorious vision: "Behold, my servant shall act wisely; he shall be high and lifted up." But right alongside this vision of glory comes a vision of, well, ugliness: "he had no form or majesty that we should look at him," Isaiah says, "no beauty that we should desire him…his appearance had been marred beyond human semblance."

This central paradox of the Servant's glory and ugliness "startles" the kings of many nations, who confess: "He was despised and rejected by men; a man of sorrows, and acquainted with grief; and as one from whom men hide their faces he was despised, and we esteemed him not" (52:15–53:3). "We didn't get it," the ancient despisers say. And they were not the only ones. My Unitarian Sunday School teacher didn't get it. My "death of God" seminary professor didn't get it. *I* didn't get it, but for the grace of God.

The song then moves to one even more marvelous feature of the Servant's suffering and grief: it was vicarious, not for his sins but for ours.

> Surely he has borne our griefs and carried our sorrows; yet we esteemed him stricken, smitten by God, and afflicted. But he was wounded for our transgressions; he was crushed for our iniquities; upon him was the chastisement that brought us peace, and with his stripes we are healed.

Finally, the song states that this vicarious suffering was not accidental, but the very will of God: "All we like sheep have gone astray; we have turned—every one—to his own way; and the LORD has laid on him the iniquity of us all."

Now, friends, let me say this—as one who bears the title "Professor of Biblical Studies"—there is no other passage like Isaiah 53 in the Old Testament. Jews in Jesus' day and down to the present, refuse to accept its clear meaning. And they are not the only ones: Jesus' own disciples missed the point. When James and John ask to sit at Christ's right hand in glory, he rebukes them, saying: "the Son of Man came not to be served but to serve, and to give his life as a ransom for many" (Mark 10:45).

I believe Jesus, and he alone, came to understand this prophecy to be referring to himself. As Jesus and his disciples journeyed toward Jerusalem for Passover, he predicted that he would be handed over to the chief priests and crucified and on the third day rise—but they did not understand him (Mark 9:32). Then on Easter evening, three days after his crucifixion, Jesus appeared at Emmaus and "opened their minds to understand the Scriptures," saying to them: "Thus it is written, that the Messiah should suffer and on the third day rise from the dead" (Luke 24:45–46). Forty days later, Jesus ascended into heaven, having told them to wait in the city until they were empowered by the Holy Spirit to preach the Gospel to the ends of the earth.

In John's gospel, Jesus conflates the crucifixion, resurrection, and ascension into one image of being "lifted up." He tells Nicodemus: "No one has ascended into heaven except he who descended from heaven, the Son of Man. And as Moses lifted up the serpent in the wilderness, so must the Son of Man be lifted up, that whoever believes in him may have eternal life" (John 3:13–15).

This is a strange yet powerful picture of the vicarious atonement: Jesus, the cursed snake, is lifted up on the Cross for the healing of the people. Again, as he entered Jerusalem on Palm Sunday, Jesus announced the coming world-historical crisis, saying, "Now is the judgment of this world; now will the ruler of this world be cast out. And I, when I am lifted up from the earth, will draw all people to myself" (John 12:31–32).

Have you noticed that there are three kinds of crosses in Christian churches? In Catholic churches the crucifix depicts the broken body of Jesus; in Protestant churches the empty cross reminds us of the empty tomb on Easter morning; and in Eastern Orthodox churches the "Christus Victor" cross shows Christ enthroned in glory and conquering the powers of darkness. In the same way, I think the Apostles' Creed expresses in one extended sentence the single "lifting up" of the Son of God: "suffered under Pontius Pilate, crucified dead and buried, risen from the dead and ascended to the right hand of God Almighty."

There is one final implication of the Isaiah passage, which Jesus foresaw. At the end of this song, God vindicates the Servant and extends the benefits of saving work to sinners. He announces:

> Out of the anguish of his soul…the righteous one, my servant, will make many to be accounted righteous, and he shall bear their iniquities. Therefore I will divide him a portion with the many, and he shall divide the spoil with the strong, because he poured out his soul to death and was numbered with the transgressors; yet he bore the sin of many, and makes intercession for the transgressors.

This is why Isaiah is called the fifth evangelist, because he preaches the justification of the ungodly through the atoning death of Christ. In our baptism, we are symbolically reenacting the death, resurrection and ascension of Christ. In our epistle today, Paul says:

> Do you not know that all of us who have been baptized into Christ Jesus were baptized into his death? We were buried therefore with him by baptism into death, in order that, just as Christ was raised from the dead by the glory of the Father, we too might walk in newness of life. For if we have been united with him in a death like his, we shall certainly be united with him in a resurrection like his.

The difference, of course, is that we are still on this side of the valley of the shadow of death, while the risen Lord is on the other side. But, Paul assures us, when we believe in Jesus Christ, when we walk by faith, we have the assurance of eternal life with him:

> Now if we have died with Christ, we believe that we will also live with him. We know that Christ, being raised from the dead, will never die again; death no longer has dominion over him. For the death he died he died to sin, once for all, but the life he lives he lives to God. So you also must consider yourselves dead to sin and alive to God in Christ Jesus.

This is the basic believing we confess as Christians. Are we putting our lives in the hands of a badman or a madman? Many in the ancient world thought it immoral and crazy to worship a crucified criminal, the so-called King of the Jews. Many in our world think so too. This is the scandal of the Gospel, as Paul expresses it:

> For the word of the cross is folly to those who are perishing, but to us who are being saved it is the power of God...For the foolishness of God is wiser than men, and the weakness of God is stronger than men. (1 Cor 1:18, 25)

What about you? Are you still a doubting Thomas? Don't let Thomas's little voice prevent you from the promise: "Blessed are those who have not seen and yet have believed" (John 20:29). As those who have been baptized into Christ and who now walk in newness of life, let us join with St. Paul in saying: "Thanks be to God for his inexpressible gift!" (2 Cor 9:15).

He Shall Come Again in Glory

DANIEL 7:9–14; 1 CORINTHIANS 15:50–58; MARK 13:23–32

May the words of my mouth and the meditations of our hearts be always acceptable in your sight, O Lord, our Rock and our Redeemer.

After a two-week intermission, I am returning today to the Apostles' Creed and in particular to the final phrase of the section on Jesus Christ our Lord, which reads: "He will come again to judge the living and the dead."

This brief phrase is a summary of what theologians call eschatology, or "the last things": death, judgment, heaven and hell. Let's begin by admitting that there is much about these last things which is a mystery. The folk singer Iris DeMent puts the matter this way:

> Everybody is a-wonderin' what and where they all came from,
> Everybody is a-worryin' 'bout where
> They're gonna go when the whole thing's done,
> But no one knows for certain and so it's all the same to me—
> I think I'll just let the mystery be.

While I agree that many of the last things are mysterious, I don't find that people are a-wonderin' and a-worryin' *enough* about where they're gonna go when the whole thing's done. Rather, I think our society is in a state of denial. If "letting the mystery be" means a kind of collective shrug of the shoulders, many are going to wake up some day to profound regret.

As Christians, we may certainly ask the questions "how," "why," "when," "where" about the last things—and I shall be coming back to these—but the fundamental question has to do with "Who" holds the future. This Person is Jesus Christ.

But did this phrase from the Apostles' Creed come from Jesus? Yes, it did. He said so repeatedly to his disciples, as is the case in our gospel text today. In the last days, he says, "they will see the Son of Man coming in clouds with great power and glory."

So how did Jesus come to know this? These past weeks I have been speaking about "Jesus becoming Jesus," how as the fully human and incarnate Word, Jesus learned about his identity and mission through the Hebrew Bible, the Old Testament. Earlier I suggested that Jesus learned from the book of Isaiah about his role as the Coming One and Suffering Servant, who would give his life as a ransom for many.

Our lesson today from the book of Daniel is a second text which I think formed Jesus' sense of his final coming in glory. Daniel chapter 7 describes a vision of the climax of world history in terms of four empires, increasingly tyrannical and culminating with a supreme horrific despot who forbids God's law, persecutes God's people, and sets an idol of himself in God's temple. This figure is the Antichrist later described in the book of Revelation as the Satanic Beast. Now back to Daniel. At the climax of the vision, God himself appears as an "Ancient of Days"—an all-powerful heavenly patriarch—coming in glory to judge these evil empires. But he is not alone when he appears:

> with the clouds of heaven there came one like a son of man, and he came to the Ancient of Days and was presented before him. And to him was given dominion and glory and a kingdom…and his kingdom is one that shall not be destroyed.

What is striking about this vision—and I think this is how Jesus understood it—is that the second figure is "a son of man," that is, he is human, not a spirit or an angel. No, he is born of a woman, he is mortal, subject to the power of death. This vision answers the question posed in Psalm 8: "What is man that you are mindful of him, the son of man that you visit him?" The answer to this question is the One who is both Son of God *and* Son of Man, Jesus Christ.

There is a second striking question raised in Daniel's vision: is this son of man ascending to the throne of the Ancient of Days or descending with him to judge the earth? Maybe both, like the angels ascending and descending on Jacob's ladder. What Jesus and the Creed are saying is that the mission of God's Son involved an ongoing movement from heaven to earth and back again, as the song says:

> You came from heaven to earth, to show the way
> From the earth to the cross, my debt to pay
> From the cross to the grave, from the grave to the sky…

And there is a grand finale to this movement: his glorious return to judge the living and the dead.

So now that we know the Who who spoke of his coming again, let's take a look at the questions: "how?" "why?" "when?" and where?" of the Last Things.

How will Christ return? The Nicene Creed adds the little phrase: He will come *in glory*. Jesus Christ is the radiance and exact imprint of the Father's glory, which he possessed before all time (Heb 1:1–4). It is the glory he suppressed when he humbled himself to be born in a stable in Bethlehem and to live the life of a servant. It is the glory which flashed forth momentarily on the Mount of Transfiguration. It is the enduring glory he received when he sat down at the right hand of the Father's throne after the resurrection.

And then there is the end. Jesus predicts an astounding explosion of that glory, saying: "Then will appear in heaven the sign of the Son of Man, and then all the tribes of the earth will mourn when they will see the Son of Man coming on the clouds of heaven with power and great glory" (Matt 24:30).

Why will Christ return? He will come again in glory "to judge the living and the dead," that is, to judge every man and woman living or dead. (This clause, incidentally, upholds the biblical and historic Christian teaching that the human person is both body and soul. The body dies and is buried; the soul lives on in some state until the Day of Judgment.)

The idea of God as judge pervades the Bible. God is good and made all things good, but there is an Enemy who has rebelled against God and tempted mankind into sin. And the wages of sin, from Eden on, is death. In his mercy, God did not leave us dead in our sins and without hope, but he sent his Son to bear the judgment that should have been ours. And now, having raised him from the dead, the Father has entrusted final judgment to his Son.

What is the basis for this final judgment? In Daniel's vision, it states "the books [plural] were opened"; the same phrase is used by John in the book of Revelation:

> And I saw the dead, great and small, standing before the throne, and books were opened. Then another book was opened, which is the book of life. And the dead were judged by what was written in the books, according to what they had done. (Rev 20:12)

Here is how I understand these account books. Those whose names are written in the book of life are the redeemed, those who have put their trust in the Lamb that was slain. Jesus is the way, the truth, and the life. No one comes to the Father except through him. At the same time, no good deed goes unrewarded in God's eyes, nor is any sin overlooked. It is my view that even for believers there is a purging, a refining of sin, but in a strange sense we shall wish to be cleansed from our impurities (cf. 1 Cor 3:12–13).

What God desires is that believers repent of evil and do good, and that unbelievers repent and come to Christ. The ultimate sin, the sin of Satan, is to know God and refuse him. So long as a person lives, the door remains open and Christ is knocking and asking to enter the heart. Without repentance, the verdict is sealed in the Second Death, which is separation from God in hell.

This leads to the next question: when will Christ come to judge? The Old Testament prophets speak repeatedly of the Day of the Lord coming at a time of God's sovereign reckoning. As for the date and time of this coming, Jesus says in today's gospel from Mark: "Concerning that day and hour no one knows, not even the angels of heaven, nor the Son, but the Father only." He goes on to say that the end will come as a complete surprise:

> For as were the days of Noah, so will be the coming of the Son of Man. For as in those days before the flood they were eating and drinking, marrying and giving in marriage, until the day when Noah entered the ark, and they were unaware until the flood came and swept them all away, so will be the coming of the Son of Man.

So stay awake, Jesus says, for you do not know on what day your Lord is coming.

Another way of looking at this question is to say that we should consider the day of the Lord's coming for us to be the day of our death. If somehow we are alive at that time, our situation before the Judge is no different. When I was a small boy, I somehow learned the prayer:

> Now I lay me down to sleep,
> I pray the Lord my soul to keep.
> If I should die before I wake,
> I pray the Lord my soul to take.

I suspect today this prayer is considered too scary for children. In earlier times and even in many parts of the world today, surviving to the next day, especially for children and the poor, is hardly to be assumed. And in any case, each one of us, young or old, has a due date with God. Forgetting this reality is part of what I am calling our collective amnesia. Think of those occupants in the condo collapse in Florida recently. They fell asleep in this world and woke up in another. So, Jesus says, keep awake with God, even as you sleep.

Now to a final question: where does the judgment take place? According to Daniel's vision, God comes "with the clouds of heaven." We naturally think of heaven as being "up there," but only silly literalists were disturbed when Yuri Gagarin, the first man in space, reported back: "I looked and looked and looked and looked, but I did not see God." Thoughtful Christians have always understood that heaven is a different dimension of reality from the up-down of our material world.

And the same distinction goes for the "where" of our final state. Going to heaven is not a change of *location* but a change of *nature*. When we speak of going to heaven when we die, we do not mean floating on clouds playing harps. The new creation, as we see in the final vision of the book of Revelation, is not fluffy like a Hallmark card but something utterly foreign, a transformation of the good world God created in the beginning into something so marvelous that it can only be described in metaphors.

St. Paul puts it this way in our epistle today:

> Behold! I tell you a mystery. We shall not all sleep, but we shall all be changed, in a moment, in the twinkling of an eye, at the last trumpet. For the trumpet will sound, and the dead will be raised imperishable, and we shall be changed. For this perishable body

> must put on the imperishable, and this mortal body must put on immortality.

In *The Last Battle*, the finale of C.S. Lewis's Narnia books, the victors find themselves in front of a door. Suddenly the great lion Aslan, the Christ-figure, appears and roars: "Now it is time!" And the door opens. As Aslan stands in the door, all the creatures come streaming toward him. Judgment happens when they enter in at the door, or turn aside; but this is just the beginning of the end. "Further up and further in!" was Aslan's cry to those pilgrims as they climb to higher and higher vistas. And as they do, they begin to meet other residents of Narnia from earlier stories and ages who are being transformed. The Apostles' Creed returns to this glorious subject in its last phrases about "the communion of saints" and "life everlasting," and we'll return to it later.

So let's come back to earth here and now. There is perhaps a proper Christian way to "let the mystery of the last things be." In the next section of the Creed, we encounter the Third Person of the Trinity, who will dwell in our hearts as we await the glorious coming of our Lord Jesus Christ.

Without forgetting the glorious hope of Christ's Return, we now return to our daily journey of faith, hope and love.

Maranatha! Come, Lord Jesus.

The Holy Spirit, God in Us

PSALM 51:1–12; ACTS 8:4–8, 12, 14–17; JOHN 3:1–16

May the words of my mouth and the meditations of our hearts be always acceptable in your sight, O Lord, our Rock and our Redeemer.

The Apostles' Creed, as we have noted, is trinitarian in shape and moves swiftly from naming God the Father, creator of heaven and earth and naming Jesus Christ, the Son of God, to the longer central narrative of Jesus' earthly work: conceived by the Holy Spirit and born of the Virgin Mary, suffered under Pontius Pilate, crucified, dead and buried, risen on the third day, ascended into heaven to God's right hand.

Now we come to a third and final section of short phrases, which reads:

> I believe in the Holy Spirit,
> the holy catholic church, the communion of saints,
> the forgiveness of sins,
> the resurrection of the body, and the life everlasting.

At first glance, this section might seem a grab-bag of miscellaneous doctrines, but at closer look it is held together by the Person of God the Holy Spirit. This section is also, for the first time in the Creed, about *us*—"us" individually and corporately as the Church. So I have titled this sermon: "The Holy Spirit, God in Us."

Of the many mysteries of the triune God, the identity of the Holy Spirit is especially mysterious. In our mind's eye, we can imagine God the Father and God the Son, because we all have experience of fathers and sons, and we can definitely imagine the historical Jesus, because he is portrayed at some length in the gospels. But the Holy Spirit is almost by definition inconceivable. Jesus himself said of the Spirit: "The wind blows where it will, and you hear its sound, but you do not know where it comes from or where it goes" (John 3:8). The closest the Bible gets to an image of the Spirit is that of a dove, but we know immediately that this is a metaphor for its movement, not its identity. (One can use "it" or "he" or even grammatically "she" for the Spirit because the Spirit is "non-representational" in a way the Father and the Son are not.)

None of this is to say that the Holy Spirit is not a real Person of the Trinity, only that he is hard to visualize. Let me try out an analogy between the divine Spirit and the human soul. Ask this question: "Who am I?" Geneticists may chart the human genome; neuroscientists may map the synapses of the nervous system and areas of the brain; computer scientists may design "artificial intelligence" programs that can talk to us and beat world masters in chess, but none of this expert knowledge explains the reality of the soul, that invisible source of our identity as creatures made in the image of God.

With great caution, I would say that the Holy Spirit is something like the *soul* of the triune God. The human soul is the source of life, of dynamism, of motivation. So also God is the "living God," the God of power, and above all, the God of love, and the Holy Spirit is particularly associated with these attributes: life, power and love.

The great church theologian Augustine spoke of the Holy Spirit as the mutual love which flows between the Father and the Son, and the Nicene Creed speaks of the Spirit as "proceeding from the Father [and the Son]."* There is a sense in which the Persons of the Trinity indwell each other, and this is why we can speak equally of the Spirit of God and the Spirit of Jesus, knowing that the Father and the Son are fully present when we experience the Holy Spirit. We seldom pray *to* the Spirit directly but rather pray *in* the Spirit; we invoke him, saying "Come, Holy Spirit."

This is as far as I dare go in explaining this unique Person of the Holy Spirit. But there is one other aspect of the Spirit as we experience him. He is *in us*, individually and corporately. From the beginning God breathed into man the breath of life, and we naturally continue to think of living and dying in terms of breathing. God's Spirit is intimately present in every soul alive and is at the same time inexhaustibly available to millions

*See the note in the Book of Common Prayer, page 109: "The phrase 'and the Son' (Latin *filioque*) is not in the original Greek text. See the resolution of the College of Bishops concerning the filioque in Documentary Foundations (page 768)."

of others at the same time. Excess population may be a problem for politicians; it is not a problem for God!

But the hope of eternal life with God was lost when our first parents tried to grasp the fruit of the tree for themselves, and this original fall is repeated in all our lives. "As in Adam, all die" (1 Cor 15:22). In our psalm today David, after his sin with Bathsheba, cries out:

> Create in me a clean heart, O God, and renew a right spirit within me. Cast me not away from your presence, and take not your holy spirit from me. Restore to me the joy of your salvation, and uphold me with a willing spirit.

Nothing but a new creation and a new Adam will do to restore salvation, which is why Jesus says to Nicodemus: "unless one is born again, he cannot see the kingdom of God." When Nicodemus objects, "How can a man be born when he is old?" Jesus repeats: "unless one is born of water and the Spirit, he cannot enter the kingdom of God." "That which is born of the flesh is flesh," Jesus says, "and that which is born of the Spirit is spirit." The sovereign work of the Holy Spirit is called *regeneration*, i.e., rebirth, not to this life in the flesh but to eternal life with God in the Spirit. And the sole condition for this rebirth is receiving God's love by faith. "For God so loved the world, that he gave his only Son, that whoever believes in him should not perish but have eternal life"—a verse which I trust you all know.

Jesus' reference to water and the Spirit suggests that regeneration has an outer accompaniment, which is baptism in water. After the Spirit descends on the Day of Pentecost, Peter concludes his sermon with this appeal: "Repent and be baptized, every one of you, in the name of Jesus Christ for the forgiveness of your sins, and you will receive the gift of the Holy Spirit" (Acts 2:38). These three responses—faith, baptism, and receiving the Spirit—are the normal pattern of conversion, but they may occur in different order. In our reading today from Acts chapter 8, we see one of these irregularities. The Samaritans, you will recall, were alienated from the Jews, but when Philip went down to Samaria and preached with signs and wonders, the Samaritans believed the Gospel and were baptized, but for whatever reason they did not receive the Spirit. Acts goes on to say:

> Now when the apostles at Jerusalem heard that Samaria had received the word of God, they sent to them Peter and John, who came down and prayed for them that they might receive the Holy Spirit, for he had not yet fallen on any of them, but they had only been baptized in the name of the Lord Jesus. Then they laid their hands on them and they received the Holy Spirit.

My own guess is that God wanted to make clear for all times and peoples that the Gospel and the Spirit were now available to every race and culture—to Jew, Samaritan, and Gentile—and that these different groups were united by the Spirit in the one apostolic faith. (A similar thing happened in Acts chapter 10 when the Holy Spirit fell on the first Gentile converts *before* they believed and then they and their households were baptized.) Note also in this episode in Samaria, the physical laying-on-of-hands accompanied the full baptism in the Spirit. This is the precedent the Church has used in the rite of confirmation.

So let me stop here and say a word about baptism as the external sign and seal of the Holy Spirit. In the early church, which experienced mass conversions, baptism usually followed repentance and faith, but as more and more households came to faith, baptism of infants and young children came to be practiced and even later became the norm. In the case of infants, the sacrament preceded adult faith; that faith was promised by parents and godparents. I do not think the Bible teaches a *causal* power in baptism (which is what Roman Catholics teach), but baptism conveys a *promissory* power to bring a child to the fulness of faith and of the Spirit. At baptism, God, as I see it, plants a seed of the Spirit in the hearts of believers' children, which they may cultivate or neglect but which remains sown throughout their lives. So Anglicans may delay baptism for young children, but they do not practice rebaptism.

There is a second external manifestation that accompanies the Spirit, and that is testimony. The risen Jesus' final words to his apostles are: "You will receive power when the Holy Spirit has come upon you, and you will be my witnesses in Jerusalem and in all Judea and Samaria, and to the end of the earth" (Act 1:8). One of the most common words in the Acts is "testify" or "witness"—the Greek word for these is "martyr." To be filled with the Holy Spirit is to be a martyr, and to be a martyr is to confess Jesus publicly. St. Paul says this about salvation: "if you confess with your mouth that Jesus is Lord and believe in your heart that God raised him from the dead, you will be saved" (Rom 10:9).

Public confession of Jesus is thus intimately linked with baptism and the Creeds. In fact, the Apostles' Creed first developed as a kind of Q&A session at baptism. If you look at the baptism service in the Anglican Prayer Book (pages 186–187), you will see the original setting. The bishop or priest asks three leading questions: "Do you believe and trust in God the Father?" "Do you believe and trust in Jesus Christ?" "Do you believe and trust in the Holy Spirit?" And the candidates answer, "I do," and then recite that portion of the Apostles' Creed.

Of course, baptism and confirmation are merely the outward sign of the Spirit's inner work, which is called sanctification. The Holy Spirit is integral to the spiritual disciplines, what one writer calls "a long obedience in the same direction." To read the Bible effectively means not only to believe that it is inspired and then to set it on a coffee table, but to read it expectantly, believing that the Spirit continues to speak to us through God's Word written. When we pray and praise with our minds—e.g., using said prayers from the Prayer Book or through psalms and hymns, the Holy Spirit is lifting our thoughts and voice to God. There is also a kind of non-verbal communication of the Spirit, either in silent meditation or ecstatic speaking in tongues in which we may participate in the depths of God.

Let me conclude with a further piece of my—I should say my and my wife's—personal testimony. I have already said that I was a convert to Christ at age twenty, while Peggy was a cradle Episcopalian. A couple years after my conversion, we both experienced "baptism in the Spirit" in the charismatic renewal in the Episcopal Church, which included our asking for the anointing of the Spirit with speaking in tongues. Anglicans have never accepted the Pentecostal idea of a second Spirit-baptism as necessary for the full Christian life. Indeed, some people experience something like a "second blessing" more than once. Anglicans believe there is in principle only one baptism (Eph 4:5), although as in the book of Acts people's experience of the one baptism may be quite varied. Anyway, looking back now on fifty years, Peggy and I both see this time as a critical moment in our walk, even as glossolalia, as it is called, has become less important in our daily lives.

During the next few weeks, we at Redeemer as a church will be preparing for the service on September 19 when Bishop Minns will come for the laying on of hands, a service of confirmation, reception, and renewal of vows. It is my hope and prayer that you will all, as individuals and a congregation, seek this occasion for a new infilling of the Spirit in your lives, wherever you are along the road of salvation.

The Bible ends with these words: "The Spirit and the Bride say, 'Come.' And let the one who hears say, 'Come.'" (Rev 22:17).

So I too conclude: *Come, Lord Jesus! Come, Holy Spirit, come!*

The Church's One Foundation

ACTS 2:41–47; EPHESIANS 4:1–7, 11–13; JOHN 20:19–23; REVELATION 7:2–4, 9–10, 13–17

May the words of my mouth and the meditations of our hearts be always acceptable in your sight, O Lord, our Rock and our Redeemer.

When I was a boy way back in the 1950s, pretty much a Sunday School drop-out, I still learned this little ditty: "Here's the church, here's the steeple. Open the doors and see all the people." Well no, that's not the Church—not the building, not the steeple, and not the comfortable pews for all those people to rest their rears on.

So what is the Church according to the Apostles' Creed? Last week I suggested that the third section of the Creed is devoted to the Third Person of the Trinity, the Holy Spirit, God in us. But who is "us"? The Creed sketches an answer to this question. "I believe in the Holy Spirit" leads naturally to the two following clauses: belief in "the holy catholic church," and "the communion of saints."

The Nicene Creed expands on the first clause, saying: "I believe in one…holy…catholic and…apostolic Church." From this definition, theologians speak of four "marks" of the Church. Let's look at each briefly.

The Church is *one*. Christian faith in one God is founded on the Old Testament confession: "Hear O Israel, the Lord our God is One" (Deut 6:4). The Apostle Paul restates this confession in trinitarian terms: "There is one body and one Spirit—just as you were called to the one hope that belongs to your call—one Lord, one faith, one baptism, one God and Father of all, who is over all and through all and in all" (Eph 4:5–6).

One prime implication of the Church's unity is *koinonia. Koinonia* is often translated "fellowship," but a stronger word is communion, and the book of Acts gives us a snapshot of what communion looks like: "And all who believed were together and had all things in common. And they were selling their possessions and belongings and distributing the proceeds to all, as any had need" (Acts 2:44–45). The word communion can also be used for Christians united in a particular tradition, such as the global Anglican Communion.

The Church is *holy*. Again, the holiness of the Church is rooted in the call of the people of Israel to be a kingdom of priests and a holy nation (Exod 19:6). "I am holy, so you shall be holy," says the Lord to Moses. Holiness is the very character of God himself, and the call to holiness sets apart each believer and the Church from the idolatry and immorality of the fallen world. The apostles began to refer to church members as "saints" both individually and corporately.

The phrase "communion of saints" in the Creed brings together these two marks of unity and holiness. As time passed and some believers died, the conviction arose that the love among brothers and sisters in Christ could not be separated by death. On November 1, All Saints' Day, we celebrate this ongoing fellowship of the Church, as the hymn puts it: "She on earth hath union with God the Three in One, and mystic sweet communion with those whose rest is won." The idea of victory over death led to the term "Church triumphant" for believers in heaven.

The Church is *catholic*, a word which means "universal." The universality of the Church follows from its unity. This universality was not self-evident on Easter Day, when Christ appeared to his Jewish disciples; but from the Day of Pentecost on, God made it clear that there is only one Church dispersed among the nations. The Church is catholic through space and time. At the Last Supper, Jesus prayed not only for those sitting with him at table "but also for those who will believe in me through their word, that they may all be one, just as you, Father, are in me, and I in you, that they also may be in us" (John 17:20–21). This extended flock includes every believer throughout the world and throughout history. Jesus was praying for them there and for us here today and for any who come to him through our witness!

The Church is *apostolic*. On the day of resurrection, Jesus breathed on his apostles and said, "Receive the Holy Spirit. If you forgive the sins of any, they are forgiven them; if you withhold forgiveness from any, it is withheld." Jesus in effect authorized his apostles to represent him. This is why Paul can speak of the Church as "built on the foundation of the apostles and prophets, Christ Jesus himself being the cornerstone" (Eph 2:20).

"Apostolic" means several things. The New Testament is authoritative because it records the memory and writings of Jesus' apostles. The Creeds are apostolic because they are "according to the Scriptures," and they refute some of the basic heresies about the Gospel. The Church's historic order, ministry, and worship—for instance, the sacraments of baptism and Holy Communion—were passed on to us through the apostles to the early Church.

So, *one, holy, catholic, apostolic*—these are the four classic marks of the Church of Jesus Christ. I want to add three other marks which I believe are unstated but implicit in the Creeds. The Church is *missionary*, the Church is *persecuted*, and the Church is *congregational*. Four plus three is seven, a good biblical number! So here we go.

The Church is *missionary*. The description of the Church at Pentecost begins and ends with these two statements: "So those who received his word were baptized, and there were added that day about three thousand souls…And the Lord added to their number day by day those who were being saved." Mission is to the Church as breath is to the body, it is said, which is not surprising, as the Spirit is the source of our individual and our corporate life. A church that does not reach out to others with the Good News and the love of Christ is no church.

The Church is *persecuted.* Jesus warned his disciples that they would be dragged before religious and secular rulers for their witness to him, and this happened from Pentecost on. Written fifty years later and reflecting one of the periodic Roman persecutions of Christians for not revering the emperor as divine, the book of Revelation contains a vision in which John is shown a countless number of believers from every tribe and nation on earth: "These are the ones," an angel tells John, "coming out of the great tribulation. They have washed their robes and made them white in the blood of the Lamb" (Rev 7:14). This is the church of the martyrs, purified in their own blood. Potentially, we are all in that number.

Today the persecuted church is more numerous and widespread on every continent than in any point in history. As you know from the Sunday liturgy, our Prayer Book now couples a petition for all who proclaim the Gospel with a petition for all who are persecuted for their faith. We in the West are experiencing a kind of cultural persecution, in which Christianity is equated with hate and injustice. To the extent these charges are true, we need to repent; at the same time, we should not be surprised when the

Church and Christians are falsely accused, for so they treated the Lord of the Church.

The Church is *congregational,* even as it is one and catholic. The Greek word *ekklesia* means a local assembly or gathering, whether sacred or secular. After Pentecost the first church in Jerusalem gathered together in one place. The first missionary churches in the Gentile world gathered in houses within various cities of the Roman world. The Reformation spawned independent congregations and in England geographic parishes. In America, the welter of denominations led to overlapping congregations, sometimes with a megachurch or a mother church overseeing smaller mission fellowships.

And that's where we come in. Redeemer was a church plant of St. Stephen's parish in Sewickley, and now we are taking steps to become an independent congregation in the Anglican Diocese of Pittsburgh.

One, holy, catholic, apostolic...missionary, persecuted, congregational. This is not the church of my childhood ditty. This is the Church of the Living God. This is the Church of the Redeemer, the Church of the Redeemed.

Let us pray:

> O God, our heavenly Father, you manifested your love by sending your only-begotten Son into the world, that all might live through him: Pour out your Spirit on your Church, that we may fulfill his command to preach the Gospel to all people. Send forth laborers into your harvest; defend them in all dangers and temptations; and hasten the time when the fullness of the Gentiles shall be gathered in, and faithful Israel shall be saved; through your Son Jesus Christ our Lord. Amen. (Book of Common Prayer, page 651)

Forgiveness, the Heartbeat of Christ and the Church

HOSEA 11:7–9; ROMANS 6:3–11; MATTHEW 18:15–35

May the words of my mouth and the meditations of our hearts be always acceptable in your sight, O Lord, our Rock and our Redeemer.

We are now approaching the end of the Apostles' Creed. The last section reads: [I believe in] "the Holy Spirit, the holy catholic Church, the communion of saints, the forgiveness of sins, the resurrection of the body, and the life everlasting. One week to go after this!

But not too fast! There is something odd here. Why is "the forgiveness of sins" placed here, next to last? Why not earlier in the Creed, which speaks of Christ's atoning death? Stick with me as I try to unravel something of this enigma.

If there is anything crystal clear in the Bible, it is God's determined will to forgive. In the Old Testament, the Lord God announces himself as a God of justice and a God of mercy. From Mount Sinai God says of himself:

> I the LORD your God am a jealous God, visiting the iniquity of the fathers on the children to the third and the fourth generation of those who hate me, but showing steadfast love to thousands of those who love me and keep my commandments. (Exod 20:5–6)

The history of God's people Israel is one of testing this steadfast love by steadfast rebellion. Time and time again, from the wilderness generation through the period of the Judges to the four centuries of Israel's monarchy, the people turned away from God to worship idols—all this, even as he warned them steadfastly of the consequences through the succession of prophets.

One of the first of the writing prophets was Hosea. Hosea's own tragic marriage to a prostitute became the prism through which he likened Israel's broken covenant with God—and God reacts to this spiritual adultery with the righteous anger of a betrayed partner. At the same time, through Hosea God reveals something of his inmost heart. It comes in our reading today from Hosea chapter 11. In this chapter, God is, in effect, talking with himself, as he did when he created man at the first (Gen 1:27). In his indignation against Israel's idolatry, he contemplates destroying the nation utterly, as he did in the days of Abraham and Lot with the so-called "cities of the plain," which included Sodom and Gomorrah and the lesser-known Admah and Zeboiim.

But then the Lord interrupts himself, saying:

> How can I give you up, O Ephraim? How can I hand you over, O Israel? How can I make you like Admah? How can I treat you like Zeboiim? My heart recoils within me; my compassion grows warm and tender. I will not execute my burning anger; I will not again destroy Ephraim; for I am God and not a man, the Holy One in your midst, and I will not come in wrath.

Here, as in the Servant Songs, we glimpse the unfathomable heart of God. He is prepared to set aside the persistent high-handedness of his people and to do so because he is God not man. Have you ever considered how strange it is that the tiny Jewish nation, which has never held power on the world stage, is still here? Where are the Assyrians, the Babylonians, the Greeks or Romans, the Mongol hordes, today? I think it is God's steadfast love, his covenant love to Israel, that has been at work to preserve the Jewish people despite the persistent history of anti-Semitism and the continuing indifference of many Jews to their God.

This is the same heart of the God who loved the world so much that he sent his Son to suffer and die for us. If there is one thing we know about Jesus, it is that his message and his ministry was one of forgiveness from start to finish. In one of his first miracles, he said to the paralyzed man on a stretcher, "Your sins are forgiven," and followed up by healing him. He taught his disciples to pray, "Forgive us our sins, as we forgive those who sin against us" and ordered them to forgive their brothers not seven times but seventy-times-seven. In the parable in our gospel today about the unforgiving steward, the sternest warning falls on unforgiveness and the failure of love for the neighbor that lies behind it. Finally, from the Cross, Jesus prayed for his persecutors: "Father, forgive them for they know not what they do."

Now let's return to the Creed. The first two sections of the Creed describe the mighty acts of God "for us and for our salvation," as the Nicene Creed puts it. The third section is about how we receive, how we appropriate that salvation. Is it not self-evident that we receive Christ into our hearts by faith? Well, I think the answer to this question is Yes and No. Yes, we are born again and saved through faith alone, by putting our trust in Jesus and him alone, as most Protestants affirm. But we are saved by faith in a context, and the context is the community of the Church, the real-life visible Church, united in love by the Holy Spirit. And the external sign of our entering the Church is baptism.

The Apostles' Creed and the Nicene Creed differ at this point. While the Apostles' Creed says, "I believe in the forgiveness of sins," the Nicene Creed adds: "We confess one baptism for the forgiveness of sins." Note the change from "I believe" (Latin *credo*) to "We believe." The Apostles' Creed was aimed at individuals coming to baptism, while the Nicene Creed was the confession of all members together as the Church. In the early church, adult converts were baptized naked in a separate hall called a "baptistery." Coming out of the water, they were clothed in white and brought into the main church to participate fully in the life of the congregation. Taken together, the Creeds make clear that baptism is a symbolic, that is, a sacramental rebirth in the life of the believer in the context of the Church. Receiving the forgiveness of sins is not a license to wander lonely as a cloud on Sunday in the woods, singing to the trees, but to gather with other Christians in a cathedral or in rented office space or under a mango tree.

The connection between baptism and forgiveness goes back to the person of John the Baptist, whose father Zechariah prophesies, saying: "You, child, will be called the prophet of the Most High; for you will go before the Lord to prepare his ways, to give knowledge of salvation to his people in the forgiveness of their sins" (Luke 1:76–77). And this is precisely what John did. Jesus himself was baptized by John in the Jordan, and he commanded his apostles to preach the Gospel to all nations, baptizing them and instructing them in all he had taught them.

And this is just what the apostles did. In our epistle today, Paul makes clear that baptism is the context of repentance and faith when he says: "We were buried therefore with him by baptism into death, in order that, just as Christ was raised from the dead by the glory of the Father, we too might walk in newness of life" (Rom 6:4).

The Anglican Church, which followed the main current of Reformation teaching, defines baptism this way:

> Baptism is not only a sign of profession, and mark of difference, whereby Christians are discerned from others that be not christened, but it is also a sign of Regeneration or new Birth, whereby, as by an instrument, they that receive Baptism rightly are grafted into the Church; the promises of forgiveness of sin, and of our adoption to be the sons of God by the Holy Ghost, are visibly signed and sealed; Faith is confirmed, and Grace increased by virtue of prayer unto God. (Article 27 of the Articles of Religion)

Almost all Christians agree that baptism is a sign of some sort, but what kind of sign? Some see it as a mere sign, like a paid-up membership card or (maybe for today's generation) like a tattoo that says, "I was saved on such and such a date." Anglicans believe that it is more than that, it is a sign of a regeneration and transformation which begins with conversion and continues throughout one's life. For this reason, baptism is a once-for-all comfort and assurance in times of doubt and temptation. Martin Luther, who made faith the heart of the Gospel, also went through many spiritual struggles, and he concluded: "The only way to drive away the Devil is through faith in Christ by saying: 'I am baptized, I am a Christian.'" Baptism and faith are two sides of the coin of salvation.

Forgiveness was signed and sealed once for all on the Cross of Calvary. Forgiveness is sealed once for all in our lives when we are born again of water and the Spirit. But forgiveness continues throughout our Christian life to the end. It is the key to personal relationships in marriage and the family. Dietrich Bonhoeffer in his wedding sermon—which Peggy and I had read at our wedding fifty-four years ago—says to the couple:

> Don't insist on your rights, don't blame each other, don't judge or condemn each other, don't find fault with each other, but accept

> each other as you are, and forgive each other every day from the bottom of your hearts.

Forgiveness in marriage, I think, includes not only things done to one another but holding against one another illusions of what the other person can never be. Sometimes it is only by kissing the toad that we discover the prince (a yucky thought, I admit).

In the Church, forgiveness includes accepting difficult and needy persons and, so it seems in our day, in resisting the temptation to judge others based on their political opinions. Forgiveness means welcoming the stranger into our midst, that neighbor who is not the person we would choose to associate with but the person for whom Christ died: the poor, the homeless, the prisoner, the social outcast.

Forgiveness is the heartbeat of Christ. It is also the heartbeat of the Church, which testifies to this forgiveness in the sacrament of Holy Baptism.

I mentioned last week that the laying on of hands service planned for September 19 will include two occasions of baptism, one on September 12 at the park and again as part of the service on September 19 itself. In the context of these baptisms, we shall be reciting the Apostles' Creed together. Let's not think of this as a mere formality but as an occasion when we as the church can celebrate the heartbeat of God in our midst, as we welcome the newly baptized with this affirmation:

> We receive you into the fellowship of Christ's Church. Confess the faith of Christ crucified, proclaim the resurrection, and share with us in the royal priesthood of all his people. (Book of Common Prayer, page 170)

As we welcome them, let us also be thankful that we are forgiven sinners and vow to extend the heartbeat of Christ to all our neighbors, for whom Christ died.

Life! Life! Eternal Life with God!

PSALM 16; 1 CORINTHIANS 15:12–26; JOHN 11:17–27

May the words of my mouth and the meditations of our hearts be always acceptable in your sight, O Lord, our Rock and our Redeemer.

So this is the final sermon on the Apostles' Creed. We've reached the end. And I must make a confession: I've enjoyed it! Truth be told, I, like a lot of people, repeat the Apostles' Creed from memory week by week—that is your assignment for the service next week—without thinking much about it. However, preaching through the Creed set me to thinking and passing it on to you. That's the price you get for employing a professor as your pastor!

Looking back now after ten weeks of sermons, I can see three things about the Creed that I had not noticed before. The first thing is that it has a *cross-shaped*, a cruciform, movement. Most obviously it moves on a horizontal axis through time, from the beginning, with God the Creator, to the end, with the resurrection of the dead and life everlasting. But it also has a vertical axis through space, as it were, reaching from heaven to earth, beginning with God himself, God the Father and God the Son, then the coming down of our Lord Jesus Christ to earth, conceived of the Holy Spirit and born of the Virgin Mary, Jesus of Nazareth, who suffered under Pontius Pilate, crucified, dead, and buried down to the depths of the underworld, from which he ascended into heaven, where he now sits enthroned at the Father's right hand. This exalted Jesus has now sent his Spirit down the same axis into the world and into our hearts, God in us. And the Spirit's coming has not only been vertical but horizontal, spreading through the mission of the one catholic and apostolic Church to the ends of the earth and to the end of time when God will judge the living and the dead. Sorry for the long sentence, but the Creed itself is a long sentence itself following the first "I believe."

The second thing I have seen is how *biblical* the Creed is, even though it never literally quotes the Bible. It unites the beginning in the book of Genesis with the end in the book of Revelation. It touches on the great Old Testament mysteries of the Suffering Servant and the Son of Man and the New Testament mysteries of the God made man and of the Church, his Body and his bride.

The third thing I have seen is how fully the Creed is incorporated in our Prayer Book. This is because prayer and worship are the work of the Holy Spirit in the Church. Last time I spoke, I asked why the "forgiveness of sins" appears in this section rather than earlier when it speaks about Christ dying on the Cross for our salvation, and my answer was that forgiveness of sin is received through the gate of baptism in the Church. Today, we the church gather in Bellevue Memorial Park around a rubber swimming pool as we baptize Makaya Martin, reciting with her the Creed as found in the Prayer Book.

With these remarks as a preface, let's turn to the final phrase in the third section of the Creed, "the resurrection of the dead and the life everlasting."

First, a little Old Testament background. From the book of Genesis on, when God breathes the breath of life into Adam, it is clear that human nature has two elements, body and soul, which are united in our earthly life. It is equally clear that body and soul are separated at death, and the body decays and returns to the dust, from which it came. But what about the soul?

Many ancient peoples believed that at death the soul descends to an underworld, a realm often called Hades, a place the Bible calls Sheol. Sheol was not a fiery hell but a kind of shadow world, and the soul in Sheol lived a kind of half-life, without the light of the eyes and the pleasures of the flesh. Above all, Sheol involved separation from God's presence, such that David frequently cries out, as in the psalm today: "Do not abandon my soul to Sheol."

Nobody, almost nobody, could escape death and the trip to Sheol. I say *almost nobody,* because ancient peoples had a few exceptions, and the exceptions were kings or heroes: in Egypt, the Pharaohs, in Greece, Hercules, in Rome the emperor. These humans were divinized and elevated into the heavens rather than going down to Hades. Among the Hebrews, a few spiritual giants like Enoch, Moses, and Elijah, were thought to have bypassed death and Sheol.

What is remarkable then is that the Creed, which follows the New Testament account, states that Jesus was not one of these heroes, rather that he died, was buried, and descended to the realm of the dead. This is the same Jesus, who was found speaking with Moses and Elijah on the Mount of Transfiguration right before his crucifixion. When Jesus died, his body decayed in the tomb for three days. He was dead and gone. Wherever we go, he went. So when the Creed goes on to say that he rose again, it means the whole man, body, soul, and spirit, everything that makes us human and then some—that "some" being God's glory—because the Jesus who appeared on Easter morning was true man raised exponentially to the nth degree.

Now, what about us? In the Old Testament times, the Hebrew people were unsure about resurrection. In a moment of hope, David says: "you will not let your holy one see corruption"; Job likewise in a shaft of light, cries out: "I know that my Redeemer lives, and that in my flesh I shall see God." In the time of Jesus, one group of Jews, the Pharisees, believed in the resurrection of the dead, and another group, the Sadducees, denied it. In our gospel lesson today, we see that Martha believes that at the Last Day, Lazarus will rise from the dead. But what Martha does not see is the connection between Lazarus's resurrection and Jesus. She sees Jesus as a miracle-worker, and indeed Jesus does bring Lazarus back from the dead (only to die again), but more importantly she comes to see Jesus as the I AM of the Creator God, who says to her.

> "Martha.... I am the resurrection and the life. Whoever believes in me, though he die, yet shall he live, and everyone who lives and believes in me shall never die. Do you believe this?" She said to him, "Yes, Lord; I believe that you are the Christ, the Son of God, who is coming into the world."

Oh, friends, this is the sweetest sound our ears will ever hear and our hearts believe. We too say, no, we sing: "Yes, Lord, Yes, Lord, Yes, yes, Lord; Yes, Lord, Yes, Lord, Yes, yes, Lord; Yes, Lord, Yes, Lord, Yes, yes, Lord. Amen."

The connection between Jesus' resurrection and ours is essential to our faith and our future. But getting it right is not always obvious, and this has been the case from the early church on. If King David and Martha of Bethany had only a distant hope of resurrection, Paul's converts in Corinth had the opposite problem. They took Paul's preaching of salvation and the coming of the Holy Spirit to mean that the resurrection had already arrived, and they were walking around as Spirit-filled gods! I have seen this kind of attitude in some "miracle" churches today where pastors teach and people believe that whatever they ask of God, he will give them, from healing of every disease to a gold-plated Mercedes, delivered by a divine Carvana to the door. Sad to say, many of these churches are in the developing world where people struggle with the basic necessities of life.

Paul's reply to the Corinthian hyper-zealousness comes when he discusses the resurrection and eternal life in 1 Corinthians 15. (Let me begin by noting that my wife has asked that this entire chapter be read at her funeral. This is St. Paul at full strength.) In the first section of the chapter, Paul recounts the evidence of Easter: the risen Jesus, he says, appeared to Peter, then to the twelve apostles—Paul doesn't even mention the women at the tomb, shame on him!—then to more than five hundred disciples at one time, most of whom, Paul notes, are still alive, then to James his brother, then to all the apostles and, last of all, Paul relates, "to me, as to one untimely born." "So we preached," Paul concludes, "and so you believed." That's Paul's testimony, his creed, as we saw ten sermons ago.

All this is great stuff (Amen?). In the next section (our text today), we find Paul the logician, moving from relating the sure evidence of Jesus' resurrection to disputing the fantastical idea that there is no need for a final resurrection because the end-time has already arrived. He argues:

> Now if Christ is proclaimed as raised from the dead, how can some of you say that there is no [further] resurrection of the dead? But if there is no [further] resurrection of the dead, then not even Christ has been raised. And if Christ has not been raised, then our preaching is in vain and your faith is in vain.

At first glance, Paul's logic may seem a bit obscure. Let me paraphrase it this way. If Jesus was resuscitated to this life only as a kind of zombie, then his bodily resurrection was fake and the witnesses to it, including Paul, are deluded or lying—worse, they are blaspheming God. And if Paul has been lying, then, he says, the Good News of the forgiveness of sins is also a delusion—"and you are still in your sinful body." And if you are still in your sinful body, then the death of that body will be all there is: end of story and end of history, no final act, no consummation, just one death and it's all over.

The author John Updike presents Paul's argument this way:

> Make no mistake: if He rose at all
> It was as His body;
> If the cells' dissolution did not reverse, the molecules reknit,
> The amino acids rekindle,
> The Church will fall.

Perhaps the poet is tip-toeing too close to the Corinthian materialist fallacy in speaking of cells, molecules and amino acids reanimating, but his main point stands: either Jesus Christ rose bodily from the dead, or our faith is in vain, and the Church deserves to wither away.

But...Paul now wraps up his case with a "but" to end all buts.

> But in fact Christ *has* been raised from the dead, the first-fruits of those who have fallen asleep. For as by a man came death, by a man has come also the resurrection of the dead. For as in Adam all die, so also in Christ shall all be made alive.

But...if the Gospel narrative is true, it dwarfs every other narrative that people live by, and it is a narrative worth selling all we have, even losing our life itself, for the sake of the glory that is to be revealed in us.

The Corinthians' error came in wanting to skip one crucial step in the narrative: resurrection comes after death of the body. They wanted to hop a ride on Christ's risen life without going through his death. They wanted to become second Adams (and Eves) without dying as the first Adam did. They wanted the reward of the divine life and power without the cost of the divine suffering and death. Paul corrects them by using the image of a harvest: the farmer has to drop the seed into the furrow, cover it over like a corpse, and wait for the new crop to spring up. The seed is this body of death; the harvest is the resurrection body and the defeat of death.

> But [Paul says] each in his own order: Christ the first-fruits, then at his coming those who belong to Christ. Then comes the end, when he delivers the kingdom to God the Father after destroying every rule and every authority and power. For he must reign until he has put all his enemies under his feet. The last enemy to be destroyed is death.

Paul goes on to explain to the walking gods in Corinth that the resurrection body will only be born when the corruptible body dies, and the resurrection body will be infinitely superior to this poor sack we carry to the grave.

This news may sound somber on one level, but in fact Paul, who has journeyed so far and endured such hardships, breaks forth in a shout of sheer joy: "Death is swallowed up in victory. O death, where is your victory? O death, where is your sting?" As the poet John Donne put it memorably: "One short sleep past, we wake eternally / And death shall be no more; Death, thou shalt die."

Paul concludes this great chapter with a prayer of thanksgiving and a word of advice:

> But thanks be to God, who gives us the victory through our Lord Jesus Christ! Therefore, my beloved brothers, be steadfast, immovable, always abounding in the work of the Lord, knowing that in the Lord your labor is not in vain. (1 Cor 15:58)

This attitude toward death and life is, I think, captured in our final hymn today, "In Christ Alone":

> No guilt in life, no fear in death,
> This is the power of Christ in me;
> From life's first cry to final breath,
> Jesus commands my destiny.
> No power of hell, no scheme of man,
> Can ever pluck me from his hand:
> Till he returns or calls me home,
> Here in the power of Christ I'll stand.

Depictions of everlasting life are the realm of the visionaries and prophets, like the book of Revelation, like Dante's *Divine Comedy*, like C.S. Lewis's *Last Battle*, and like John Bunyan's *The Pilgrim's Progress*. Bunyan's Christian Pilgrim, as he leaves the City of Destruction in this world, cries out "Life, life, eternal life." And that, friends, is what we are headed toward, together as Christ's Body the Church.

Brothers and sisters, we have now arrived at the end of the Apostles' Creed and at the moment of entry of one young citizen of the Kingdom as she begins, or perhaps better, takes a step forward toward life, life, everlasting life.

[Baptism by immersion followed.]

Incarnational
Sermon Cycle

THE TRUE LIGHT
COMING INTO THE WORLD

Advent Ingathering: The Coming of the Son of Man

PSALM 50; LUKE 21:25–33

May the words of my mouth and the meditation of our hearts be always acceptable in your sight, O Lord, our Rock and our Redeemer.

This past weekend has brought together a constellation of times and seasons. This past Thursday marked Thanksgiving for the harvest of the fields and the last gasp of autumn, and today we begin a new year in the church calendar—Advent. Three weeks from now—at the winter solstice—we'll look forward to increasing longer days, and perhaps with the Groundhog's help, an early spring.

As it is a transition time of the seasons, so also it will be a transition time in my sermons. I'm calling this new series of sermons "The True Light Coming into the World."

In my last sermon I spoke about stewardship of time. I mentioned that there are two visions of time in the Bible. There is the *circular* or *cyclical* vision which we saw in the book of Ecclesiastes.

> The sun rises, and the sun goes down, and hastens to the place where it rises. What has been is what will be, and what has been done is what will be done, and there is nothing new under the sun. (Eccles 8:8–9)

This is also the vision of the annual harvest: "all is safely gathered in, ere the winter storms begin." About this time every year, I complete preparing my garden for winter. As the first frost approaches, I pull up the dead zinnias and border flowers, cut back the peonies and hydrangeas, take down the hanging baskets and give a final buzz haircut to the lawn.

As I grow older (and older), I have this additional thought as winter approaches: "Hope goes underground in the bulbs and trees and shrubs, and they will burst out in spring—but maybe I won't be here to see it." The cycle of the seasons now intersects with another vision of time, the *linear* timeline that runs from birth to death, the deadline, if you will. This vision is also found in the Preacher of Ecclesiastes, who says: "A generation goes, and a generation comes, but the earth remains forever" (Eccles 1:4). This is sober wisdom for the elderly, with or without the Covid threat. We are not going to live forever, true for every mortal, whatever your age.

This is why I spoke last week in terms of our "working to a deadline." For a Christian, it is a doubly good thing to work to a deadline: it motivates a person to make the most of his time here in this age, but it is also good because we know that something better lies ahead. And this something better is the coming of the Lord. And that is the meaning of the word Advent and why the harvest hymn continues this way:

> For the Lord our God shall come,
> and shall take the harvest home;
> from the field shall in that day
> all offenses purge away.

In my sermon series on the Apostles' Creed last summer, I noted that the phrase "he shall come in glory to judge the living and the dead" is an essential belief of the Church. Why is it essential? Because Jesus himself said so. Jesus' word is not a casual remark, a "maybe I will and maybe I won't" kind of statement. Jesus says repeatedly in the gospels that the "Son of Man *will* return in the clouds," that is, in divine glory.

When he speaks of the "Son of Man," he is specifically referring to his own mortality, a mortal nature that is transformed when he descends to the dead and rises on Easter morning and ascends into heaven forty days later, where he is now seated at God's right hand, and from where he will descend at the Last Day.

My friends, you cannot believe in Jesus' first coming without also believing in his Second Coming. He makes this point in our gospel today by appealing to a common observation:

> Look at the fig tree, and all the trees. As soon as they come out in leaf, you see for yourselves and know that the summer is already

> near. So also, when you see these things taking place, you know that the kingdom of God is near.

The fig tree was an early-blooming tree, like the forsythia bush in our climate, the harbinger of coming spring. So also, Jesus says, there are signs of the end-time, visible to the eyes of faith: "Now when these things begin to take place straighten up and raise your heads, because your redemption is drawing near."

And what a difference redemption makes—note this well, you Redeemed! It makes all the difference in the world in how we view our mortal lives, how we use our time, how we work, how we love. Jesus puts it this way:

> For what does it profit a man to gain the whole world and forfeit his soul? For what can a man give in exchange for his soul? For whoever is ashamed of me and of my words in this adulterous and sinful generation, of him will the Son of Man also be ashamed when he comes in the glory of his Father with the holy angels. (Mark 8:36–38)

Note the accounting language here: profit and loss and exchange of goods. He tells the story of the corporate magnate who is not satisfied with his billions and decides to tear down his business and build a "metaverse" in its place. "But God said to him, 'You fool! This night your soul is required of you, and the things you are planning, whose will they be?'" (Luke 12:20). In the case of this man, the day of accounting is the day of his death. Like the rich fool who despises the beggar Lazarus, he finds out to his horror there is an unbridgeable chasm between hell and heaven, with no ghosts of Christmas past, present, and future to warn him.

While death may be a personal deadline, there is also a deadline for the world, something the Old Testament prophets called the Day of the Lord. It is the moment when cyclical time will cease and a new era of time will begin—call it eternity, or the end-time. Jesus uses cosmic imagery to portray this deadline: the powers of the heavens are shaken, the normal time-bearers, sun and moon and stars fail, and the normal boundaries of sea and land collapse.

What are we to make of these signs of the end-time? Here is how I see it. Jesus was a prophet, and he spoke the language of the Old Testament. What made him more than a prophet is that he came to understand that all these prophecies were referring to his coming, first in the days of King Herod and Pontius Pilate and then at the Second Coming. The end had dawned in the midst of time. The meaning of linear history was fully revealed at the Cross, when Jesus cried: "It is finished." A new era had dawned, which is why Christians divide history into BC, "before Christ," and AD, *anno domini*, which we could translate "the age of our Lord," or "world without end," as the Prayer Book puts it.

Jesus used dramatic language for this dawning age: "Truly, I say to you, this generation will not pass away until all has taken place." This prediction has troubled Christians from the first generation to the present. Here we are, sixty-some generations after Christ, and he has not returned. Once again, Jesus was a prophet. The Old Testament prophets always addressed *a* particular moment in their time, like the destruction of kingdoms of Israel and Judah and the exile to Babylon. But their prophecies were not just cancelled out when the events had come to pass. Rather, they were projected onto a future scenario of God's coming to judge his people.

Likewise, Jesus made two concrete predictions in his own day: that he would be handed over by the Jews and crucified by the Romans; and that these same Romans would destroy the Jewish temple. Both these predictions came to pass. He was crucified under Pontius Pilate in 30 AD, and in 70 AD the Romans destroyed Jerusalem and the temple once and for all. Within one generation, the greatest monotheistic religion and the greatest pagan nation had foundered on the stumbling block of God's Son, although it took 400 years more for Rome to meet its demise.

I would extend "this generation" to mean "this age." Why the delay? I think Jesus himself gives the reason. In the verse before our passage, he says:

> Jerusalem will be trampled underfoot by the Gentiles, until the times of the Gentiles are fulfilled. (Luke 21:24)

And in Matthew's gospel he says something similar:

> This gospel of the kingdom will be proclaimed throughout the whole world as a testimony to all nations, and then the end will come. (Matt 24:14)

The reason for the delay is God's merciful outreach to all peoples and tribes and languages and nations with the saving Gospel. There is indeed a wideness in God's mercy, like the wideness of the sea. Who are we to restrict the mercy of God to millions of souls yet to come?

Having said this, there is a warning and a promise. The warning is this: no one knows the timing of God, "not even the Son," the earthly Jesus says (Mark 13:32). The end of linear time, or so I think, will be just as mysterious as the beginning, with its billions of years and light-years.

The promise is this: though the precise date of the end is a mystery, the certainty of the end is not. As this same Jesus said: "Heaven and earth will pass away, but my words will not pass away." Jesus Christ will come again in glory, that is the rock on which our hope is built.

So while we continue to live within the cycles of time—seedtime and harvest—we have this hope as the anchor of our souls, that the risen Lord has gone ahead of us to prepare a garden place for us, and he will surely return with his angels for the final harvest, taking us back to our hymn:

> Even so, Lord, quickly come,
> bring thy final harvest home;
> gather thou thy people in,
> free from sorrow, free from sin…

May it be so, as we give thanks for the year that is past and look forward to the coming year as we begin this Advent season. Come, Lord Jesus, come!

John the Baptist: The Wrap-Around Prophet

PSALM 126; MALACHI 3:1–5; LUKE 3:1–6

May the words of my mouth and the meditation of our hearts be always acceptable in your sight, O Lord, our Rock and our Redeemer.

Last week I spoke about the intersection of two dimensions of time. There is the *circular* dimension, the natural rotation of the heavenly spheres, the rising and setting of the sun, the seed-time and harvest of the seasons, the life cycle of the generations. And then there is the *linear* or straight line dimension, which marks out the individual lifespan from birth to maturity to death—the "riddle of the Sphinx" (*Question*: What goes on four feet in the morning and two at noon and three in the evening? *Answer*: Man). This dimension also marks out history from the beginning of creation to the end-time. But truth be told, these two dimensions intersect one another, at least for mankind, because we have minds that can look backward (memory) and look ahead (prophecy). And human history—which is really the only history there is—also contains both dimensions, with repetitive patterns.

What is unique about biblical history is that there is an end-point in the midst of time with the coming of Jesus Christ. Advent is the season of the Church Year when we vividly recall this: "In the fullness of time, God sent forth his Son." And so we remember his first coming—his birth, life, death and resurrection and ascension to heaven. But also we remember that he will come again in glory to judge the living and the dead, as he told us.

This is why I call the season of Advent the wrap-around season. Do you all remember as kids—do they still do this?—when we cut construction paper strips and glued them in rings of a chain for the Christmas tree?

Today we shall see two examples of this wrap-around dimension of God's revelation. The first is the Bible. The Bible is a wrap-around book. Let's look at today's Scripture collect.

> Blessed Lord, who caused all Holy Scriptures to be written for our learning: Grant us so to hear them, read, mark, learn, and inwardly digest them, that by patience and the comfort of your Holy Word we may embrace and ever hold fast the blessed hope of everlasting life, which you have given us in our Savior Jesus Christ; who lives and reigns with you and the Holy Spirit, one God, for ever and ever. Amen.

This Prayer Book collect, written by Archbishop Thomas Cranmer, is one of the finest prayers ever written. It beautifully summarizes the Christian, and the Anglican, understanding of the Bible as "God's Word written."

God has inspired the Scriptures *uniquely*—they are "holy," as he is holy.

God has inspired them for a *purpose*—"for our learning." "All Scripture is breathed out by God and profitable for teaching, for reproof, for correction, and for training in righteousness" (2 Tim 3:16).

God has inspired *all* the Scriptures, i.e. all 66 books from Genesis to Revelation.

We have to apply our minds and hearts to understand the Bible, which includes *reading* it, in church and at home; *marking* it, comparing text with text; *learning* passages by heart; and *applying* it to our lives.

The goal of our learning is to *hold fast* the promise of salvation through Christ.

Now here is the wrap-around character of the Bible. Although God is, from all eternity, the Father, the Son, and the Holy Spirit, he has revealed himself in two acts or chapters over two periods of history. We call these acts and chapters the Old and New Testaments. And we can put dates on the end of the first act, the return from exile in 500–400 BC, and the beginning of the second act from the Christmas story: "In those days a decree went out from Caesar Augustus that all the world should be registered" (that's at the turn of the first century from BC to AD).

We can also see this seam in the story with the last book of the Old Testament, Malachi, and the first book of the New Testament, the Gospel of Matthew. Half a millennium has intervened, but even more importantly, God is coming into history in a new way: the advent of Jesus.

In our lesson today from Malachi, you are reading the last chapter of the Old Testament. Malachi is the last of the "succession of prophets," beginning with Elijah. In this chapter, God personally promises to send his messenger before the "great and terrible day of the Lord," before the end-time. In fact, he calls this messenger Elijah, and there was a tradition that since Elijah was taken directly into heaven and did not die, he would return again personally to usher in the Day of the Lord.

The gap between Malachi and the gospels is bridged by our wrap-around figure, John the Baptist. Mark's gospel makes an immediate connection of Old and New Testaments. He begins this way: "The beginning of the gospel of Jesus Christ, the Son of God, as it is written: "Behold, I send my messenger before your face, who will prepare your way" (Mark 1:1–2). Luke gives more background information by linking the conception and birth of the cousins Elizabeth and Mary, the mothers of John and Jesus.

John himself always confessed that he was a forerunner: "After me comes he who is mightier than I, the strap of whose sandals I am not worthy to stoop down and untie" (John 1:27). But even after baptizing Jesus, John was not sure Jesus was the One. Later when John was imprisoned by Herod Antipas, John sent Jesus a message saying: "Are you the one who is to come, or should we look for another?" Jesus replied: "Go and tell John what you hear and see: the blind receive their sight and the lame walk, lepers are cleansed and the deaf hear, and the dead are raised up, and the poor have good news preached to them" (Matt 11:4–5). Jesus goes on to say this of John: "Truly, I say to you, among those born of women there has arisen no one greater than John the Baptist. Yet the one who is least in the kingdom of heaven is greater than he."

So John is the wrap-around prophet, the last of the line of Old Testament prophets, the second coming of Elijah, and yet his ministry was transitional. He is of the old dispensation, yet unlike the other Old Testament prophets, he is alive in time to announce the new age, the age of repentance from sin and forgiveness of sin. Jesus himself received John's baptism on our behalf, and through him it became the Church's chief sacrament of entry.

So what does the wrap-around Bible and the wrap-around Prophet mean to us? A few implications.

First, regarding the Bible. We ourselves are living in a wrap-around age, though not the same period as John the Baptist. We live in the *already* of the Kingdom: Jesus has come once and for all, has died and risen, has sent his Spirit. But we also live in the *not yet*, in a world where the world, the flesh, and the devil are active, not only in society but in our own fallenness.

For this reason, we need to read the whole Bible, both Old and New Testaments. Going back to the Scripture collect, we need to read, mark, learn and inwardly digest the wonderful stories of the Old Testament, read the Psalms as our hymnbook, ponder the wisdom of Solomon, and yearn for the Second Coming of the Messiah much as Isaiah and Malachi did.

Secondly, because we have a foot in both ages, we need to examine our own lives and confess our sins as much as the Jewish people did who went to the Jordan to be baptized by John. Forgiveness of sin does not exempt us from the demands of holiness and righteousness; in fact it heightens the cost of discipleship.

Thirdly, we must be prepared to give our all, to become fools for Christ as John was, and to pay the ultimate price for the truth of the Gospel, as John did.

Yesterday we commemorated the eightieth anniversary of Pearl Harbor Day, December 7, 1941, "a date which will live in infamy," as President Roosevelt memorably put it. In the war that followed, nearly a half million Americans were killed, another half million wounded, and countless millions affected, including the Holocaust of the Jewish people in Europe and the final blow struck by the atom bombs at Hiroshima and Nagasaki. Imagine the abrupt shock and change in perspective which the "greatest generation" experienced that Christmas in 1941.

In our day we can be certain that times of personal and historical tribulation lie ahead of us as a nation and as a church. There may be times where we as Christians will find ourselves outcasts, as even millions of Christians are throughout the world today. We may see many signs that Jesus spoke of concerning the end times.

As I said last week, the one thing we know for sure about the Second Coming is that it will happen. And this is the other side of the wrap-around message. We live in faith and hope of the new age, the day of redemption. Despair is overcome by hope. Jesus said of the last times: "Now when these things begin to take place, straighten up and raise your heads, because your redemption is drawing near" (Luke 21:28).

Imagine the joy of the end of the war in 1945, the crowds jubilant, the girls kissing strangers, the soldiers' relief sailing past the Golden Gate

Bridge: "We made it home alive." Then multiply that by eternity. This is the joyful message of our psalm today:

> When the Lord restored the fortunes of Zion,
> we were like those who dream.
> Then our mouth was filled with laughter,
> and our tongue with shouts of joy…
> He who goes out weeping,
> bearing the seed for sowing,
> shall come home with shouts of joy,
> bringing his sheaves with him.

Brothers and sisters, let us embrace this wrap-around season, with repentance and sobriety, and with expectation and joy.

Stephen, John, and the Holy Innocents: Witnesses to Christ

ACTS 8:54–60; JOHN 21:20–25; MATTHEW 2:16–23

May the words of my mouth and the meditation of our hearts be always acceptable in your sight, O Lord, our Rock and our Redeemer.

Merry Christmas! Ok, precisely, Merry Day after Christmas.* Actually on the church calendar this is the First Sunday after Christmas. And to be sure, merry Stiller Sunday, if you are perhaps online and also on TV.

Let me try again. Happy Holidays! Because there are *three* holy days in the Church Year that occur right after Christmas. These are called red-letter days because they commemorate major events or persons in the life of Jesus Christ. You can find these on pages 691–712 in the Book of Common Prayer, and like cars linked to a locomotive, they fall on December 26, 27, and 28, following Christmas Day on December 25.

These three holy days commemorate St. Stephen, St. John, and the Holy Innocents. I want to speak of these three as "witnesses to Christ," who was the light coming into the world.

Stephen, Deacon and Martyr

Today is St. Stephen's Day. When my parents named me, I doubt they imagined me preaching in a church or blogging under the name "Contending Anglican." Stephen was indeed a contentious man, speaking to a Jewish audience:

* We at Redeemer celebrated Christmas on December 19 with a Festival of Lessons and Carols. Many young people were away on Christmas Day (Saturday) visiting parents.

> You stiff-necked people, uncircumcised in heart and ears, you always resist the Holy Spirit. As your fathers did, so do you. Which of the prophets did your fathers not persecute? And they killed those who announced beforehand the coming of the Righteous One, whom you have now betrayed and murdered.

This portrait of Stephen reminds me from my student days of an old evangelist named Hubert Lindsey—"Holy Hubert," students affectionately called him—who set himself up on a soapbox near Sather Gate in Berkeley, California, the site of many student riots and protests. His wiki-bio reads: "Lindsey was confrontational, even combative, humorous and hyperbolic, and relentless in his preaching. His signature line was 'Bless your dirty heart,' a phrase which he used as the title of a 1973 autobiography." I am not sure how many students came to Christ from Holy Hubert's preaching, but I do know he was part of a motley Jesus Movement that emerged in the late sixties and seventies.

Stephen too had few converts we know of, but one of them would change the world: Saul of Tarsus. This Saul, Paul the Apostle, later confessed:

> And when the blood of Stephen your witness was being shed, I myself was standing by and approving and watching over the garments of those who killed him. And [the Lord] said to me, "Go, for I will send you far away to the Gentiles." (Acts 22:20–21)

In his steadfast faith and forgiveness of his enemies, Stephen became a watchword of the early Christians: "the blood of the martyrs is the seedbed of the Church."

St. John the Evangelist

The second feast tomorrow is of St. John the Evangelist. John was not, so far as we know, a soapbox evangelist but rather a theologian—the Orthodox call him the Theologian—and an author of at least four books of the New Testament (the gospel and three letters, and perhaps the book of Revelation). John saw himself as a *witness* to the light of Jesus Christ. Much as John the Baptist was forerunner of the Messiah, so John the Evangelist lived almost to the end of the first century and was the last apostle to write his gospel. It was said of him:

> So the saying spread abroad among the brothers that this disciple was not to die; yet Jesus did not say to him that he was not to die, but, "If it is my will that he remain until I come, what is that to you?" This is the disciple who is bearing witness about these things, and who has written these things, and we know that his testimony is true.

Yet even more significant than the length of his apostleship was the depth of his knowledge of Jesus. He is called the Beloved Disciple, the one who laid his head on Jesus' chest at the Last Supper and who, alone of the disciples, stood at the foot of the Cross. In his gospel, one might say, he writes from the heart of God to our hearts. John's soapbox was his gospel, and many, many have been converted simply by reading it.

The Holy Innocents

The third day—the Feast of Holy Innocents—seems hardly something to celebrate: the genocide of the children of Bethlehem:

> Then Herod, when he saw that he had been tricked by the wise men, became furious, and he sent and killed all the male children in Bethlehem and in all that region who were two years old or under, according to the time that he had ascertained from the wise men.

The Church calls them "innocent," not that they were born into the fallen race of Adam without sin, but in the sense that they were too young to have committed conscious sins. If you wish, they were the quintessential victims.

It is hard not to think of the children one sees on TV screens at Christmas, cooped up in refugee camps, begging on the streets, and trafficked by pimps. We think in particular of persecuted Christians around the world.

Herod was a truly despicable man, killing his own wife and sons, but he was merely a pawn in a larger drama of evil in the high places, even the spirit world. Here is how John sees it in his apocalypse:

> And a great sign appeared in heaven: a woman clothed with the sun, with the moon under her feet, and on her head a crown of twelve stars. She was pregnant and was crying out in birth pains and the agony of giving birth. And another sign appeared in

> heaven: behold, a great red dragon, with seven heads and ten horns, and on his heads seven diadems. (Rev 12:1–3)

There is a spiritual source of evil, Satan, who is called the "prince of this world," the Tempter, a murderer from the beginning. Jesus has exposed this source of evil and conquered it on the Cross. The blood of these innocent victims cries out for justice. By recalling the Holy Innocents, the Church stands in solidarity with all these people.

And that cry receives an ultimate reply from God. Matthew cites the following passage from the Old Testament prophet Jeremiah:

> Thus says the LORD: "A voice is heard in Ramah, lamentation and bitter weeping. Rachel is weeping for her children; she refuses to be comforted for her children, because they are no more." Thus says the LORD: "Keep your voice from weeping, and your eyes from tears, for there is a reward for your work, declares the LORD, and they shall come back from the land of the enemy." (Jer 31:15–16)

In the midst of the greatest personal tragedy, a mother weeping for her lost children, God promises hope: "they shall come back." This is the word of hope to all who mourn. God who did not spare his own Son, will he not give us all good things? This is my personal view with regard to the lost innocents of our day, those cut off from the womb. They will see the light of God.

Brothers and sisters, these three holy days remind us of three ways Christians can witness to the Christ child: through lives of bold evangelism; through lifelong study and meditation on God's Word; and through extending a hand of mercy—a cup of cold water—to the many millions who are victims of the principalities and powers of this age.

So as we keep these feasts of Jesus' birth, let us also be counted among those who have witnessed to the true Light that has come into the world.

JESUS: THE EARLY YEARS

The Name Made Flesh: The Circumcision and Naming of Jesus

GENESIS 17:7–13; PHILIPPIANS 2:5–11; LUKE 2:15–21

May the words of my mouth and the meditations of our hearts be always acceptable in your sight, O Lord, our Rock and our Redeemer.

Last Sunday I opened with Merry Day-after-Christmas! Today it's Happy Day-after-New Year's! Peggy and I encountered a new custom when we lived in Uganda: everyone greeted their neighbors with "Happy New Year!" once, no matter how late in the year it was. Could even be July 1!

So with these greetings in mind, I am proposing a series of sermons to look at "Jesus: the Early Years," as found in the New Testament.

Two of the gospels—Mark and John—are silent about Jesus' early years. This should not be so surprising when we realize that neither Peter, from whom Mark derived his gospel, nor John knew Jesus until he was an adult.

Here is where the other two gospels—Luke and Matthew—come in. Each includes a genealogy of Jesus and then several stories about the birth of Jesus and his early years. Where did they get this testimony? Most likely, one of them—Luke's gospel—came from Jesus' mother, who, the text says, "treasured up all these things, pondering them in her heart" (Luke 2:19). What an amazing thought that one testimony to Jesus comes from a man who lay on Jesus' breast, and another testimony comes from a woman who nursed Jesus at her breast! The other account in Matthew's gospel, I think, comes from Jesus' other parent, from Joseph, as I'll explain in a later sermon.

My plan for this sermon series is to look at the glimpses of Jesus' early years, from his birth to his baptism in the Jordan River. The series will cover the major events of the Christmas and Epiphany seasons, though I shall reorder the specific texts and weeks in the Prayer Book lectionary.

The topic for today is the Circumcision and Holy Name of Our Lord Jesus Christ, which is a red-letter holy day for January 1. So instead of "Happy New Year!" it's "Happy Circumcision Day!"

This takes us into some rather messy territory. In the story of *The Best Christmas Pageant Ever*, the scruffy Herdman kids hear the Christmas story for the first time and perk up at the news Mary was "great with child." "Pregnant!" Ralph Herdman cries. "Mary was pregnant!" The prissy young Alice Wendleken takes offense at this: "I don't think it's very nice to say Mary was pregnant," she whispers. Imagine her reaction had they asked what was meant when the text says, "Jesus was circumcised on the eighth day"!

Circumcision is the practice of removing the foreskin of the male phallus with a knife. Circumcision is a medically neutral act. In some cultures, circumcision is practiced at puberty, as a recognition of a boy becoming a man. Among some tribes in Uganda, it is a public ceremony with parades through town! Other cultures, such as the Romans of Jesus' day, considered it disfiguring the body and shameful.

But for the Jews, it is an identity marker, the outer sign of being a covenant partner with God. As commanded in our first lesson from Genesis, normally circumcision was done on the eighth day after birth. God's promise to Abraham that his offspring would be God's own people was to be inscribed in the flesh and blood of every Jewish boy.

So Jesus became a son of the covenant by circumcision. Jesus was a Jew through and through and took that sign in his flesh to the Cross. Judaism is the mother of Christianity, and Jewish Christians were and are circumcised. However, once Jesus had shed the blood of the covenant once and for all, circumcision became a secondary matter. It took some Jewish believers time to realize the change, but Paul taught that true circumcision is inscribed on the heart by the Spirit (Rom 2:29). This is not to say that external signs are now useless, for indeed baptism now replaces circumcision as the sign of the new covenant in Christ's blood for Jew and non-Jew alike. Paul puts it this way:

> In him also you were circumcised with a circumcision made without hands, by putting off the body of the flesh, by the circumcision

> of Christ, having been buried with him in baptism, in which you were also raised with him through faith in the powerful working of God, who raised him from the dead. (Col 2:11–12)

As you are aware, some Christians baptize infants as a sign of God's sovereign grace, which comes before a child is morally responsible and which they must confirm by faith at a later age. Others delay baptism for those old enough to confess Christ publicly as a sign of faith. Both practices, as I see it, testify to the Gospel truth that "by grace you have been saved through faith, and that is not of your own doing; it is a gift of God" (Eph 2:8).

Back to Jesus' circumcision. He received not just a mark in the flesh but a name as part of his identity. As our gospel text today puts it: "he was called Jesus, the name given by the angel before he was conceived in the womb." Both Matthew and Luke record that the name Jesus was given by an angel. "I would have named him Bill," Imogene Herdman interjected. She was not all wrong. Jesus, Joshua, Yeshuah, was a common name among Jews. Of course, Jesus had a great prototype in the Joshua who led God's people into the Promised Land. Further, like many Jewish names, "Joshua" meant something—"Yahweh saves." But, to be fair, there were bad Yeshuahs in Jewish history who pretended to liberate the people. What this passage teaches is that, unlike most families where the parents choose a child's name, in this case God chose the name Jesus.

Of course, no one knew the full significance of the name at the time, not even Mary and Joseph, nor even Jesus himself. He was simply Jesus of Nazareth, the carpenter's son. But that's just the point of the Gospel. The name is planted like a seed in the soul of Jesus, along with his circumcised body, but we only come to know him as he grows to full manhood.

The Christian Gospel has a dogma, but it is dogma based on a story. We can only really understand the full message when we look back from the end of the story. Like most great stories, people repeat the narratives from start to finish, even when they know the ending, that "they lived happily ever after."

In one of the most powerful expressions of this unfolding drama—our second lesson today—St. Paul urges believers to

> have this mind among yourselves, which is yours in Christ Jesus, who, though he was in the form of God, did not count equality

> with God a thing to be grasped, but made himself nothing, taking the form of a servant, being born in the likeness of men. And being found in human form, he humbled himself by becoming obedient to the point of death, even death on a cross. Therefore God has highly exalted him and bestowed on him the name that is above every name, so that at the name of Jesus every knee should bow, in heaven and on earth and under the earth, and every tongue confess that Jesus Christ is Lord, to the glory of God the Father.

Paul is addressing the Church, those who are "in Christ Jesus" as if they are beginning the divine story with a clean slate. He does not name Jesus but speaks of "one who was in the form of God" from all eternity. This figure, Paul continues, "emptied himself," literally "made himself nothing" by voluntarily taking upon himself "human form." Paul is here touching on the supreme mystery of the Incarnation, how the utterly transcendent God could become someone "in human likeness." Paul is referring to the race of Adam, mankind created in God's image. Through Adam's disobedience, this race has been enslaved in sin. Adam the servant has become Adam the slave. And therefore it was necessary for God to send a servant in Adam's likeness and for this servant to live the life of a slave, paying the penalty of sin by dying on the Cross.

The story is only half-told, though. Paul goes on to say that God exalted this man—remember the "lifting up" of Christ from the Cross to the grave to the divine throne. And God "bestowed on him the name that is above every name."

What was that name? Stop! Don't run ahead or you may miss something. In Judaism, the name of God—YHWH—was never pronounced because it was considered too sacred. When Jews came upon this name, they would substitute *ha-shem*, literally "the name," or if they spoke Greek they might say *kyrios*, "the LORD" (most English Bibles follow this convention for the sacred name).

So when Paul finally reveals the name—Jesus Christ the Lord—it refers to the Jewish man Jesus of Nazareth, the promised Messiah, Son of Abraham and David, and the Lord, the Second Person of the Trinity. This Jesus is the co-equal with the Father of glory. God and God alone could name his Son, and he chose to name him Jesus. Case closed; sorry, Imogene, Bill won't do!

The combination of the circumcision of the flesh and the naming of Jesus is now clear, and we retell the story every year. We do this as the Church, the Body of Christ. We ourselves are flesh-and-blood residents of this world, in particular of Bellevue and the North Boroughs. It may seem too much to think that God cares about our little assembly here. But this is the same God who cared about Mary and Joseph and their child. What we are called to do in our day is to be obedient to God's Word and God's Way, just as they were in circumcising their son and naming him Jesus.

I've mentioned the story *The Best Christmas Pageant Ever* a couple times, so I'll end on this note. After the pageant, Imogene Herdman, who played Mary, asked for the picture of Mary from the Bible-storybook, and "she said that it was exactly right, whatever that means." Imogene's younger sister, Gladys, who had played the role of the Christmas angel, went out onto the street after the service, shouting: "Hey, everyone! I bring you good tidings of great joy! It's Jesus!"

Can we at Redeemer do less?

THE FIRST SUNDAY OF EPIPHANY — JANUARY 9, 2022

Jesus: Messiah for the Gentiles

MICAH 5:2–6; EPHESIANS 3:1–13; MATTHEW 2:1–12

May the words of my mouth and the meditations of our hearts be always acceptable in your sight, O Lord, our Rock and our Redeemer.

This is the second sermon in the series "Jesus: The Early Years."

How little we know about world-historical individuals: in ancient history we know about the exploits of Julius Caesar in his adult years; in the Bible, we know about David as a young man. But they are unusual and even with them we know little about their younger years. There are two reasons for this, I think. Ancient societies did not cultivate childhood in the way moderns do. Furthermore, history was about kings and gods, not about commoners, and if perchance a commoner came to the throne, he often tried to suppress his lowly origins.

With this in mind, let me pose some "Epiphany Jeopardy Questions on early US Presidents":

- This President is said to have cut down a cherry tree. "Who is....?
- This President had been the first vice president. "Who is....?
- This President wrote the Declaration of Independence. "Who is....?
- This President is the architect of the US Constitution. "Who is....?
- This President is known for his doctrine concerning South America. "Who is....?
- This President was the son of a president. "Who is....?
- This President was born in a log cabin in Kentucky. "Who is....?

Here is the difference between hindsight and foresight. In 1807, when Abraham Lincoln was born at the mid-point of the first six presidents, all of them were from Virginia or Massachusetts, and from eminent and relatively well-to-do families. No one in America at that time could have imagined that the barefoot boy reading by candlelight in Kentucky would be one of the greatest, if not the greatest president in American history, and for much of his life Lincoln himself suppressed his lowly origins, later reinventing himself as a "log-cabin Republican."

So now we come to the gospel text for today, the three visitors to the baby Jesus. Who were these men? Sometimes they are called wise men, sometimes kings, as in "We Three Kings." The word in the New Testament is *magi*. We get our word magic from this word, but they were not performing magicians, pulling rabbits out of a hat. Probably the best word is astrologers. Throughout most of human history, people have looked to the stars and tried to find signs and meaning in them. There was a religious side to astrology; often the stars have been associated with gods and goddesses—think of the names of our planets. But astrology could also be a kind of proto-science, and I think the best way to describe the magi would be professional star-gazers. As such, they had discovered a particular configuration in the heavens that they interpreted as pointing to the birth of a new age, with the birth of a new king. They were not kings themselves, but they were king-searchers, and, we might say, king-finders. We still find Christ through them when we read the Christmas story.

The magi had travelled a long distance from their home. While they were not Jews, they had learned from their research that the Jews were expecting a great king, a Messiah. So they set off, guided by the star, to Jerusalem, the center of Jewish religious and political power. When they arrived and announced they were looking for a newborn Messiah, King Herod and his circle did not receive this as good news, but "were greatly troubled."

Let me say a word about Herod. Herod was a great builder. If you travel to Israel today, you will find that some of the oldest remains are the palaces and fortresses of Herod the Great. He had even rebuilt the temple in Jerusalem, and you can see its magnificent foundations today. Herod's main claim to greatness was the fact he was a client of Caesar Augustus, the first and greatest Roman Emperor, who was even worshiped as a god. Herod was a power-hungry, ruthless man, who murdered any competitor, even his own wife and children. He was only half-Jewish by birth and not religious at all, so the prophecy about the birthplace of the Messiah was probably as much a surprise to him as to the magi, but more like an alarm bell. Herod's interest in their finding the child was not in order to worship him but to kill him. (I spoke two weeks ago about Herod's vicious slaughter of the innocent children after the magi were warned to go home another way.)

The prophecy from the book of Micah is significant because it highlights God's sovereign grace in salvation. David, the last son of Jesse, came from a tiny village outside Jerusalem. (Bethlehem is still small and war-torn to this day, as Peggy and I found out when we went there on Christmas Eve 2007, with Palestinian guards perched on all the rooftops of Manger Square.) In the same way, the Scripture says, from this humble village, tucked away from the lights of the royal city Jerusalem, God will raise up a leader for his people from the lowliest birthplace.

But this is not the whole story of Christmas and Epiphany. Despite the prophecy, none of the Jewish leaders went with the magi to check it out. It's as if they were blinded by their own city lights or the awesome beauty of Herod's temple, because it says that as the magi left the city, the star reappeared and led them to the very spot where Mary, Joseph, and Jesus were. The star represents the natural order known to people by reason and experience. It took them as far as Jerusalem, but only after they heard the Word of God did it lead them further. Those Jewish leaders, who had the biblical revelation, refused to follow it to its logical conclusion, which is the Word made flesh, the child in the manger. Thirty years later, their offspring cried, "Crucify him," and Herod's successor Pontius Pilate carried out the sentence.

Not so, the magi. Their reaction was joy, worship, and thanksgiving. "They rejoiced with exceeding, great joy"; they prostrated themselves before the Christ Child; and they gave their best gifts in thanksgiving (which I would suggest is the best reason we give Christmas gifts to those we love). Their returning home by another way is a sign of the new way of salvation that God offered them and us through Jesus the Messiah.

The story of the magi is remembered because Jesus Christ was not only the expected Messiah of the Jewish people but the Savior of all nations ("Gentiles"). The word "epiphany" means the "shining forth" of Jesus as the Light of the World. Interestingly, Jesus himself only gave glimpses of this role throughout his earthly ministry. In fact, Matthew records that he once said to a Gentile woman: "I was sent only to the lost sheep of the house of Israel" (Matt 15:24). He died on a Cross that read "the King of the Jews." It was important for Jesus to fulfill the promise of God's covenant with the Jewish people before he shone forth to the nations.

To this day, there are Jews who honor Jesus as a great rabbi, based on his teachings in the Sermon on the Mount in Matthew's gospel. The problem is, those Jews have not read to the end of the story. This same Gospel of Matthew ends with the risen Jesus' Great Commission: "All authority in heaven and on earth has been given to me. Go therefore and make disciples of all nations, baptizing them in the name of the Father and of the Son and of the Holy Spirit" (Matt 28:18–19).

This same risen Jesus appeared to Saul of Tarsus, a zealous Jew if ever there was one, on the road to Damascus, and this Jesus commissioned him to preach the Gospel to the Gentiles "to open their eyes, so that they may turn from darkness to light and from the power of Satan to God" (Acts 26:18). In our epistle today, Saul, now called Paul, himself describes his commission this way:

> For this reason I, Paul, a prisoner for Christ Jesus on behalf of you Gentiles—assuming that you have heard of the stewardship of God's grace that was given to me for you, how the *mystery* was made known to me by revelation, as I have written briefly. When you read this, you can perceive my insight into the *mystery of Christ*, which was not made known to the sons of men in other generations as it has now been revealed to his holy apostles and prophets by the Spirit. This *mystery* is that the Gentiles are fellow heirs, members of the same body, and partakers of the promise in Christ Jesus through the gospel. (Eph 3:1–6)

Three times Paul describes his gospel as the revelation of a *mystery*, that is, something that Jews under the Old Covenant did not expect or understand. Paul says not only that the Gentiles have been included in the new covenant but that they have been joined as "members of the same body." Through this Body, the Church, he goes on to say, "the manifold wisdom of God might now be made known to the rulers and authorities in the heavenly places."

Dear friends here at Redeemer, we here today are beneficiaries, the offspring of this mystery. Few if any here have Jewish ancestry: we come from European, African, and Asian backgrounds. We are the heirs of the magi, who are traditionally portrayed as having different ethnicities. We are also people with different opinions on many matters of the day. For Christmas, I got a book called *Think Again: The Power of Knowing What*

You Don't Know. The author is a social psychologist who looks at ways people with strongly held beliefs can open themselves to communicate with those who hold equally strong beliefs and opinions to the contrary and perhaps in the process rethink their own views.

Take the relatively simple matters surrounding the current pandemic. Is it a world-changing event, or will it soon pass and be forgotten? Should the government intervene with mandates or allow freedom of choice? How does one weigh the health benefits of masks and lockdowns with the social and educational losses of isolating people, especially schoolchildren?

Anglicans are heirs of a tradition which says "In essentials unity; in secondary matters difference; in all things charity." I'd like to suggest the magi as role models in this regard. First of all, they were "wise men," who knew the science of the stars, who also sought the "why" of the world as well as the "how": a new king was to be born. This led them to Jerusalem, where they heard the Word of God and set off for Bethlehem. Finally, they encountered the Christ Child himself, and their response was worship.

The New Testament word for "rethinking" is "repentance." It is not always easy to discern what things are essential and what things are secondary. The author of *Think Again* says: "rethinking is not just a skill set but a mindset," and he goes on to call for "confident humility," which is more than mere compromise but less than unbending certainty. I would suggest that "confident humility" is another way of saying "charity." We must have confidence in the truth of the Gospel and love of the Father in order to walk in the light but also realize that we continue to be sinners constantly being tested and tempted to enthrone our own ideas as if they were God's. We need each other, we need "the other," the neighbor, in the Body of Christ to discern the light that God gives through his Son.

As we celebrate the Day of Epiphany and the season named for it, let us join the magi and journey once again to the crib of the Christ Child, "in whom are hidden all the treasures of wisdom and knowledge" (Col 2:3). O come let us adore him!

Jesus and Mary: Flesh of Our Flesh and Blood of Our Blood

EXODUS 13:2, 13B–15; HEBREWS 2:14–18; LUKE 2: 22–40

May the words of my mouth and the meditations of our hearts be always acceptable in your sight, O Lord, our Rock and our Redeemer.

This is the third sermon in the series "Jesus: The Early Years." I am using the "proper" lessons, as they are called, for the holy day which normally falls on February 2. No, Yinzers, it is not Groundhog Day, though the weather today certainly reminds me of Bill Murray and Andie MacDowell frolicking in front of the weather map.* Rather, the day is named "The Presentation of Christ in the Temple."

The Feast has a second name: "The Purification of the Blessed Virgin Mary." The choice of "presentation" or "purification" is not a Protestant versus Catholic thing. It's not a matter of Jesus versus Mary. They go together, just as the virginal, if you wish the immaculate, conception of Jesus by the Holy Spirit in the womb of his mother goes together with his altogether natural birth in the stable in Bethlehem. Hence my theme: Jesus and Mary share the same flesh and blood, and yes, it's our flesh and blood. Praise God!

Let's look at the text of today's gospel from Luke, chapter 2. The first thing to notice is that purification is "according to the Law of Moses." It's hard to get one's mind around the rationale of this Law. In fact, there is something of a "yuck" element to purification, just as there was with circumcision. As the Law sees it, the mother's bloody afterbirth—the pla-

* "Yinz" is the Pittsburgh version of "y'all." The protagonists of the movie *Groundhog Day* are part of a Pittsburgh weather team that gets caught in a snowstorm and a time-warp in Punxsutawney, Pennsylvania. As it turned out, our service this day was snowed out and I posted the sermon on our Facebook page.

centa—renders her "unclean" for forty days. This is not a matter of hygiene calling for a scrub nurse. The rationale for this law goes something like this: blood is the principle of life—"life is in the blood," the Law says (Lev 17:11)—but blood in the wrong place, outside the body, is a sign of disorder and death. Think of the spilt blood of Abel, the son of Adam and Eve, crying out from the earth (Gen 4:10). But unlike the sin of murder, a woman's vaginal blood is morally neutral and can be cured by the passage of time and a sacrificial offering. In the case of a new mother, both are at work. After forty days, she comes to the temple and offers a sacrifice—a lamb for the well-to-do, two turtle doves for the poor. The priest then declares her clean again.

Now we come to the second aspect of the Law in this gospel passage: the presentation of the first-born son. God says to Moses: "Consecrate to me all the firstborn. Whatever is the first to open the womb among the people of Israel, both of man and of beast, is mine...Every firstborn of man among your sons you shall redeem."

There is a second principle at work here: God has a claim on the first-born offspring as token of the truth that God has a claim on all life. This claim on the first-born has a basis in God's creation of man—God is our ultimate Father, and we are not our own: we were made and bought with a price (1 Cor 6:20). Presenting one's first-born son at the temple is a symbolic way of offering him back to God. This act may be more than symbolic. In the Old Testament, Hannah made a vow to dedicate her first-born to serve in the temple. God opened her womb and Samuel became a great priest and prophet in Israel. It has been a custom among many Roman Catholics to "dedicate" their eldest sons (often in a large family) to the priesthood.

Equally, the dedication of the first-born is a reminder of God's salvation of his people at the Red Sea. The Old Testament text goes on:

> And when in time to come your son asks you, "What does this mean?" you shall say to him, "By a strong hand the LORD brought us out of Egypt, from the house of slavery. For when Pharaoh stubbornly refused to let us go, the LORD killed all the firstborn in the land of Egypt, both the firstborn of man and the firstborn of animals. Therefore I sacrifice to the LORD all the males that first open the womb, but all the firstborn of my sons I redeem."

Here we see another connection between the blood of purification and the blood of redemption. The wages of sin, of our rebellion against God, is death, and Pharaoh and the Egyptians paid this price on Passover night, when all the first-born of Egypt died. But God spared his people, his adopted son, by redeeming them through shed blood on the doorposts. Now God's true Son is born and presented at the temple, along with two small birds, the humblest of offerings. These birds foreshadow the offering of Christ on the Cross, who emptied himself and became nothing for our sake.

The presentation of the baby Jesus, which probably occurred amongst milling multitudes at the temple, does not go unnoticed. Two elderly figures, "waiting for the redemption of Israel," break forth in song and prophecy. Just as the pagan magi had prostrated themselves before the Messiah, so now the pious Jew Simeon takes the baby in his arms and cries out:

> Lord, now let your servant depart in peace…for my eyes have seen your salvation that you have prepared in the presence of all peoples, to be a light to lighten the Gentiles and for your people Israel.

Simeon goes on:

> Behold, this child is appointed for the fall and rising of many in Israel, and for a sign of opposition (and a sword [he says to Mary] will pierce through your own soul also), so that thoughts from many hearts may be revealed.

The prophecy of the dawn of salvation is accompanied by a dark shadow—for Jesus, for Mary, and for the Jewish people. It is another foreshadowing of Calvary, of Mary at the foot of the Cross, though it includes the promise that this same Gospel of Christ crucified will penetrate the hearts of many down through time to the present day.

The second witness at the presentation is the prophetess Anna, a Jewish centenarian, who had been widowed for eighty-four years. Anna is, I think, the patron saint of the retired but not tired, for it says of her:

> She did not depart from the temple, worshiping with fasting and prayer night and day. And coming up at that very hour she began

> to give thanks to God and to speak of him to all who were waiting for the redemption of Jerusalem.

Anna fasted, Anna prayed, Anna praised, and Anna evangelized.

And so Luke concludes his story of the Holy Family, saying "when they had performed everything according to the Law of the Lord, they returned into Galilee, to their own town of Nazareth." This verse leaves out part of the story, which we shall come to next week: the flight into Egypt.

So what are we to make of this glimpse into Jesus' first visit to the temple in Jerusalem? This brings me to the reading today from the Epistle to the Hebrews:

> Since therefore the children share in flesh and blood [of their parents], he himself likewise shared in these same things…and it was necessary that he was like his brothers in every respect.

Last year I was quite struck by a fine song written by our own Melissa McKinney titled "The DNA of God." This is from the first stanza about the angel's announcement of Jesus' birth:

> Earthly mother, foster father, they rejoiced,
> For that word brought her
> A baby with the DNA of God.

Now I am no geneticist but my understanding is that DNA comprises a protein which contains a digital code that opens up the amazing complexity of human nature. However God the Holy Spirit worked in the womb of the Virgin Mary, it was her DNA, her flesh and blood, that was shared by Jesus. And in turn, Mary's DNA had descended from *her* parents and grandparents, all the way back to Adam, fallen Adam and Eve, and is shared with us today.

And that, my friends, is the Good News of the Word become flesh. Hebrews goes on to say:

> Therefore, so that he might become a merciful and faithful high priest in the service of God, he made propitiation for the sins of the people. For because he himself has suffered when tempted, he is able to help those who are being tempted.

This is Good News indeed because the flesh and blood of Jesus Christ is the flesh and blood of a Savior. The early Christians used the fish symbol *IXTHYS* for the Gospel. The Greek letters spell: Jesus Christ, Son of God, Savior. Unless he is Son of God, he cannot save. Unless he is Savior, there is no Good News to tell and, as Paul puts it, we believers are the most pitiable of men.

So yes, the purification of Mary and presentation of Jesus does have a "yuck" element because we weak mortals, we creatures of flesh and blood, are yucky, and we need One who has become like us in every way.

Earlier this afternoon, I went to the gravesite of a little baby who was born one year ago today and died two weeks later. A year ago, the parents had been bereft, like the mothers of Bethlehem in Jesus' day, and I had tried to console them with the prophetic words: "Keep your voice from weeping, and your eyes from tears…declares the LORD. There is hope for your future." This year, the mother is pregnant again and hoping to deliver a baby soon.

Christian hope is founded on the Gospel truth that God spared not his own Son but gave him up, flesh and blood, for us all (Rom 8:32). And on that first Easter Day, as Melissa ends her song:

> Mary recognized his visage
> Folded graveclothes, with his Image
> Imprinted with the DNA of God.

May we have this hope imprinted in our hearts this day as well, for we too like Mary are sharers of the blood of Jesus and the DNA of God.

Jesus: The Return of the Refugee

EXODUS 4:19–23; JUDGES 13:1–7; MATTHEW 2:11–13, 19–23

May the words of my mouth and the meditations of our hearts be always acceptable in your sight, O Lord, our Rock and our Redeemer.

In my snowed-out sermon last week I spoke about an event that happened forty days after Jesus' birth: the purification of Mary and the presentation of the baby Jesus at the temple in Jerusalem. Then, according to Luke's gospel, the Holy Family went home to Nazareth. It is hard to fit Luke's version easily into Matthew's version of the visit of the magi, Herod's genocide of the children of Bethlehem, and the Holy Family's escape into Egypt. Rather than try to harmonize Luke and Matthew into one seamless account, I am suggesting that each evangelist had separate sources, Luke's through Mary, and Matthew's through Joseph.

Matthew's perspective is more masculine than Luke's. He begins with a patriarchal genealogy down from Abraham to David to "Joseph, the husband of Mary, of whom Jesus was born." Joseph is the principal actor in the first two chapters. He is a *just* and *courageous* man, willing to bear the scandal surrounding Mary's pregnancy. He is a *spiritual* man, who receives dreams and angelic visions from God, and it is he who names Jesus. He is an *energetic* and *resourceful* man, leaving Bethlehem abruptly by night with his wife and young child on an arduous journey. He is a *well-informed* and *prudent* man, choosing to return to Nazareth rather than locate in Judea, where danger still lurks under Herod's son Archelaus.

Whatever the differences in perspective between Luke and Matthew, they are agreed that the central figure of the narrative is Jesus, who is the long-awaited Messiah. Luke highlights Jesus' arrival through living prophets in the present, Zechariah, Mary, Simeon, and Anna. Matthew punctuates Jesus' life as the fulfilment of proof-texts from the past, Isaiah ("a virgin shall conceive"), Micah ("you, O Bethlehem"), Jeremiah ("Rachel weeping for her children"), and the two texts for today: "Out of Egypt I have called my son" and "He shall be a Nazarene."

So let's take a look at these two texts: the first, "out of Egypt I have called my son," is taken from the prophet Hosea, who was, along with Amos, the first writing prophet to warn the nation of a coming exile. In this prophecy, the Lord God speaks as a heart-broken father about his wayward son: "When Israel was a child, I loved him, and out of Egypt I called my son. The more they were called, the more they went away; they kept sacrificing to the Baals and burning offerings to idols" (Hos 11:1–2). In referring to the nation corporately as God's son, Hosea is recalling God's instruction to Moses: "You shall say to Pharaoh, 'Thus says the LORD, Israel is my firstborn son…Let my son go that he may serve me'" (Exod 4:23). But just as surely as the Lord names Israel as his son, just as surely this prodigal rebelled against God, beginning with the golden calf and on down to its persistent worship of Canaanite idols.

Despite this grim track record, Matthew sees hope in the prophecy because now God's true Son has come into the world. In the context of Herod's persecution, the family's exile to Egypt is part of God's provision for his Son. This was true of the first Joseph, who was taken as a slave to Egypt as part of God's plan to prepare a place for the people. Egypt was later a place of refuge when the Babylonians invaded the land. Many exiles remained in Egypt, which became a center of Jewish life and learning.

The word "refugee" has two senses. There is the sense of *loss*: loss of one's home, one's family and friends, one's identity. Think of the pitiable condition of millions of refugees around the world today, living in tents and cardboard shanties, with poor water, food, medicine, and education, and little hope for the future. Some of these camps have existed for decades, and children have been born and grown to adulthood without experiencing anything like a normal life.

But there is another sense of *refuge*: a place of relative safety from tyranny, brutality, and death in the home country. Refugees have chosen refuge, and at times they have been welcomed by their host nation. The Bible gives special instructions for treatment of sojourners: "You shall not wrong a sojourner or oppress him, for you were sojourners in the land of Egypt" (Exod 22:21). Today host nations and international aid agencies give refugees a place to live and wait for a time when they may either return home or emigrate to a new homeland. Refugees experience hardship and uncertainty; they also live in hope of a better day to come. And for believers, this hope is grounded in God himself, as the psalms say so eloquently: "God is our refuge and strength, a very present help in trouble. Therefore we shall not fear" (Psalm 46:1–2).

I titled this sermon "Jesus: The Return of the Refugee." Matthew is telling us that the Holy Family's flight to Egypt was reenacting Israel's four-hundred-year sojourn in Egypt. The child Jesus is born in a stable in a strange town, he travels through the wasteland of Judea, and we have no idea where he spent his first few years. On leaving Egypt he takes a detour to find safe space in Nazareth. And because he has become like us in all things, Jesus is our refuge.

Now I want to turn to the second part of this passage: Return from refuge. Matthew says of Joseph: "being warned in a dream he withdrew to the district of Galilee, and he went and lived in a city called Nazareth." Why Galilee? Why Nazareth? Of course, because Nazareth was Joseph and Mary's adopted home town (it seems likely that their families had migrated there from Bethlehem). I think Matthew is also drawing a connection between Bethlehem and Nazareth. Both were insignificant villages, one in the Jewish heartland, the other in the mixing bowl of Galilee. Even within Galilee, Nazareth was an obscure village—"Nowheresville," one commentator calls it.

Today tourists drive several hours north within the state of Israel from Jerusalem to the Sea of Galilee. That was not true in Jesus' day. In Old Testament times, the Land had been divided into a northern kingdom (Israel) and a southern kingdom (Judah and Jerusalem), and in 721 BC, the Assyrians conquered the northern kingdom and deported most of its population and replaced them with refugees from other nations. For this reason, this region was known as "Galilee of the nations." In Jesus' day, Galilee was a crazy quilt of Jews and Greeks and Samaritans, and the elite leaders in Jerusalem considered its people impure. "What good can come out of Nazareth?" they sneered.

Yet, as St. Paul puts it, "God chose what is foolish in the world to shame the wise; God chose what is weak in the world to shame the strong" (1 Cor 1:27). The exiled family of Joseph may have even been considered outsiders by the people of Nazareth, as seen years later in Jesus' hostile reception at the synagogue there. But Matthew contrasts their "impure" status, even in Nazareth, with Jesus' pure spirituality, as prophesied: "He shall be a Nazarene."

Matthew makes this connection by means of a word-play, linking the name of the town Nazareth with the Hebrew word *nazir* or "nazirite." A nazirite in the Bible is a person who takes a special vow to devote himself to God's service. He signals his vow by abstaining from alcohol and leaving his hair uncut. Usually a nazirite vow was for a limited time, but Samson is an exceptional case, as the angel says to his mother: "the child shall be a nazirite to God from the womb to the day he dies." While the nazirite vow did not include abstaining from sex, in the case of Samson, women were his downfall, dallying with the Philistine Delilah and getting a haircut for his troubles.

There are other hints in the Old Testament that, despite the general command to "increase and multiply," God honors those who remain single in his service. In the courts of kings, eunuchs were unsexed to serve as body guards. Although their status violated Jewish laws of purity, the prophet Isaiah says this of such people:

> Let not the eunuch say, "Behold, I am a dry tree." For thus says the Lord to the eunuchs who keep my Sabbaths, who choose the things that please me and hold fast my covenant: "I will give in my house and within my walls a monument and a name better than sons and daughters; I will give them an everlasting name that shall not be cut off." (Isa 56:3–5)

Jesus himself echoes this exceptional view in his teaching on marriage, saying: "For there are eunuchs who have been so from birth, and there are eunuchs who have been made eunuchs by men, and there are eunuchs who have made themselves eunuchs for the sake of the kingdom of heaven" (Matt 19:12).

It is well-known that Jesus was unmarried, and there is no evidence that he ever looked at a woman lustfully, though he could warn others not to. It is clear that Jesus was totally dedicated to his Father. Thus he was a nazir, a "eunuch for the kingdom of God."

This is no irrelevant fact about Jesus. Just as he had a miraculous conception through the flesh and blood of Mary, so also he was not the biological father of any child. While he had half-brothers according to the flesh, he is the adoptive brother of all who come to the Father through him. He made this clear when his mother and brothers came looking for him, and he looked at his disciples and said: "Here are my mother and brothers!" Let us praise God for this! As we come to the Lord's Table to-day, know that the Lord is present and saying to us, "Welcome to the wedding feast! You are my brothers and sisters, born again into my family."

Now let me conclude by linking Jesus the Nazarene with Jesus the refugee. The entire mission of the Son of God was to take on our human nature even at its lowliest status and to lift it up on the Cross. "God became man that man might become God," said the great bishop Athanasius. When Jesus humbled himself to be born in a stable and to be exiled to Egypt and to forgo the normal pleasures and duties of husband and father, he did so for us. And our primary response to this self-emptying is thanksgiving, which is what we offer in the Holy Eucharist.

O the deep, deep love of Jesus,
Love of every love the best;
'Tis an ocean vast of blessing,
'Tis a haven sweet of rest.
O the deep, deep love of Jesus,
'Tis the heaven of heavens for me;
And it lifts me up to glory,
For it lifts me up to Thee.

Jesus the Adolescent

1 KINGS 3:5–15; LUKE 2:39–52

May the words of my mouth and the meditations of our hearts be always acceptable in your sight, O Lord, our Rock and our Redeemer.

This is the fourth and final sermon in the series "Jesus: The Early Years." I'll be continuing next week with "Jesus: The Ministry Begins."

Let me begin this sermon about Jesus the Adolescent with a couple points of personal privilege. First point: as of next Sunday, Peggy and I shall be the grandparents of five teenagers, five out of our total seven grandchildren, three of them living with us in Sewickley. This situation reminds us of a time thirty years ago when we had four teenaged children in the same household.

Here is the second point. Peggy and I were the prototypical adolescent Baby Boomers, born right after the Second World War. Our generation grew up in a dominant, wealthy and peaceful country with relatively stable two-parent families and with a vague sense that God was in his heaven and all was right with the world. Personally, I look back at my adolescence as a blessing from God, even though for much of that time I did not even know him to give him thanks. I cannot be so positive about my generation as a whole. Too many of my generation, some still hanging on to power, have indulged their adolescent privilege and have never come to grips with the dark shadow they have brought over the generations that followed.

Turning now to the text, I admit that speaking of Jesus as an adolescent is anachronistic. The modern concept of adolescence posits a distinct period between childhood and adulthood. Many cultures past and present regard growing up in two stages: children and adults. Think of St. Paul's famous line: "When I was a child, I spoke like a child, I thought like a child, I reasoned like a child. When I became a man, I gave up childish ways" (1 Cor 13:11).

This twofold view is reflected in the gospel passage today, where St. Luke tells us about an event in the life of the twelve-year old Jesus. Up to this point, both Matthew and Luke refer to Jesus as a "child." We don't know how long the Holy Family remained in Egypt, but when the time arrived, Matthew reports the angel saying to Joseph: "Rise, take the child and his mother and go to the land of Israel, for those who sought the child's life are dead" (Matt 2:20). Luke refers to the "child" Jesus at his circumcision after eight days and presentation after forty days, and he covers the next twelve years in one sentence: "And the child grew and became strong, filled with wisdom. And the favor of God was upon him."

If we were to paraphrase this last verse, we might say something like: Jesus was a child prodigy, a spiritual prodigy. We are accustomed to noting musical prodigies, mathematical prodigies, and athletic prodigies, I'm not sure we would recognize a spiritual prodigy. That Jesus was a spiritual prodigy should come as no surprise, since unlike any other human child, Jesus was conceived by the Holy Spirit. Even so, as I see it, the Spirit's work in the child Jesus was developmental. The baby Jesus did not start speaking Hebrew in the cradle, nor did the boy Jesus cast out demons or walk on water or read the thoughts of others. No, he grew in wisdom and favor with God as he grew in age and stature.

In looking for parallels with Jesus' early years, I was drawn to the example of Solomon. "King Solomon," Scripture says, "excelled all the kings of the earth in riches and in wisdom" (1 Kgs 10:23). Our Old Testament lesson today tells the story of the young Solomon praying in the temple, thanking God for blessing his father David and his kingdom, and asking for one supreme good: "an understanding mind to govern your people." The text goes on to say that Solomon's prayer "pleased God," and he promised Solomon not only wisdom but riches and honor beyond any king of his day.

Like the young Jesus, Solomon grew in wisdom and favor with God, and his wisdom was so world-renowned that the Queen of Sheba traveled from Africa to Jerusalem to learn from him. But the Bible casts a shadow over Solomon. God's promise comes with a condition: "that you walk in my ways, keeping my statutes and my commandments, as your father David walked." Sadly, Solomon did not continue to walk in God's ways, but "loved many foreign women"—seven hundred wives and three hundred concubines (*whew!*)—"and his wives turned his heart." Unlike his father David, who also had a woman problem, Solomon never repented, and after his death the kingdom was divided in two and was plagued by idolatry down to its end two hundred years later.

How was the young Jesus different from Solomon? To begin with, the young Jesus had none of Solomon's *worldly* advantages: he was not born in Jerusalem in a royal palace nor raised in a king's court but was born in a manger in Bethlehem and raised a refugee in Egypt and then later as a carpenter's son in Nazareth of Galilee. But Jesus had *great* advantages over Solomon: his father Joseph, as I noted last week, was a just and upright man, a man of courage and prudence; his mother was a handmaid of the Lord, pondering the destiny of her son in her heart; and his relatives were godly folk like Zechariah, Elizabeth and John the Baptist, yearning for the coming of the Messiah. So it is not surprising that Jesus' coming of age occurred on an annual pilgrimage to Jerusalem for Passover.

Adolescence is often associated with rebellion against parents. And so it seemed with Jesus: "The boy Jesus stayed behind in Jerusalem, and his parents did not know it." We observe this moment from his parents' perspective, reminding me of the "Kevin!" moment in the movie *Home Alone*. "Son, why have you treated us so?" his mother scolds him. "Your father and I have been searching for you in great distress." Of course, unlike Kevin, Jesus was not pulling pranks on some clueless burglars but sitting in the temple among the rabbis, listening to them and asking them questions.

By age twelve, Luke tells us, Jesus was no longer a child but a man. He had grown in wisdom and favor with God, with knowledge of the Scriptures equal to or beyond the rabbis, and he had become aware that his true Father was in heaven, not in Nazareth.

Having given a glimpse of Jesus' adult identity, Luke lowers the curtain again, saying only that "he went down with his parents and came to Nazareth and was submissive to them." Indeed he remained there for about twenty years with his mother and brothers, being known as "the carpenter's son," even after Joseph's death.

In the coming weeks, I shall speak about Jesus' further education in Sonship, as Luke repeats the phrase that "Jesus increased in wisdom and in stature and in favor with God and man." This sounds a lot like Solomon's success story, but there is a dark foreshadowing in the phrase: "his mother treasured up all these things in her heart." This is the same Mary who was forewarned that "a sword will pierce your soul." The education to come will be preparation for the Suffering Servant, and the foreshadowing will be in the shadow of the Cross.

Now let me return to the question of Jesus' coming of age and ours here at Redeemer. It has been about a year since Seth Zimmerman announced his departure and the church had to decide whether to return to the mother congregation in Sewickley or to strike out on its own. At Easter, the executive team/vestry announced that Redeemer would become its own congregation, and I became its interim rector. This was the toddler stage. Over the next months the congregation changed: some left and some came. In September, when the bishop visited for confirmations, receptions, and rededication and later when the diocese met, Redeemer got its Anglican identity markers. The final stage of childhood was the search for a permanent pastor, and I want to commend the church leadership, the search committee and vestry, for carrying out an excellent professional search. The process is not over, but we may see the end in sight.*

In this context, I want to offer you our new membership directory. I'd like to think of it as a kind of graduation gift from me to you. As I assembled it, I was touched by the names and faces of so many of you gathered here. In Uganda, we would call you the pioneer class. There will no doubt be many changes as Redeemer enters its next stage of growth. But I think it is the right point to celebrate "the far we have come"—another African phrase (cf. 1 Sam 7:12 NIV).

However, when all is said and done, let us remember as a church that we are nothing but a sounding brass and a tinkling cymbal without the encompassing love of Jesus Christ, who has gone before us as our pioneer and who has travelled through every stage of human life and growth, even to the Cross. To him be glory now and forever!

* In fact, on January 30, the finalist and his wife were visiting from Rwanda and present in the congregation. Three days later, the vestry issued him the call.

JESUS: THE MINISTRY BEGINS

Jesus: Man of the Spirit

ISAIAH 42:1–9; LUKE 3:15–28, 38

May the words of my mouth and the meditations of our hearts be always acceptable in your sight, O Lord, our Rock and our Redeemer.

Today I am beginning yet another sermon series on the Lord Jesus Christ, titled "Jesus: The Ministry Begins." Yet it is a continuation of what has gone before and follows roughly the readings for the Church Year. That year begins in the Advent season with the theme of the coming of God's Son as the light of the world, as prophesied in the Old Testament and by John the Baptist, and it culminates in the birth of Jesus on Christmas Day. The twelve days of the Christmas season take us to Epiphany, the revelation of Christ to the Gentiles, as represented by the three magi.

In the previous series, I have rearranged some episodes in order to look chronologically at Jesus' early years—his circumcision and naming after eight days, his presentation in the temple, along with his mother's purification after forty days, his refuge in Egypt and return to Nazareth after several years, and his coming of age when he was twelve years old and stayed behind in Jerusalem dialoguing with the rabbis.

We now move to a new stage, his coming out. Jesus' public ministry begins with his baptism (today's topic), which is normally observed on the first Sunday after Epiphany but which happened decades later when he was thirty years old. We know this is a new stage because all four gospels stop and record Jesus' baptism, and Mark's gospel and the earliest sermons of the apostles begin by telling the story of this baptism (Acts 10:36–38). But even here, Jesus' public ministry unfolds step by step. His baptism leads immediately to his temptation in the wilderness, then to his return to the synagogue in Nazareth, and then on to his first public sign at a wedding in Cana. When we get to the end of these four episodes, we'll be ready for the season of Lent, his road to the Cross.

So let's turn to today's gospel reading from Luke. Luke's account of Jesus' baptism is the shortest among the four gospels, only two lines. Luke surrounds these central lines with two blocks of information in chapter 3: the first block about the public ministry of John the Baptist (verses 1–20) and the second block (verses 23–38) about Jesus' ancestry. Sandwiched between these blocks are these verses:

> Now when all the people were baptized, and when Jesus also had been baptized and was praying, the heavens were opened, and the Holy Spirit descended on him in bodily form, like a dove and a voice came from heaven, "You are my beloved Son; with you I am well pleased." (verses 21–22)

One might expect to hear some important conversation between Jesus and John—which the other gospels record—but Luke ushers John off-stage by mentioning that he was arrested and imprisoned by Herod Antipas. Luke's focus now moves exclusively to Jesus. As John himself said: "He must increase and I must decrease" (John 3:30).

A new actor now appears on stage, not John the Baptist, but the Holy Spirit, who comes upon Jesus as he prays. In the Church's later reflection on the doctrine of the Trinity, the Person of the Holy Spirit was the last piece of the puzzle to fall into place, some seeing the Spirit simply as a force or manifestation of God. But here in Luke, I think, we see something striking: the Holy Spirit descends in bodily form as a dove. What does this mean? Clearly the Spirit is not a bird! But neither is he simply a force like wind or like fire, two other images associated with him. We are into a deep mystery here, but could we say this moment refers to the embodiment of the Spirit in Jesus? Jesus was conceived by the Spirit, and now his adult self is indwelt by the same Spirit. John's gospel puts it this way: the Spirit descended on Jesus and remained on him (John 1:32–33).

From this point on, Jesus was to be directed by the Spirit in all he said and did, until he finished his saving work and gave up his spirit on the Cross. At the same time, Jesus was Lord of the Spirit, as Peter later put it: "He went about doing good and healing all who were oppressed by the devil, for God was with him" (Acts 10:38). And from this point on, the Church has always linked the Son with the Spirit who, we say in the Nicene Creed, proceeds from the Father and the Son, or some would say from the Father through the Son. Put another way, there is no Spirit who is not the Spirit of Jesus, and no Jesus who is not the man of the Spirit.

The descent of the Spirit on Jesus was accompanied by the voice of the Father: "You are my beloved Son; with you I am well-pleased." In Luke's account, this voice was received inwardly by Jesus, in prayer. The Father's words echo several important Old Testament Scriptures. There is God's promise to the Messiah in Psalm 2:7: "You are my Son; this day I have begotten you." Then there is God's word to the Servant in Isaiah, today's reading: "Behold my servant, whom I uphold, my chosen, in whom my soul delights; I have put my Spirit upon him." In both these Scriptures, there is an incredible intimacy of the Father and the Son: "I have begotten you"; and "My soul delights in him;" and "I have put my Spirit upon him." It is hard to see any historical figure—prophet, priest or king like David—coming close to fulfilling these words. Only one who is born of flesh and blood and of the Spirit can possibly suffice. And that One is Jesus Christ! Praise the Lord!

And this is just the point of the second block of information given us by Luke when he says: "Jesus, when he began his ministry, was about thirty years of age, being the son (as was supposed) of Joseph" (verse 23). Here we link up with the story of Jesus the adolescent. While ancient peoples did not envision adolescence as an extended childhood, they did distinguish between "young" and "old" men and women. Youths still needed guidance from "elders" who had reached full adulthood (think the book of Proverbs). While Jesus likely was about thirty when he was baptized, the more important point is that he had achieved "mature manhood."

Not only was Jesus accounted an adult but he was also the first-born and heir of Joseph, his "supposed" father, who by this time had certainly died. Luke goes on at this point to attach a genealogy of Jesus through Joseph. Matthew also has a family tree, which goes back to David and Abraham, but Luke's tree goes back even further to "Seth, the son of Adam, the son of God." The details of the ancestry are not so important as the truth that Jesus shared the DNA of every human being that ever lived. The phrase "Adam, the son of God" is interesting because Adam was never called "son" in the Bible. Adam had no human father but was a creature of dust, into whom God breathed the breath of life. But Jesus did have a human mother and was therefore a "son of man." Finally, Adam was created without sin, but after he fell, all his offspring inherited the curse of sin and death, including Jesus. When Jesus was baptized, he voluntarily accepted that curse even though he had not personally sinned. (Is it possible to see Jesus in this sense as taking upon himself the "innocence" of the slaughtered children of Bethlehem, and other such little ones down the ages?)

Jesus' atoning death on the Cross is foreshadowed in the Father's announcement. It recalls another time when God commanded Abraham: "Take your son, your only son Isaac, whom you love, and go to the land of Moriah, and offer him there as a burnt offering on one of the mountains of which I shall tell you" (Gen 22:2). When Abraham obeyed to the letter, God substituted a ram caught in a thicket. This time, though, it will be God the Father who does not spare his beloved Son but gives him up for us all, the Lamb that was slain. "Oh, the depth of the riches and wisdom and knowledge of God! How unsearchable are his judgments and how inscrutable his ways! But thanks be to God who gives us the victory through our Lord Jesus Christ!" (Rom 11:33; 1 Cor 15:57).

So Luke places Jesus' baptism in the clear context of Jesus' humanity and mortality. But the baptism signals something new: Jesus is also "son of God" through the Holy Spirit. Jesus is the "man of the Spirit" unlike any other person in human history. From his conception in the womb by the Spirit, Jesus had the DNA of God, but at his baptism the Spirit came to dwell in him in a new way. We might even say that he was born again. He was now empowered for his life ministry, for preaching with power, for healing the sick, for casting out demons, and for forgiving sin. From his baptism on, Jesus was not only the recipient of the Spirit but the giver of the Spirit. For this reason, St. Paul can say: "The first man Adam became a living being; the last Adam became a life-giving spirit" (1 Cor 15:45).

So what does Jesus' baptism mean for *us*, for our lives as individuals and as a church? Let me say that this Epiphany sermon series as a whole is meant to increase our understanding and appreciation of the fullness of the Father's love and of Jesus' self-emptying for us. In the words of the famous hymn: "O love, how deep, how broad, how high, how passing thought and fantasy, that God, the Son of God, should take our mortal form for mortals' sake!"

Let's note three ways in particular that Jesus' baptism is for us. First, he accepted John's baptism of repentance for us even though he had no sin to repent of. Luke's account hardly mentions the water of baptism, but Jesus himself went with the people to be baptized. When he commissioned the Church, he commanded it to evangelize and baptize in the name of the Father, the Son and the Holy Spirit. Any faithful church will baptize, whether infants or adolescents or adults, and will hold baptism in honor. This truth is not just for the Church but for us as individual believers. Remember Martin Luther's watchword: "The only way to drive away the Devil is through faith in Christ by saying: 'I am baptized, I am a Christian.'"

Secondly, Jesus' baptism was the fulcrum for the coming and power of the Holy Spirit. Though the Holy Spirit was with Jesus from the moment of his conception, at age thirty he experienced an infilling of the Spirit, who remained with him and in him throughout his ministry, and after his resurrection and ascension into heaven, he dispenses his Spirit to those who, like him, wait in prayer and hear the Father's voice saying: "You are my son," adopted by grace through faith. Again, for us Christians, the seed of the Spirit has been planted in baptism, but we need to be filled, baptized with the Spirit, and to tend and water that seed by asking, asking again and again in prayer. And to those who ask, Jesus promises: "If you then, who are evil, know how to give good gifts to your children, how much more will the heavenly Father give the Holy Spirit to those who ask him!" (Luke 11:13)

Finally, Jesus' baptism transformed what it means to be human. He took on our human flesh and blood and bore it on the Cross, but he also lived a new human life as a "man of the Spirit." This is what we call sanctification. It is also what we call discipleship, walking the way of Christ, the way of the Cross. We who believe have only received the first-fruits of the Holy Spirit—we remain sanctified sinners—but we live in hope that at the Last Day our transformation will be complete, and while we can barely imagine what that looks like, we know it is distinctly human and distinctly Christ-like. We too will be revealed as men and women of the Spirit, partaking of the divine nature and sharing, as it were, the DNA of God (2 Pet 1:4).

The Temptation of Jesus: Satan's Big Ask

1 CORINTHIANS 10:1–14; LUKE 4:1–13

May the words of my mouth and the meditations of our hearts be always acceptable in your sight, O Lord, our Rock and our Redeemer.

We began a new sermon series last week on "Jesus: The Ministry Begins" with the first sermon on Jesus' baptism. I made the point that even though Jesus was conceived by the Holy Spirit and was a kind of "spiritual prodigy" in his adolescence, his baptism at the age of thirty was a decisive moment that set him on a course of ministry that would end with death on the Cross three years later.

His baptism, I said, was not primarily a baptism in water but a baptism in the Holy Spirit, who descended on him in bodily form as a dove, accompanied by the voice from heaven that announced: "You are my Son, with whom I am well-pleased." According to today's gospel, Jesus from this point on was "full of the Holy Spirit" or as I put it, Jesus was now the man of the Spirit, directed by and directing the power of the Holy Spirit, who dwelled or "remained" in and with him. From now on, Jesus preached with divine authority, cast out demons, healed the sick, performed dramatic signs and knew the inner thoughts of others. It was the Spirit, now his Spirit, who led him from baptism in the Jordan to be tempted by the devil in the wilderness.

A word about the devil. I titled my podcast this week, "I believe in Satan," by which I mean "I believe that Satan exists." This should be a no-brainer for those who read the Bible, but it isn't. Even Evangelicals often feel uncomfortable and fudge the matter of the devil as a personal being whose goal is to separate souls from God and consign them to everlasting destruction with him in hell. My main purpose today is not to focus on Satan but on Jesus and how he was prepared for his ministry by this encounter with Satan.

First of all, I think Jesus' baptism flushed Satan out into the open. Satan, you see, prefers to operate as an undercover agent, pulling the strings of fleshly and worldly temptation. He is also ashamed and angry at his fallen identity. When Satan was cast out of heaven, he lost his angelic body and became a bodiless spirit, roaming the earth to see whom he could mislead. The appearance of Jesus as a man filled with the Holy Spirit posed a threat to Satan's secrecy and petty pride, but he imagined an opportunity: maybe he could expel the Holy Spirit and occupy the empty room of Jesus' soul. A kind of reverse exorcism. If this was Satan's hope, it showed how deluded he was about God's Son. When Satan kept probing Jesus with "If you are God's Son," he was actually arming Jesus for his ministry to come. In fact, according to Matthew's gospel, it is Satan himself who is exorcised when Jesus finally says: "Begone!"

So let's look at the three temptations in our text: turning stones into bread, becoming world ruler, and throwing himself off the Temple Mount. Often these temptations are associated with "the world, the flesh, and the devil" that Christians renounce at baptism.

The first temptation—to become *the Great Humanitarian*—was the result of Jesus' forty-day fast in the wilderness. In one sense, Jesus was reenacting the forty-year wilderness journeys of the people of Israel under Moses. He was also taking up the rigorous life of John the Baptist. Jesus was not known as an ascetic; in fact he was accused of being something of a party-goer, and later he did host two huge feasts in the wilderness. But in this test, Jesus took to heart the Scripture that "man shall not live by bread alone" (Deut 8:3). The centrality of eating for all human beings makes food the first temptation of the flesh. For many of us, fasting even for one day is a difficult feat. Yet for many around the world hunger is a daily companion. Trusting God for our daily bread and hungering and thirsting for righteousness is a first step in our life with God. Jesus, as I said several weeks ago, was a "Nazarene" who had dedicated his bodily desires—food and sex—to God. He now proved this before Satan. One gospel says that after the forty days "angels ministered to him." I think that included providing him with food, though probably not the Duncan Hines angel-food cake variety.

The second temptation was the offer to become *the Caesar to end all Caesars*. Glimpsing the totality of the regimes of world history, Satan vows: "To you I will give all this authority and their glory, for it has been delivered to me, and I give it to whom I will." Like most of Satan's lies, there is a half-truth here: the fallen world is under corrupt world rulers, from the greatest tyrant to the lowliest politician or police chief, but it is also true that, as Paul puts it, "there is no authority except from God, and those that exist have been instituted by God" (Rom 13:1). Jesus himself will confess before Pilate: "You would have no authority over me at all unless it had been given you from above" (John 19:11). We should not minimize the temptation to political power. In our day, not only tyrants like Hitler and Stalin but various utopians think they can save the world by means of one scheme or another. The first step in these schemes is to tear down the existing order, which though fallen, is God's domain.

There is no doubt that a man of Jesus' prodigious gifts could have ascended to the throne of Caesar and "made the world a better place." But instead he chose the role of a street preacher in a backwater district of a petty Roman province, announcing "The kingdom of God is at hand." And even now in the hindsight of history, who made the largest and best impact on human history—Caesar or Jesus—not to mention the world to come?

Now to the third temptation—to become *the P.T. Barnum of all Showmen* by staging a grand miracle. Matthew's and Luke's accounts here differ on the order of the temptations. Matthew puts the offer of secular dominion last, but Luke puts religious dominion in that place. The devil challenges Jesus to perform a miracle at the very heart of Judaism, the temple. Even today a visitor to Jerusalem can see the sheer drop from the Temple Mount to the Kidron Valley below. What a spectacle if Jesus, like an acrobat falling from the high wire, had been buoyed up in an angelic safety net. What better way to demonstrate that the true Messiah had come? Here's another spectacle: the Messiah hanging from a Roman cross outside the city wall with the title "King of the Jews." When did Jesus come to understand that his way was the one headed toward Calvary? Perhaps this last temptation of the road not taken was the beginning of Jesus' conviction that "the Son of Man must suffer many things and be rejected by the elders and chief priests and scribes, and be killed, and on the third day be raised" (Luke 9:22).

Let's sum up. I titled the sermon "Satan's Big Ask." What was it? I think it went like this: Jesus, I stand at the door of your heart and knock. Let me in and I'll give you anything and everything a human being could ever want: food, sex, money, power, fame, and immortality. All you have to do is exchange your soul, your spirit, for my spirit.

In ages to come, this "ask" would become known as the Faustian bargain, named after the brilliant Dr. Faustus (no, not Dr. Fauci), who sold his soul to the devil. The truth is that Satan did not have any idea who the Son of God truly is, or the Holy Spirit who had ignited Jesus' soul. The irony is that Satan's malice served as an instrument to prepare Jesus for his coming ministry and the road to the Cross.

Luke's account ends this way: "When the devil had ended every temptation, he departed from him until an opportune time." Jesus never again encountered Satan face to face but only his minions, the demons who oppressed poor vulnerable people and whom he cast out. The opportune test came in the Garden of Gethsemane—this time with the Father—when he prayed: "Father, if you are willing, remove this cup from me. Nevertheless, not my will, but yours, be done" (Luke 22:42). Unlike the earlier temptations, Jesus accepted the Father's verdict on what lay ahead.

What is the relevance of Jesus' temptation for our lives? Our lesson today from 1 Corinthians 10 can give us some insight into this question.

Let's begin by noticing that this little homily by Paul was occasioned by a dispute that was splitting the congregation in Corinth—one of many, it seems—this one about sharing food at church. Imagine that after our weekly Communion services we had suppers like the one two weeks ago but that only tithers or members of fellowship groups were welcome. Paul makes a big deal about this exclusiveness, likening it to Israel's temptations in the desert, which were a kind of object lesson plan for the dysfunctional church.

In particular, Paul saw three temptations in Israel's past: a temptation to false worship, i.e., idolatry; a temptation to false sexuality; and a temptation to broken fellowship by grumbling and gossip. These three temptations were epitomized in the golden calf incident where the people grumbled about Moses's whereabouts (he was talking to God on Mount Sinai) and so they made an idol and they ate and drank and danced and rose up to play (think spring break).

Paul calls these temptations to mind and then challenges the congregation: "We must not put Christ to the test, as some of them did and were destroyed by serpents, nor grumble, as some of them did and were destroyed by the Destroyer." A church, Paul is saying, can be undermined by Satan the Destroyer when its members consciously or unconsciously turn from the way of Christ, the way of the Cross, and in effect put him to the test. The beginning of temptation, Paul warns, is complacency: "Therefore let anyone who thinks that he stands take heed lest he fall." There is no point in the Christian life when one can simply lean back and say, "I've made it. Time to retire to a spiritual Florida and play golf." Better to say: "Teach us to number our days that we may get a heart of wisdom" (Psalm 90:12).

Having warned the Corinthians, Paul has good news as well.

> No temptation has overtaken you that is not common to man. God is faithful, and he will not let you be tempted beyond your ability, but with the temptation he will also provide the way of escape, that you may be able to endure it.

Jesus' defeat of the devil in the wilderness was once for all, just as his death on Calvary was once for all. There is no sin that we can commit that he cannot forgive. There is no point, even to the moment of death, when a person cannot turn to the Lord and be saved. The only real Enemy is despair, doubting the fullness of God's grace. This is the sin of Judas and of Dr. Faustus.

At this point, I want to commend you Redeemer folk for the mature way you have conducted the search for a rector. I think that your unity in the search and in the decision has avoided the kind of divisions that have often happened, even in our parent bodies. But, "take care when you stand, lest you fall" and trust in the One who alone has been tempted in every way without falling.

Jesus' First Sermon: Propelled into Mission

PSALM 67; LUKE 4:14–30

May the words of my mouth and the meditations of our hearts be always acceptable in your sight, O Lord, our Rock and our Redeemer.

In my sermon series about Jesus' early years, we saw how the baby Jesus travelled from Bethlehem through the Judean desert to Egypt and then back to Nazareth. Now, as he begins his ministry, the pattern repeats: Jesus is baptized in the Jordan River, is driven into the desert to be tempted by Satan, and then returns to Nazareth.

What is it about Nazareth? Of course, it is Joseph's immediate hometown, and it was Joseph who directed the first journey. But thirty years later, Joseph is dead, and Jesus' journey is directed by his heavenly Father through the Holy Spirit. Nazareth was hardly a town, but merely a village of several hundred residents. Jesus was almost certainly well-known to all of them, maybe even a local celebrity, which is perhaps why they handed him the scroll of Isaiah to read at the Sabbath service.

Remember that there were no Bibles in Jesus' day; rather, each biblical book was copied on a papyrus scroll. One of the best preserved of the Dead Sea Scrolls is the twenty-four-foot-long Isaiah scroll, including all sixty-six chapters. Isaiah is also the most theologically powerful Old Testament prophetic book, with references to the Messiah in the early chapters and references to the Suffering Servant and the herald of salvation at the end.

Jesus chooses a short portion of this herald prophecy to outline his coming ministry:

> The Spirit of the Lord is upon me, because he has anointed me to proclaim good news to the poor. He has sent me to proclaim

> liberty to the captives and recovering of sight to the blind, to set at liberty those who are oppressed, to proclaim the year of the Lord's favor. (Luke 4:18–19; cf. Isa 61:1–2)

His ministry will include evangelistic preaching—"proclaiming good news." It will involve exorcisms—liberating the captives of Satan; and healing—opening the eyes of the blind. These acts will usher in a new era of God's favor.

This new era is based on the law of the jubilee in the book of Leviticus. According to this law, every fiftieth year (a sabbath of sabbath years) was designated a time of cancelling debts and bonds of servitude and of restoring homesteads to their original owners. It also was a *sacred* year, holy to God and characterized by joy and thanksgiving. The jubilee was a time of jubilation. In this law the prophet Isaiah foresees a final and coming year of the Lord, a jubilee of jubilees, which will be ushered in by the Messiah. This was Isaiah's gospel, good news!

Jesus puts his own stamp on this text. It says:

> And he rolled up the scroll and gave it back to the attendant and sat down. And the eyes of all in the synagogue were fixed on him. And he began to say to them, "Today this Scripture has been fulfilled in your hearing."

What did Jesus mean by this action and "today" comment? I think it meant this: Today the Scripture has been fulfilled. Today the future begins. Today is the day of jubilee. Today the Old Covenant has been superseded. I am not a prophet like Isaiah. I am the One Isaiah was prophesying about. I am he. I am the Messiah, the Son of God, who has come to inaugurate the kingdom of God.

Friends, we are part of that today, that jubilee. Praise the Lord!

How did the congregation in Nazareth receive this announcement? It says: "their eyes were fixed on Jesus." What were they thinking as they looked on this man whom they had known from boyhood as the carpenter's son? Perhaps there was an element of amazement at his newly acquired spiritual power, at "the words of grace coming from his mouth." Perhaps they were secretly thinking of their reputation: "Can anything good come out of Nazareth?" Perhaps there was an element of envy, having heard that this Jesus had made his reputation elsewhere before coming home.

Whatever the reasons, the men of Nazareth were hearing the Good News Jesus was bringing with their outer ears, but their inner ears were locked shut against his message. This should not surprise us. It had not surprised Isaiah, whom God warned in advance: "Make the heart of this people dull, and their ears heavy, and blind their eyes; lest they see with their eyes, and hear with their ears, and understand with their hearts, and turn and be healed" (Isa 6:10).

And it did not surprise Jesus. Having sensed their inner thoughts, he rebuked them: "Doubtless you will quote to me this proverb, 'Physician, heal yourself.' What we have heard you did at Capernaum, do here in your hometown as well." To paraphrase: "If you won't perform miracles for us, then to hell with you." In Mark's version of this story, it says: "he could do no mighty work [in Nazareth], except that he laid his hands on a few sick people and healed them" (Mark 6:5). What an amazing statement! Jesus could do no mighty work because of their stubbornness, oh yes, except for healing a few sick people!

Jesus goes on to link the deafness of his fellow villagers to the history of the people of Israel, who repeatedly rejected the prophets. Yet there is a silver lining in this refusal. When Israel rejected the prophets, God sent them to others outside Israel, like the widow in Sidon and Naaman the Syrian. The Good News of the coming jubilee cannot be contained. If God's chosen people reject God's favor, it overflows to those who will embrace it in faith: to the poor, the sick, the blind, the imprisoned, the exiles—and to those outside the covenant.

Not surprisingly, Jesus' rebuke antagonized the Nazarenes all the more: "When they heard these things, all in the synagogue were filled with wrath. And they rose up and drove him out of the town and brought him to the brow of the hill on which their town was built, so that they could throw him down the cliff."

Some years ago, Peggy and I visited Nazareth. There is not much there to see—no carpenter's shop, no synagogue. The entire town is built on a hill, so it's not clear where they intended to stone him, and it is also unclear how he slipped away—but he did. And where did he slip away to? I suspect it was to Cana, another village less than five miles away. We'll come back to Jesus' reception there next week.

His time was not yet, but I think it fair to say that Jesus foresaw in the visages of his fellow townsmen the faces of those who three years later would welcome him to Jerusalem with "hosannas" and palm fronds and then turn on him, crying, "crucify, crucify!" and who mocked him on another hill, saying "he saved others; himself he cannot save!"

Jesus left Nazareth never to return again. His rejection propelled him to a wider mission to "the lost sheep of the house of Israel." And afterward on yet another hill—the Mount of Olives—the risen Lord would commission his disciples to preach the Gospel to the ends of the earth.

It is this Great Commission that we commemorate on this World Mission Sunday. I want to add one further thought to you Redeemer folk as we prepare for a new stage, yes, let's call it a jubilee in our life as a congregation. Under a new rector, this congregation will change. I commended you last week for the remarkable unanimity that has characterized the formation of this congregation and the search for a new rector to lead it. You are the planting, and the soil has been prepared. But if Redeemer is to grow, to fulfill the Great Commission, it will need to reach out beyond those of us here—to reach out to the poor, the blind, the prisoners of our day.

Let's not be like the Nazarenes. Let's be like those who celebrate the year of the Lord's favor in our midst—and invite others to join us!

Jesus' First Sign: The Wedding at Cana

SONG OF SONGS 8:1–7; JOHN 2:1–11

May the words of my mouth and the meditations of our hearts be always acceptable in your sight, O Lord, our Rock and our Redeemer.

Who is Jesus? This is the most important question the world needs to ask. It is the most important question *we* need to ask. Over the past weeks, we have been looking at the story of Jesus' early years and call to ministry in the Gospels of Luke and Matthew.

John's gospel approaches the question from 30,000 feet up—well actually from heaven downward: "the Word became flesh and dwelt among us, and we have seen his glory, glory as of the only Son from the Father, full of grace and truth" (John 1:14). As John presents it, the Son shared the glory of the Father from all eternity, but in humbling himself to become man, he manifested that glory through time and human experience, which John lays out in a series of signs.

When we first meet Jesus in John's gospel, he is already an adult, baptized by John and full of the Spirit. The first sign occurs at a wedding in the village of Cana in Galilee. Prior to Cana, the Synoptic Gospels suggest, Jesus had called the disciples and began to work miracles at Capernaum near the Sea of Galilee. *The Chosen* series shows Jesus liberating Mary Magdalene from the demonic and amazing Peter with a boatload of fish. These miracles, the show suggests, were relatively private and personal, whereas Cana was witnessed by a large crowd of wedding guests.*

I would suggest another explanation for why Cana was the first sign. Let's look at the brief interchange between Jesus and his mother:

* After the service, we had a viewing in the parish hall of the episode about the Wedding at Cana.

> When the wine ran out, the mother of Jesus said to him, "They have no wine." And Jesus said to her, "Woman, what does this have to do with me? My hour has not yet come." His mother said to the servants, "Do whatever he tells you."

At the human level, Jesus is saying quite naturally, "Mother, why are you bothering me with this trivial problem?" When he goes on to comment "My time is not yet," we may imagine that Jesus foresaw that at some point he would have to "manifest his glory," as John puts it, in some irreversible way. But surely not at a village wedding. The show implies—and I see no reason to object to it—that it is his mother who first senses that this is Jesus' decisive moment when she says "they have no wine," and then goes on to tell the attendants, "Do whatever he tells you." Is it too much to think that she who conceived the Son by the Holy Spirit might have been inspired by the same Spirit to give him a nudge toward the next stage of his ministry?

Why would "they have no wine" be the turning point in Jesus' ministry? Here's a thought. Changing water into wine is impossible according to nature. Jesus' early works of healing and exorcism, wonderful though they were, were extensions and intensifications of natural processes of body and mind. Even a sudden catch of fish can be accidental, an "act of God," as the insurance policies put it. In John chapter 2, Jesus laughs when Nathanael calls him Son of God simply because he saw him sitting under a fig tree. Was this event a case of super-vision, or maybe Jesus just saw him from a distance?

But no one has ever turned water into wine! True, wine is the product of water and the vine, and true, water and wine are both drinks that quench thirst, but no chemist or alchemist can turn a flask of water into a flask of wine, not to mention 150 gallons of it at a go! When Jesus asked the servants to fill the stone water jars with water, he knew that this miracle would be different from the others. This miracle is of a piece with his feeding the five thousand from scraps or his walking on the water or his raising of Lazarus, whose body was already decaying.

This very public sign of Jesus' power over the created order set the clock ticking on his ministry, which was to end on Good Friday and Easter morning. A simple problem—"they have no wine"—gave opportunity for a sign that manifested Christ's glory. A normal ceremony—"I, John, take you, Mary"—looked forward to the marriage of heaven and earth. The

Cross and resurrection are the ultimate manifestations of God's glory in Jesus Christ. The Wedding at Cana was the first manifestation of that glory.

What is it about a wedding, what is it about wine that makes it a fit sign of God's glory? In many cultures, including Jewish culture, a wedding is the culmination, the consummation of a process of courtship, engagement (betrothal) and marriage. It is a family matter, as two families offer up their son or daughter to make a new family. It is a sexual matter, as bride and groom anticipate sleeping together for the first time. It is a spiritual matter, as somehow they recognize that matrimony is holy even as it is mundane, blessed by a good Creator. For all these reasons, the wedding feast is an intoxicating and intoxicated affair.

Let's look for a moment at the Old Testament reading from the Song of Solomon, also known as the Song of Songs. There are many ways to interpret this strange book of the Bible. Let me propose this way. I described in my podcast this week how Peggy and I often spent Saturdays in Uganda with the surround sound of ululations and choruses of "Here Comes the Bride," living as we did next door to the local cathedral. We also attended quite a few engagement ceremonies and wedding receptions. In all these cases, there were many speeches, even when there was no wine present (Anglicans in Uganda are teetotalers and don't dance the *hora*). My proposal is that the speeches or songs of the man and woman throughout the Song of Solomon are wedding boasts. The bride and the bridegroom tell exuberantly the story of their love from their first meeting in the countryside to their entry into the bedchamber.

These are young lovers, but their love has matured like fine wine. The bride warns her younger siblings, "Do not stir up or awaken love until the time is right." The bridegroom, acknowledging the gift the Bride's mother has given him, promises fidelity to his wife, to be a seal upon her heart and flesh, "for love is strong as death, jealousy is fierce as the grave." Marriage is to be a life-long covenant until death do us part.

And beyond? The Old Testament uses the startling imagery of marriage to portray God's enduring love of Israel. St. Paul picks up this imagery when he says marriage is a mystery of Christ and the Church. Finally, John looks to a consummation, the union of believers in heaven with Christ.

> "Let us rejoice and exult and give him the glory, for the marriage of the Lamb has come, and his Bride has made herself ready;

> it was granted her to clothe herself with fine linen, bright and pure"—for the fine linen is the righteous deeds of the saints. And the angel said to me, "Write this: Blessed are those who are invited to the marriage supper of the Lamb." And he said to me, "These are the true words of God." (Rev 19:7–9)

Perhaps Jesus chose the wedding to reveal his glory because "God is love." Just as he chose the Jubilee as the model for God's peaceable kingdom, so here he chooses the joy of a wedding feast to reveal the glorious union of the triune God with his people in the bond of love. In the scene from *The Chosen*, we see Jesus playing games with children, laughing and joking, and dancing the *hora* with all the guests. Who wouldn't want to be in that number in the kingdom of heaven?

I think there is another reason, a somber one, that Jesus chose wine for his first sign. Wine is double-edged. While mild intoxication may at times promote good cheer and sociableness, drunkenness—draining the cup to the dregs—is associated with anger and violence. In the classic cowboy Western movie, it is usually in the saloon that arguments turn to gunfights, and someone ends up dead. Wine can also be an image of God's righteous anger and punishment of his enemies, domestic and foreign; "for in the hand of the LORD," says the psalmist, "there is a cup with foaming wine, well mixed, and he pours out from it, and all the wicked of the earth shall drain it down to the dregs" (Psalm 75:8).

Wine is also red, blood red, the sign of sacrifice. Just before he died on the Cross, Jesus drank the sour wine offered him and shortly thereafter from his pierced body flowed water and blood. And of course, Jesus foretold his atoning death at the Last Supper, when he offered his disciples the cup, saying, "This is my blood, which is poured out for you and for many, for the forgiveness of sin."

When we come to Holy Communion, we share in the duality of this sign. The Anglican poet George Herbert wrote this incredible verse about Jesus' agony: "Love is that liquor sweet and most divine, which my God feels as blood; but I, as wine." The same duality occurs when Holy Week culminates on Good Friday: what was supremely bad for Jesus was supremely good for us.

Let's come back to Cana. The final verse begins: "This, the first of his signs, Jesus did at Cana in Galilee, and manifested his glory." Did Jesus know what was going to happen when he and his disciples showed up in

Cana and where it would lead? Was this first sign also the last piece of Jesus' own preparation for ministry? The text does not say. In the video version of the climactic moment with the stone jars, Jesus asks to be alone. Looking up to his Father, he cups his hand in the water jar and scoops up—wine! His time had now come, the way that would lead to the Cross.

And was this also a turning point for the disciples? The verse concludes "…and his disciples believed in him." This is the first time John's gospel says they believed in him, they put their trust in him. It has often been noted that at Cana the stone jars for purification are replaced by the living vessel of Christ's Body and Blood. By the same token, we may foresee in this miracle another miracle: that the lifeless and repetitive rituals of the Law are being replaced by the living water of faith in Jesus Christ.

Who is Jesus? As readers of the gospel, we have to read on, but from this first sign, we know the answer:

> Now Jesus did many other signs in the presence of the disciples, which are not written in this book; but these are written so that you may believe that Jesus is the Christ, the Son of God, and that by believing you may have life in his name. (John 20:30–31)

This concludes my series on Jesus. Next week I turn to the second towering figure from the New Testament, St. Paul. In the letter to the Galatians, Paul will be wrestling with the second implication of Jesus' coming and dying for our sins. How do we receive this salvation? Paul's answer is the classic defense of justification by faith, the doctrine, Martin Luther claimed, on which the Church stands or falls.

Let us turn our hearts this Lent to God's Word and to the repentance that leads to faith in the One who came to offer his life as a sacrifice for many.

Evangelical Sermon Cycle

WHAT IS THE GOSPEL?
ST. PAUL TO THE GALATIANS

The Apostle's Call: No Other Gospel

GALATIANS 1

May the words of my mouth and the meditations of our hearts be always acceptable in your sight, O Lord, our Rock and our Redeemer.

In Epiphany I asked, "Who is Jesus?" Now in Lent we look at the question, "Who is Paul?"

I suspect Paul would object to the way this question is framed. Who am I, he would say, but a servant of Jesus Christ? True enough, but it is also true that God set Paul apart from his mother's womb, the risen Lord commissioned him to preach the Gospel to the nations, and the Holy Spirit inspired the writing and collection of his letters that are an integral part of the Bible, the Word of God written.

So let's meet St. Paul. We do this in two ways. One way is through the Acts of the Apostles, in which he is the major character from chapter 9 on. Acts was written by St. Luke, who was Paul's traveling companion for many years and recorded a first-hand narrative of Paul's missionary work. Let me urge you, as part of this Lenten exercise, to read Acts chapter 9 (Paul's conversion) and chapters 13 and 14 (his first missionary journey to Galatia), which is our focus in this sermon series.

Then there is the letter to the Galatians. Unlike our series on Jesus' early years and ministry, we are meeting Paul in mid-career. The year is 48 AD. It has been more than fifteen years since his conversion on the road to Damascus, and he has been recognized as a leader in the church in Antioch, the eastern capital of the Roman Empire at that time. He and Barnabas have just completed a pioneering mission trip up-country in a region called Galatia (today that's in southern Turkey), where they have planted four young congregations. But now they hear some disturbing news about the Galatians, and Paul puts pen to paper in what will be the first of a corpus of writings that will change the world. Let's follow along in chapter 1.

"Paul an apostle" introduces himself in the first four verses as the sender of the letter. The title "apostle" literally means "one who is sent," but in this case it means that the sender has been authorized by and the letter franked by "Jesus Christ and God the Father, who raised him from the dead." By referring to the resurrection, Paul reminds the Galatians that his authority as an apostle stands or falls on his encounter with the risen Lord. As he says later to the Corinthians: "If Christ has not been raised, then our preaching is in vain and your faith is in vain" (1 Cor 15:14). Of course he follows on immediately: "But in fact Christ has been raised from the dead, the first-fruits of those who have fallen asleep" (1 Cor 15:20). *Without* Christ's resurrection: no eternal life with God, no resurrection, and Paul is a fraud, as are all the apostles. *With* his resurrection: a whole new world and new life opens up—for him and for us 2000 years later. This is the basis of Paul's gospel, plain and simple.

He goes on to greet the Galatian churches with a distinctive formula "Grace and peace"—in Greek and Hebrew, *charis* and *shalom*, respectively. By *grace* we know the Gospel is God's free gift to sinners; by *peace*, we sinners accept that gift by faith and have "peace," a clear conscience before God. The grace comes from God the Father through the Lord Jesus Christ. In this first letter, we see already Paul's teaching on the distinction and unity of the divine Persons, the seedbed of the doctrine of the Trinity.

We also see the centrality of Jesus' sacrificial death, who "gave himself up for our sins to save us from this present evil age." In this one sentence, Paul gives a summary answer to the question: "What is the Gospel?" In his great commentary on Galatians, Martin Luther does not let us slide past Paul's mention of "our sins."

> You must learn from Paul here to believe that Christ was given, not for sham or counterfeit sins, nor yet for small sins, but for great and huge sins; not for one or two sins but for all sins, not for sins that have been overcome [e.g., by New Year's resolutions], but for invincible sins. And unless you are part of the company of those who say "our sins," that is those who hold this doctrine of faith, and teach, hear, learn, love and believe it, there is no salvation for you.

Ash Wednesday without Good Friday is a mere exercise in self-absorption. But Lent with Good Friday is unspeakably Good News. Luther continues:

> Practice this pronoun "our" in such a way that this syllable once believed may swallow up and absorb all your sins, that you may be certain that Christ has taken away not only the sins of some men but your sins and those of the whole world.

We now move to verses 6–11, the middle section of chapter 1, the meat in the sandwich. Having introduced himself as an apostle of the crucified and risen Lord, Paul now abruptly turns on the Galatians: "I am astonished that you are so quickly deserting him who called you in the grace of Christ and are turning to a different gospel."

On Ash Wednesday, I woke up from a little dream about a greeting card, one of those humorous ones. When I opened it up, a boxing glove popped out and punched me in the nose. That's pretty much what Paul is doing here. Again, Luther says that Paul "erupts" in this letter. The same zeal which led Paul to persecute Christ is now directed toward those who would compromise the Gospel. Notice how the messenger and the message are inseparable. If you turn away from Paul's gospel, you turn away from God himself and are still in your sins.

This verse is the first time Paul uses the word "Gospel"—"Evangel"—and then he keeps using it, five times in five verses. Paul's rebuke is not so much a punch in the nose as a series of body blows to bring the Galatians to their knees.

To understand the force of this middle section of chapter 1, it's good to know something about Paul's early years. Paul was raised in Tarsus, a small but influential city in Asia Minor (modern-day Turkey) on the trade route between East and West. Tarsus was known for its high Greco-Roman culture. Paul himself spoke Greek as his first language and no doubt was trained up in the classical education of grammar, logic, and rhetoric. But he was also a Jew, who as a young man was sent to Jerusalem to study Torah under the great Rabbi Gamaliel. Like Jesus, Paul knew the Scripture inside and out—the Law and the Prophets—and he could argue like a rabbi and preach like a prophet.

In verse 6, Paul speaks of the Galatians turning to "another gospel," but he immediately undercuts this idea, saying "not that there is another one." To speak of another gospel, Paul suggests, is as ridiculous as speaking of another God. "One Lord, one faith, one Gospel" was clearly part of Paul's teaching in Galatia. And since there is only one true God, so also there is only one truth of the Gospel.

That leads Paul to conclude that the Galatians have been deceived: "there are some who trouble you and want to distort the gospel of Christ." Paul knows something about being deceived and being a deceiver. It took the blinding light of the risen Lord on the Damascus Road to turn Saul the persecutor into Paul the Apostle. From this experience, Paul learned to be a pastor, and here he is warning the sheep while hunting down the wolves.

In chapter 2, we'll learn more about these false teachers, but for now it is clear that they claimed to be Christian, i.e., they used "gospel" language and twisted it. It is against these heretics—if I may use a later term—that Paul calls down a curse: "But even if we or an angel from heaven should preach to you a gospel contrary to the one we preached to you, let him be accursed" (verse 8).

Paul includes himself rhetorically in "*we* or an angel from heaven" as potential heralds of a false gospel, and indeed he does believe that Satan is at work "in this evil age" to pervert God's word, just as he did in Eden. But what about Paul himself? Could he have succumbed to temptation and be preaching a false Gospel? That is what some in Galatia were saying.

This insinuation leads Paul to the third section of chapter 1 (verses 11–24), the story of his conversion and call to preach. Paul moves smoothly from argument to narrative, making his case like a lawyer summoning a witness to the stand. In this case, the witness is Paul himself. Paul's testimony here is not self-absorbed but God-absorbed. In the rest of chapter 1 and on into chapter 2, Paul is going to make the case, hammer-blow by hammer-blow, that his gospel did not come by any human means but only by a revelation of God. There is nothing in my resume, he says, that would explain how I changed from being a denier of Christ and persecutor of the Church to being his slave and his apostle. There is only one explanation: God!—"he who had set me apart before I was born, and who called me by his grace, was pleased to reveal his Son to me." This is the testimony of the Jewish man, a Hebrew of Hebrews as he calls himself, who was thrown to the ground by a flash of light and heard a voice saying: "Saul, Saul, why are you persecuting me?" and the man who asked: "Who are you?" and was answered "I am Jesus, whom you are persecuting" (Acts 9:3–5).

Why should we believe Paul? You decide, but let me tell you of one modern convert. Heinz Cassirer was the son of a scholar renowned for his study of Immanuel Kant, one of the chief philosophers of Enlightenment rationalism. Heinz embraced his father's and Kant's rationalism for fifty years, until, somewhat by accident, he began reading St. Paul and was converted to Christ. Here is his explanation:

> Although St. Paul's nature was indeed a most unusual one, what strikes one particularly about it is this: he was the sort of man one would least expect to renounce self-will and to give up control of his own life to another...He was the very last man to fall victim to self-deception...and in consequence, I find it impossible to entertain seriously the idea that his spiritual pilgrimage had hallucinatory experience for its starting point.

My brothers and sisters here at Redeemer, let's be clear. Just as it is said of Jesus: either he was mad or he was bad or he was God, so also it is true of St. Paul: either he was deluded or he was lying or he was telling the truth about God. And if he was telling the truth, then there is no other Gospel than the one which Paul received on the Damascus Road and has passed on to us in his letters. There is no Gospel-and, no Gospel plus x, y, or z.

At the end of the day, of course, our reason takes us only so far, and we are faced with a matter of trust. Do we trust Paul's gospel? Do we trust Jesus Christ? That will be the continuing subject of the letter to the Galatians.

Justified by Faith Alone

GALATIANS 2

May the words of my mouth and the meditations of our hearts be always acceptable in your sight, O Lord, our Rock and our Redeemer.

What is the Gospel? Let's note that Evangelical Christianity has taken the name "Gospel"—"*Evangel*" as its hallmark and has identified the central tenet of the Gospel to be justification by faith alone. This view is held by Evangelical Anglicans, as expressed in the Thirty-nine Articles:

> We are accounted righteous before God, only for the merit of our Lord and Savior Jesus Christ by Faith, and not for our own works or deservings: Wherefore, that we are justified by Faith only is a most wholesome Doctrine, and very full of comfort… (Article 11)

This doctrine is clearly expressed in two key texts of the Bible. The first is from one of Paul's later letters, to the Romans:

> For I am not ashamed of the gospel, for it is the power of God for salvation to everyone who believes, to the Jew first and also to the Greek. For in it the righteousness of God is revealed from faith for faith [that is, for faith alone], as it is written, "The righteous shall live by faith." (Rom 1:16–17)

The second text is from our Galatians reading today, one of his earliest letters:

> We know that a person is not justified by works of the law but through faith in Jesus Christ, so we also have believed in Christ Jesus, in order to be justified by faith in Christ and not by works

> of the law, because by works of the law no one will be justified. (Gal 2:16–17)

The Romans passage is like a thesis statement at the beginning of a treatise. The Galatians passage, however, comes at the climax of Paul's dramatic story of his conversion. Let's step back a bit and see how he gets there.

The first section of our passage today (chapter 2, verses 1–10) continues on from chapter 1, Paul's account of God revealing his Son to him on the road to Damascus. As described in the book of Acts, Paul encountered a blinding light from heaven and heard a voice, saying "Saul, Saul why are you persecuting me?" Paul had to be led by the hand to the house of Judas, the Christian, where Ananias laid hands on him and the scales fell from his eyes (Acts 9:17–18).

After his conversion and a brief visit to Jerusalem, Paul says, he went "into Arabia." Let's imagine the Pharisee-turned-Christian praying alone in the desert, trying to put his life back together. I think that all the pieces of the mature Gospel that we find in his letters came from the outworking of that one singular encounter with the risen Lord. He sums up this revolution in his letter to the Philippians:

> If anyone else thinks he has reason for confidence in the flesh, I have more: circumcised on the eighth day, of the people of Israel, of the tribe of Benjamin, a Hebrew of Hebrews; as to the law, a Pharisee; as to zeal, a persecutor of the Church; as to righteousness under the law, blameless. But whatever gain I had, I counted as loss for the sake of Christ. Indeed, I count everything as loss because of the surpassing worth of knowing Christ Jesus my Lord. For his sake I have suffered the loss of all things and count them as rubbish, in order that I may gain Christ and be found in him, not having a righteousness of my own that comes from the law, but that which comes through faith in Christ, the righteousness from God that depends on faith. (Phil 3:4–9)

No one knows how long it took for the full meaning of this revelation to sink in, but it seems when Paul returned from Arabia to Damascus and Antioch, he began preaching this Gospel to mixed congregations of Jews and Gentiles. This message came as a particular shock to many Jewish Christians.

Let me pause for a moment and clarify which Jewish groups we are talking about. The largest group of Jews Paul encountered on his missionary journeys when he preached in synagogues were not Christians at all; indeed they were hostile to Paul and often tried to shout him down or even to kill him. But in Antioch, Paul preached to *Jewish Christians*—we might call them messianic Jews—who had not processed the full meaning and implications of the Gospel. One group of Jewish Christians, often called *Judaizers*, saw Jesus as the Messiah of Israel, who had come to include Gentiles in the covenant—if they would submit to circumcision and observe the Law of Moses. Another group, represented by James, the Lord's brother and head of the Jerusalem church, saw the Gospel as running along two tracks: a faith track for Gentile Christians and a law track for Jewish Christians. They did not, for instance, require Paul's Gentile companion Titus to be circumcised.

But all Jews, Christian and non-Christian, held one conviction in common: that their relationship with God, their righteousness, was conditioned on their keeping the Law. In a sermon last year, I mentioned that Jews identified 613 ordinances in the Law of Moses. The glory of the Jews was keeping the whole Law. When Paul describes his former conduct as blameless with regard to the Law, he means "I kept every one of the commandments." In Galatians Paul labels this Jewish view as observing "the works of the Law."

As Paul's narrative continues in chapter 2, he reports his visit to Jerusalem, for the first time after fourteen years, to meet with James and Peter and the leaders of the mother church. The outcome of that meeting, it seems, was a tactical success:

> when they saw that I had been entrusted with the gospel to the uncircumcised, just as Peter had been entrusted with the gospel to the circumcised ...they gave the right hand of fellowship to Barnabas and me, so that we should go to the Gentiles and they to the circumcised. (verses 7, 9)

We now come to the second section of this passage (verses 11–14). The Jerusalem agreement had papered over a basic question: what is the Gospel that Paul and Peter were proclaiming to Gentiles and Jews? The question came to a head "when Peter came to Antioch." Here is how Paul reports the matter:

> But when Cephas [Peter the Rock] came to Antioch, I opposed him to his face, because he stood condemned. For before certain men came from James, he was eating with the Gentiles; but when they came he drew back and separated himself, fearing the circumcision party. And the rest of the Jews acted hypocritically along with him, so that even Barnabas was led astray by their hypocrisy.

Why did Paul blow his top and call Peter and even Barnabas hypocrites? At the basic level of fellowship, Peter had dissed the Gentile Christians by first joining in their meals and then withdrawing from them. But beyond the discourtesy lay a much larger question. Are there two Gospel tracks for following Christ—faith and law-keeping—or only one? Peter had eaten like a Gentile one day and then jumped the tracks and turned back to kosher food the next. Paul called him out.

Peter, the leader of Jesus' band, had missed the point—yet again! It was Paul's insight that changed Christianity from being a Jewish sect to a worldwide religion: "Now," Paul says in Romans, "the righteousness of God has been manifested apart from the law, although the Law and the Prophets bear witness to it" (Rom 3:21).

This brings us to the third and climactic section of the chapter (verses 15–21). Paul begins with a rhetorical head-fake by talking like a Pharisee (he should know how): "We ourselves are Jews by birth and not Gentile sinners," he says. The Christian Judaizers might be thinking: "Right on, Paul. Sock it to those unclean Gentiles. Dogs are not welcome at our table!" But then Paul turns the tables on them: "yet we know that a person is not justified by works of the law but through faith in Jesus Christ" (verse 16). This is not the Pharisee speaking but Paul the Apostle, and this phrase—"we know"—is basic Christian teaching that both he and Peter would affirm. Being right with God, Paul says, doesn't have two tracks: law-keeping and faith. No, there is only one way to be right with God and that is faith in Jesus Christ. And if this is basic Christianity, then it follows that "by the works of the law no one will be justified."

In the next verse Paul takes the pejorative phrase "Gentile sinners" and turns it on its head. "In seeking to be justified in Christ, we too were found to be sinners." Yes, he says, Gentiles are sinners—and so are we Jews! He puts it this way in Romans: "All have sinned and fallen short of the glory of God" (Rom 3:23). The doctrine of justification by faith presupposes the universal bondage of sin, original sin. For Paul, this bondage is not just a doctrine but his life experience: Seeking to be right with God had led him—Mr. Perfect—to persecute the Son of God. What he found on the Damascus Road was not what he was seeking but what God revealed to him by pure grace in the crucified Messiah.

Paul concludes his argument with the Jewish Christians this way: "I do not nullify the grace of God, for if righteousness were through the law, then Christ died for no purpose" (verse 21). In light of the Cross, Paul says, the two-ways teaching of right standing with God—faith and the Law—is impossible, even an abomination. Only the truly desperate state of fallen man could explain or justify God giving up his Son on the Cross.

The Cross is a sign of contradiction: No to every form of self-justification, Yes to a new life in Christ alone. Hence the famous line: "I have been crucified with Christ. It is no longer I who live, but Christ who lives in me. And the life I now live in the flesh I live by faith in the Son of God, who loved me and gave himself for me." This is the true Good News, which caused Bunyan's Pilgrim to flee the City of Destruction, crying, "Life, life, eternal life!"

Paul tells the story of his confrontation with Peter to the Galatians because he sees the same double-mindedness infecting their church and tempting people to compromise the Gospel in favor of a Jewish half-way house. And Paul knows from experience that that house is built on sand.

This is where Martin Luther comes in as a bridge to our day. In his commentary on Galatians, Luther makes a fundamental distinction between *active righteousness*, sometimes called "works righteousness" and *passive righteousness*, which is the righteousness of faith. In the case of faith, Luther says, "we work nothing, render nothing to God; we only receive and permit someone else to work in us, namely God."

Active righteousness wants something, even a crumb, to boast about. Passive righteousness says: "Nothing in my hand I bring, only to Thy Cross I cling." Active righteousness prays with the Pharisee in Jesus' parable: *God, I thank you that I am not like other men*; passive righteousness prays like the publican: *Lord, have mercy on me, a sinner* (Luke 18:12, 13). Active righteousness, like Martha, busies itself with much serving; passive righteousness, like Mary, sits at Jesus' feet and listens to his teaching (Luke 10:39–42).

The doctrine of justification must be lived out in each of our lives. Living by faith is not a matter of reclining in a spiritual La-Z-Boy. Paul and Luther were hardly slackers. But the season of Lent offers us a way to come apart with Jesus, to listen to his Word, to repent of our sins and to take up our cross and follow him. Let us use this season to reorient our lives as Paul himself did in Arabia and as he challenged his people in Galatia to do.

Faith and the Law

GALATIANS 3

May the words of my mouth and the meditations of our hearts be always acceptable in your sight, O Lord, our Rock and our Redeemer.

How do you justify yourself? Honestly, if you ask yourself that question, or if you listen to others, you will find that everyone has an answer and a story, sometimes a sad story, to tell.

Some people justify themselves in terms of *identity or origin*. I am an American, or I am African American or, I am Gen X, or I am a Hebrew of Hebrews, or I am an Anglican.

Some justify themselves by *family*. I come from a happy family, or a broken family. I am adopted. I am single and satisfied. My children have attended Ivy League colleges. I have helped my husband battle cancer.

Some people justify themselves by their *work*: they are building a resume with highlights of education, military service, work experience, honors received, recommendations from people of influence. For others, their resumes are a "chronicle of wasted time."

Some people justify themselves by *mammon*: their net worth, homes, cars and savvy investments, donations to charity. Or maybe they barely scrape along from day to day.

There are many who justify themselves by their *hardships*. I had an unhappy childhood, I never had a chance to go to college. I have an alcohol problem. I have screwed up so many times I can't get out of this hole.

And then there are the *religious and irreligious* justifications. I grew up in the church and have never doubted God. I don't need God as a crutch. I rejected God in my teens until I got converted in midlife. I have been ordained fifty years and a missionary overseas. "I fast twice a week; I give tithes of all that I get."

Finally, there are *moral* justifications. I've never been arrested. I am as good as anyone else. I'm a winner. I'm a victim. After all, no one is perfect.

These answers are what Paul calls "works of the Law" and what Martin Luther called *active righteousness*, and they have their necessary place in our lives. Everybody has an ego—a strong ego, a weak ego. Everyone "loves himself" in some sense; everyone has a life story and a resume, long or short, written or unwritten. Everyone has a conscience, even if it is distorted or buried deep within. Everyone has an awareness of God, even Vladimir Putin, especially Vladimir Putin, and they have some sense, some dread, that they will be ultimately accountable to him.*

But here's the thing: none of these active justifications makes us righteous before the holy God. This is what Paul learned on the Damascus Road; this is why he says he counts all his merits and demerits to be rubbish. He has thrown the account books into the trash bin. If there were works of the law that could satisfy God, Paul now says, God would not have sent his Son to the world to die on a Cross and rise from the dead.

The opposite of active righteousness, according to Martin Luther, is *passive righteousness*, the righteousness of faith. Active righteousness begins with "I"; passive righteousness begins with God and ends with "me." "God have mercy on me, a sinner." "Not I but Christ lives in me."

So let's now turn to Galatians chapter 3. Paul is addressing the converts from his first missionary journey in Asia Minor. The four congregations are the fruit of his preaching in synagogues where there were Jews and Gentile "God-fearers." After Paul had returned home, some Jewish converts—we call them Judaizers—were telling these new Christians that they could have it both ways: believe in Jesus *and* be justified by keeping the Law of Moses. The next step, they said, was that new Christians should—no, they *must*—be circumcised and take on the yoke of the Law.

So let's see how Paul responds to this situation in the first section (verses 1–6). Paul, who had been "astounded" by this false turn in chapter 1, now says: "O foolish Galatians! Who has bewitched you!" Here Paul is chastising them, but he does so as children who have forgotten the ABC's of their Christian experience. And the ABC's are these:

Paul's vivid preaching of Christ crucified: "It was before your eyes that Jesus Christ was publicly portrayed as crucified" (verse 1).

* Russia had invaded Ukraine one month before, and Putin had justified the invasion as a crusade.

The power of the Holy Spirit in their midst: "Does he who supplies the Spirit to you and works miracles among you do so by works of the law, or by hearing with faith?" (verse 5).

Suffering for their faith: "Did you suffer so many things in vain—if indeed it was in vain?" (verse 4). Paul and Barnabas had been beaten nearly to death and their followers had been shunned by Jews and pagans alike.

Tell me, Paul says, do you deny these things happened? And if they are for real, how did you experience these things—by following all the peccadillos of the Jewish Law, or by hearing with faith? For shame, children, wake up lest you lose it all! Paul links their experience of faith with the patriarch Abraham, who "believed God, and it was counted to him as righteousness" (verse 6; cf. Gen 15:6).

In the second section (verses 7–18) Paul portrays Abraham as the father of faith, over against those Jews who claimed him as father of circumcision and the Law. As Paul interprets Scripture, God was announcing the Gospel beforehand—literally "pre-preaching the Gospel"—when he said to Abraham: "in your seed will the nations be blessed" (verse 8; cf. Gen 22:18). The covenant with Abraham was based on an unconditional promise, and it looked forward to a coming "seed" or offspring, who would be a blessing to all nations (verse 16). The promised seed was Jesus, the Son of God, and the blessing was the forgiveness of sins and the gift of the Holy Spirit. Circumcision was the seal on the covenant, and a sealed covenant cannot be revoked by subsequent law. Hence when Abraham "believed God," he was showing the true way of receiving the promise of God.

What Paul learned on the Damascus Road was that his idea of perfect law-keeping was a deception, because all attempts to justify oneself, even by God's Law, treat only the outer shell of the human heart, whereas the human heart is desperately corrupt, infected by sin. He explains it this way in the letter to the Romans:

> The law is holy…righteous and good…and I delight in the law of God in my inner being, but I see in my members another kind of law waging war against the law of my mind and making me captive to the law of sin that dwells in my members. (Rom 7:12, 22–23)

This other kind of law is the bondage of sin. After meeting Christ, Paul came to see the Law as bringing a curse, indeed the curse of death. But he also saw in the risen Jesus the promised seed, the one who had paid the price of sin for us:

> Christ redeemed us from the curse of the law by becoming a curse for us—for it is written, "Cursed is everyone who is hanged on a tree"—so that in Christ Jesus the blessing of Abraham might come to the Gentiles, so that we might receive the promised Spirit through faith. (verses 13–14)

This blessing is the Gospel, seen from afar by Abraham, the promise of being put right with God by God's own doing through the Cross of Christ. This blessing was not earned by any works, whether the Law of Moses or any of our hand-crafted justifications—but through simply trusting Jesus. This, my friends, is the Gospel! "It's so sweet to trust in Jesus, just to rest upon his promise." "Leaning, leaning, safe and secure from all alarms, I'm leaning on the everlasting arms."

In the final section of chapter 3 (verses 19–29), Paul asks: "Why then the Law?" This is surely the question which Paul asked himself when he retreated to Arabia to pray and ponder. "Why was I, why were my fellow Jews, so wrong about seeking to justify ourselves by keeping the Law?"

Paul approaches this question vertically and horizontally—it's cross-shaped, if you will. Vertically, to the question "Why the Law?" he answers: "because of transgressions" (verse 19). At the root of every transgression is sin, and sin is fundamentally rebellion against the holy God. We don't see it that way, because we have a built-in excuse mechanism—"nobody's perfect"—or we internalize our guilt and just "try harder."

Paul recalls the giving of the Law on Mount Sinai and how the people were terrified by the glory of God and asked Moses to be their mediator (verse 20). The Law, Paul says, was an accommodation to human sinfulness. At times, it may put brakes on our worst inclinations; at other times it may actually stimulate our wrong-doing and give us a guilty conscience. But in no case does it purify our hearts and make us worthy to stand before God. So Paul concludes: "For if a law had been given that could give life, then righteousness would indeed be by the law" (verse 21). But it can't!

Horizontally, Paul looks to salvation history. There was a 430-year gap between the promise to Abraham and the giving of the law to Moses and then another thousand years before the promise was fulfilled under Pontius Pilate. The Old Testament is a record of man's repeated transgressions and God's repeated judgments, from the Garden of Eden to the tower of Babel to the golden calf to the exile, to the crucifixion. Paul likens this history of sin to a long imprisonment "until the coming faith would be revealed" (verse 23).

The role of the Law in this history, Paul says, is that of a "pedagogue" (cf. "pedagogy"), translated "guardian" in our text (verse 25). A pedagogue was a household slave who accompanied the child of a Roman household around town and attended to his early education. He acted a bit like a music master who makes sure the child practices his scales, or like a nun who raps his hand with a ruler, saying "Wake up, and repeat your multiplication tables!" The pedagogue was allowed to treat the child as a slave until the time the child grew up and inherited his place in society as a free citizen. This image explains Paul's final vision of faith. "But now that faith has come, we are no longer under a guardian [a pedagogue], for in Christ Jesus you are all sons of God, through faith" (verses 25–26).

In chapter 4, Paul is going to continue his analogy of the son becoming an heir—and I'll return to that next week. For now I want simply to note the way Paul highlights "faith" here—"until faith came" (verse 24). For Paul, the Gospel requires a decision between two ways: faith and law. Law brings with it a righteousness of sorts, but because of our deep-seated sin, we find ourselves on the wrong side of the Law's judgment, which is condemnation. In the eyes of the law, "all our righteousness," even our achievements, "are filthy rags" (Isa 64:6). Faith, on the other hand, makes no claim to righteousness but rather looks to the righteousness of Christ, who clears our account by his blood on the Cross. It is faith alone that justifies.

So, how do you justify yourself? Which account, which narrative do you wish to stake your life on? Your own justification, in whatever way you wish to frame it—or the righteousness of faith that trusts in the one who loved me and gave himself for me? My friends, ponder this question deeply during this Lent.

Next week we'll follow Paul in noting two results of justification by faith: freedom and equality, both Christian fruits that have passed into our Western culture.

Not Slaves but Sons

GALATIANS 4

May the words of my mouth and the meditations of our hearts be always acceptable in your sight, O Lord, our Rock and our Redeemer.

Last week our family drove to Hershey for the state basketball finals, in which our grandson Daniel was playing for Quaker Valley High School. The day before the game, the team was given a police escort out of Sewickley, with sirens and horns blaring. We were standing and waving on the sidewalk when the team bus passed by, and for a moment Daniel stuck his head out the window and waved and smiled. I had this eerie sense that this boy whom I had baptized and who had grown up near us on the hills of Uganda and who shared our home here for the last seven years, this Daniel had become a man, had changed status before my eyes.

The theme of Galatians, justification by faith, involves the change of our status, our standing before God brought about by the death and resurrection of Jesus Christ.

We have been looking at the life of St. Paul alongside his first letter, to the Galatians. Paul experienced a change of status on the road to Damascus in two dimensions: vertically from heaven to earth; and horizontally, as an act in salvation history.

Vertically, as Paul himself put it, "God revealed his Son to me." Like the apostles, Paul was granted a glimpse of heaven, with the risen Lord seated at the right hand of God. In this same flash of light, Paul saw that the Law, which had been his guiding light, was only a "pedagogue," an intermediary, preparing him for the service of God but also humbling him to see himself as a sinner desperately in need of saving grace. From that moment on, Paul sought one thing only, "to be found in him, not having a righteousness of my own that comes from the law, but that which comes through faith in Christ" (Phil 3:9).

Horizontally, Paul came to realize that he was a witness to the decisive act of history when "in the fulness of time, God sent forth his Son." Paul not only *witnessed* the risen Christ reigning in heaven at the change of the ages from BC to AD, but he was *commissioned* to be a change agent in this new age by taking this Gospel out to the pagan world, beginning with four small congregations in Galatia.

So let's turn to today's text. I need to back up a few verses to the end of chapter 3, where Paul describes the change of status of believers through three examples: from child to heir, from slave to free, and from godless to Spirit-filled.

The first example of a change of status is from child to heir:

> But now that faith has come, we are no longer under a guardian, for in Christ Jesus you are all sons of God, through faith. For as many of you as were baptized into Christ have put on Christ. There is neither Jew nor Greek, there is neither slave nor free, there is no male and female, for you are all one in Christ Jesus. And if you are Christ's, then you are Abraham's offspring, heirs according to promise. (3:25–29)

Earlier Paul had reminded the Galatians of their experience of the Spirit when they had first heard the Gospel and had witnessed signs and wonders. Now he reminds them of another experience—baptism. "As many of you as were baptized into Christ have put on Christ." The language here is of putting on a garment. In the early church, baptism often involved a person taking off all their clothes (men and women separately) before entering the baptismal pool and then being clothed in a white garment as they emerged from the pool. They had symbolically died to their old sinful self and been clothed in Christ's righteousness.

By putting on Christ in baptism, believers were entering a new community, the Church, the Body of Christ. Membership in the Church—and remember, "member" has to do with body parts—confers a new identity in which "there is neither Jew nor Greek, there is neither slave nor free, there is no male and female." This new identity is distinct from that of the Jew under the Old Covenant. A well-known Jewish prayer goes like this: "Blessed are you, O God, for not making me a Gentile, or a slave, or a woman." It's not hard to imagine this prayer in the mouth of the Pharisee in Jesus' parable for whom it was a boast, or in the mouth of Saul, the Hebrew of Hebrews and persecutor of the Church.

That's how different the new identity in Christ is. The new identity has to do with dying to self in the waters of baptism and arising a "new creation." Its boast is that of the publican in Jesus' parable: "God have mercy on me, a sinner." It is not a declaration of exclusivity, nor is it a declaration of individual rights (though Christian belief was the seedbed of modern democracy), but it is a declaration of solidarity. I am a brother and sister in Christ, a member of the family of God.

The second example of a change of status is from slave to free. Paul continues:

> I mean that the heir, as long as he is a child, is no different from a slave, though he is the owner of everything, but he is under guardians and managers until the date set by his father. In the same way we also, when we were children, were enslaved to the elementary principles of the world. But when the fullness of time had come, God sent forth his Son, born of woman, born under the law, to redeem those who were under the law, so that we might receive adoption as sons. (4:1–5)

Paul had already likened the status of Jews living under the Law to a child living under a household slave. Now he expands the imagery to Gentiles, who are living under "the elements of the world," the powers of darkness and superstition characteristic of pagan societies. Because of human sin, the Law and superstition from time immemorial have worked in tandem to hold a person's soul prisoner and enemy of God. But, Paul says, now in the midst of time, Christ has come to redeem the prisoners by his blood and to grant them status of adoptive sons and daughters.

The ancient world knew very well the difference between slave and freeman, much as American slaves like Frederick Douglass proclaimed his escape from slavery and sought it for his race. Redemption in Christ, Paul says, is like civil emancipation, but it is a redemption that goes beyond to include union with God and adoption into his family the Church. (Again, this Christian concept underlies the American civil creed, and our failure to live up to that creed is one of the scandals of our history.)

Freedom in Christ has important ramifications which Paul will turn to in the next chapter.

The third example of the change of status is from godless to Spirit-filled:

> And because you are sons, God has sent the Spirit of his Son into our hearts, crying, "Abba! Father!" So you are no longer a slave, but a son, and if a son, then an heir through God. Formerly, when you did not know God, you were enslaved to those that by nature are not gods. But now you have come to know God, or rather to be known by God. (verses 6–9)

To "put on Christ" is to enter into relationship with the triune God, to be filled with the Holy Spirit, and to pray "Abba, Father." This relationship is not some intellectual puzzle but a dynamic of believing and receiving, of knowing God as the one who knew you and loved you from all eternity. This knowledge includes the hope of eternal life with God and sharing in the inheritance of the saints in light! Praise the Lord!

Paul was not only a great missionary and great theologian. He was a great pastor. If you read the middle verses of chapter 4 (verses 10–20), you will see Paul appealing to the Galatians in highly emotional terms as their spiritual father to hold fast the Gospel: "my little children, for whom I am again in the anguish of childbirth until Christ is formed in you!" (4:19).

With these words in mind, let me speak personally and say that while my time here has been fairly brief and is not quite over, I have enjoyed getting to know many of you individually. I am convinced that God has a good purpose for each of you and for Redeemer as a congregation. I am confident that you have made a good choice in calling Ethan Carlson as your full-time rector. He is a young pastor and you are a young congregation. That is part of your appeal, and no doubt will bring its share of challenges. Only "stand fast in the liberty whereby Christ has set us free"—the topic of next week's sermon.

I have seen the Gospel bus pass by and your faces in the window. Peggy and I shall continue praying for you on your journey.

For exposition of Galatians 4:21–31, see the podcast for March 22.

Walking in the Freedom of the Spirit

GALATIANS 5

May the words of my mouth and the meditations of our hearts be always acceptable in your sight, O Lord, our Rock and our Redeemer.

Over the past weeks, we have been examining the Gospel as it is found in Paul's letter to the Galatians and captured in this phrase: "The righteous shall live by faith." This brief definition covers two dimensions of faith: status and action. As it refers to our status, our standing with God, we can read the phrase this way: "He who has been made righteous by faith in Christ will find life." This is what Martin Luther calls "passive righteousness": there is nothing that I can do because Jesus did it all on the Cross.

But when we think of action, we may read the phrase as answering this question: "how now shall we who are justified live our lives?" And the answer is: We are to live by faith. Here faith is not passive reception but active deeds of love and service.

Paul spells out this duality of status and action more fully in these famous lines (Eph 2:8–10):

> For by grace you have been saved through faith. And this is not your own doing; it is the gift of God, not a result of works, so that no one may boast. [*status*]

And he continues:

> For we are his workmanship, created in Christ Jesus for good works, which God prepared beforehand, that we should walk in them. [*action*]

With this distinction in mind, let's turn now to Galatians, chapter 5. The first section (verses 1–6) talks about freedom. Many of Paul's letters are divided between a theological focus (status) and an ethical focus (action). In the case of Galatians, this division happens at chapter 5, and freedom is the word that bridges the gap. "For freedom Christ has set us free..." Being set free is a status, emancipation from slavery. Once freed, we now are free to act, free for some good deed. Paul's civil status was that of a free Roman citizen, and he made use of this status to travel freely along Roman roads to found churches and at times to appeal to Roman magistrates for protection.

Paul's supreme status as a freeman was not civil but spiritual. He puts it this way:

> For through the Spirit, by faith, we ourselves eagerly wait for the hope of righteousness. For in Christ Jesus neither circumcision nor uncircumcision counts for anything, but only faith working through love. (verses 5–6)

Active faith is motivated by the Holy Spirit working through hope and love. Hope is the confidence we have in our status as God's sons that nothing in heaven and earth can separate us from his love and that our faith will be rewarded, come what may. Hope is the sure and steadfast anchor of the soul that frees us to love others. Love is faith's companion on the road, summing up the moral commandments of the Law toward God and neighbor, but whereas the Law channels our actions, love is the source, the wellspring of those actions in God, who is love.

In the second section (verses 7–12), we get a glimpse of Paul as the model pastor. He says: "You were running well. Who hindered you from obeying the truth? This persuasion is not from him who calls you" (verses 7–8).

Paul's approach, given his former life as a model Pharisee, is utterly amazing. He does not condemn the Galatians for disloyalty nor command their obedience. He speaks to them as fellow citizens in the kingdom of God and seeks to persuade them to resist the Judaizers and to turn to God. The term we usually use for this approach is exhortation. "You were running well," Paul says, "now return to your first love." You already know the truth and the truth will set you free. You already have received the Holy Spirit. Just listen to him—and to me.

If I may say so, exhortation is exactly the approach Christian preaching takes. I am not here to force my views or the doctrine of the Church upon you. I am here to explain the Gospel and the Scripture and the faith of the Church in such a way that you are motivated to follow Christ.

Of course, exhortation includes warning. There is a spiritual battle going on, with false teachers who are troubling the congregations in Galatia, leavening the lump by claiming that faith requires something more—circumcision. If circumcision is so important, Paul replies cuttingly, let these guys go all the way and emasculate themselves (verse 12).

In the third section (verses 13–16), Paul returns to the theme of freedom. He begins: "For you were called to freedom, brothers. Only do not use your freedom as an opportunity for the flesh, but through love serve one another" (verse 13).

The flesh is the X factor that complicates Christian freedom. Paul speaks of "flesh" in two ways. The naturalistic way is simply recognizing our created bodily existence: "the life I now live in the flesh I live by faith in the Son of God" (Gal 2:20). The fleshly body is morally neutral, although it is weak, corruptible and mortal. But that's only part of the story, which begins in Eden. Because of the Fall, the flesh is also morally corrupting. It is subject to sinful, call them carnal desires. Paul puts it this way in Romans: "For while we were living in the flesh, our sinful passions, aroused by the law, were at work in our members to bear fruit for death" (Rom 7:5).

If there is any doubt about how sin is rooted in our inner desires, just turn to the master psychologist, Jesus, who says this in our gospel lesson today:

> There is nothing outside a person that by going into him can defile him, but the things that come out of a person are what defile him… For from within, out of the heart of man, come evil thoughts, sexual immorality, theft, murder, adultery, coveting, wickedness, deceit, sensuality, envy, slander, pride, foolishness. All these evil things come from within, and they defile a person. (Mark 7:16, 21–23)

Or take a fine line from today's collect: "Almighty God, who alone can bring into order the unruly wills and affections of sinners…"

Freedom in Christ does not exempt us from living our lives in the flesh. When at baptism we renounce the world, the flesh, and the devil, we don't receive a get-out-of-jail-free-from-sin card. Rather we are given a wonderful resource, the Holy Spirit poured into our hearts, crying "Abba, Father." So Paul concludes this section: "But I say, walk by the Spirit, and you will not gratify the desires of the flesh" (verse 16).

In the fourth and final section (verses 17–26), Paul contrasts spiritual freedom with carnal bondage:

> For the desires of the flesh are against the Spirit, and the desires of the Spirit are against the flesh, for these are opposed to each other, to keep you from doing the things you want to do. But if you are led by the Spirit, you are not under the law. (verses 17–18)

Law, Paul says, attempts to control your passions by fear and guilt, but that becomes a kind of bondage. "Don't do that or you'll be damned!" The law of the policeman may be necessary to maintain civic order, but it does not reach a person's inner being, and it often stores up self-pity, resentment and, worse, violence. This is the problem of recidivism, as when released prisoners return to their crimes.

Paul gives a catalogue of vices and virtues, the works of the flesh and the fruit of the Spirit. All works of the flesh are distortions of some natural desire. The first three—sexual immorality, impurity, sensuality—involve abuse of the God-given desire for sexual union. Sorcery and idolatry involve false religion that perverts the true worship of God. Enmity, strife, jealousy, fits of anger, rivalries, dissensions, divisions—these are all social sins and the opposite of loving one's neighbor. These vices pop up in congregations, then and now, and are a central concern in Paul's letters, "lest you bite and devour each other," as he puts it in verse 15. The final grouping, drunkenness and orgies, involves abuse of the body and the natural urges to eat and drink, whether individually or collectively. The fleshly life is fundamentally disordered, a chaos of competing desires, as noted in our collect, with one sin leading to another and all together tending toward death and judgment. So Paul can warn that "those who do such things will not inherit the kingdom of God."

The works of the flesh explode like buckshot from a shotgun. The virtues, by contrast, are like organic fruit ripened until harvest time, as the Holy Spirit guides and governs a person's life. While they are manifold—love, joy, peace, patience, kindness, goodness, faithfulness, gentleness, self-control—they are ordered from the top, from love, love of God and neighbor, and regulated by careful self-control. While each believer, each saint, presents a particular combination of spiritual gifts and fruit, together they offer what Paul calls "an aroma of Christ to God" (2 Cor 2:15). Against such a person, such a congregation, Paul says, there is no need for law.

Perhaps at this point, we may wonder if such a life for each of us and for this congregation is possible or sustainable. And we would be right to do so, especially when we think of the frailty of our works. And this brings us back to justification by faith. We are accounted righteous, even in our unrighteous and imperfect deeds, by the atoning blood of Christ. Paul concludes this section by saying that "those who belong to Christ Jesus have crucified the flesh with its passions and desires" (verse 24). Strange as it may sound, it is only in the Cross that we find perfect freedom.

Next Sunday will be Palm Sunday, or the Sunday of the Passion, when we walk again with our Lord on the *via dolorosa*, the way of the Cross. We shall conclude this series in chapter 6 with Paul's claim to the righteousness of faith: "Far be it from me to boast except in the cross of our Lord Jesus Christ, by which the world has been crucified to me, and I to the world" (Gal 6:14).

Boasting in the Cross

GALATIANS 6

Lord, take my lips and speak through them; take our minds and think through them; take our hearts and set them on fire with love for yourself, Lord Jesus.

One of the odd features of Paul and his gospel is his claim that the utter need for God's grace in Christ can be a ground for boasting. This same Paul who speaks of himself as the "least of the apostles" because he persecuted the Church, this "wretched man," as he calls himself, who ripped up his resume and tossed it in the trash, this man can repeatedly talk about boasting (cf. 1 Cor 15:9; Rom 7:24; Phil 3:20).

Let me begin by noting that what St. Paul means by "boasting" is not the same as the modern synonym "bragging." In fact, the word means something like one's testimony, what you stake your life on. So let's keep an open mind when he uses it three times in our passage today.

Chapter 6, as I see it, has two main sections: the first section completes his teaching on Christian moral behavior, and in the second, which begins at verse 11, he puts his signature on his gospel. In order to look at the first section fully, it's best to back up to chapter 5, verses 24 and 25: "And those who belong to Christ Jesus have crucified the flesh with its passions and desires. If we live by the Spirit, let us also walk by the Spirit."

I mentioned last week that these verses are or should be really daunting. How many of us can truthfully say we have crucified our flesh and its passions? How many of us can say we are walking in the Spirit as we should? How much, rather, do we find ourselves unsteady and ever-changing, what used to be called giddy.

Paul is hardly blind to personal giddiness (go to Romans chapter 7), but in these verses he is talking to the church community as a body—those who have "put on Christ" by faith and in baptism. Even this community is by no means perfect, but Paul sees hope in its communal life:

> Let us not become conceited, provoking one another, envying one another. Brothers, if anyone is caught in any transgression, you who are spiritual should restore him in a spirit of gentleness. Bear one another's burdens, and so fulfill the law of Christ. For if anyone thinks he is something, when he is nothing, he deceives himself. (5:26–6:3)

This is the same church which Paul had accused of turning away from the Gospel, and one can hardly read any of his other letters without recognizing flawed and failing sinners like ourselves. Crucifying the flesh and walking in the Spirit includes the weak helping the weak, or the strong helping the weak, or the weak helping the strong, knowing that they are equally subject to temptation, just as Paul told the Corinthians: "No temptation has overtaken you that is not common to man" (1 Cor 10:13). We are, in Martin Luther's phrase, at the same time saints and sinners.

In applying Paul's moral teaching, let me introduce a distinction from the field of ethics: "first-person perspective" and "third-person perspective." First-person perspective is when you apply a moral command to yourself; third-person perspective is when you apply it to someone else. Our natural tendency is to see the splinter in someone else's eye and miss the log in our own eye. Paul turns this tendency upside down. In verses 4–5, he says: "Let each one test his own work, and then his reason to boast will be in himself alone and not in his neighbor. For each will have to bear his own load."

Paul is saying: Hold yourself to the highest standard, not by comparing your conduct with that of your neighbor. Here we encounter the word "boast" for the first time. Boast in this case means one's self-understanding, or rather one's standing before God. Now here is the marvelous thing about Christian freedom. Because we are justified by Christ, we are free to aim at our best self, free to love our neighbors as ourselves, free not to judge them. We can seek to carry our own load, without comparing it with our neighbor's.

Verse 6, I think, is a parenthesis but a relevant one then and now. Paul says: "One who is taught the word must share all good things with the one who teaches." Ministers of the word, he says, are not burdening the congregation in getting support for their work. Paul himself refused payment so that he could preach without cost, but this was his personal choice as an apostle, not a rule for others. It's not just about money, either. There is an old saying: "Reverend, you've just moved from preaching to meddling." Done well, meddling is the clergy's right and duty. I hope when Pastor Ethan arrives, you will be quick to hear and slow to judge.

Paul now returns to the theme of first-person accountability:

> Do not be deceived: God is not mocked, for whatever one sows, that will he also reap. For the one who sows to his own flesh will from the flesh reap corruption, but the one who sows to the Spirit will from the Spirit reap eternal life. (verses 7–8)

It is all too common to shift our personal failures onto others, or onto God. Blame-shifting goes way back, to the Garden of Eden: "The snake tempted me and I ate"; "the woman You gave me, she gave me the apple…" Just as the tempter is the father of lies, so all our temptations are based on falsehoods, fantasies and fictions about ourselves. "If only I had this or that, money, education, parents or husband or wife…I couldn't help myself…"

The Collect for Purity, with which we open our Communion service, sets us on the straight path of reality: "Almighty God, to whom all hearts are open, all desires known and from whom no secrets are hid…" God knows our hearts, and he will not be mocked. However, he will, if we ask him "cleanse the thoughts of our hearts by the inspiration of his Holy Spirit" and aid us to "perfectly love him and worthily magnify his holy Name."

From this sense of our right standing with God, Paul urges his Christians to continue on with good works:

> And let us not grow weary of doing good, for in due season we will reap, if we do not give up. So then, as we have opportunity, let us do good to everyone, and especially to those who are of the household of faith. (verses 9–10)

The early church was known for its works of charity. We get an image of the Church's care for its poor, its widows and orphans from the pages of the New Testament. Even hostile pagans commented on the Christians not committing fraud, theft, or adultery and for taking in abandoned children. Friendship evangelism—the "art of neighboring"—was one of the most common ways that the Gospel spread then and now. The old hymn says:

> If you cannot preach like Peter,
> if you cannot pray like Paul,
> you can tell the love of Jesus,
> who died to save us all.

That, friends, is a word for Redeemer now and going forward. "Don't grow weary!"

At verse 11, we come to the second section of chapter 6, which is the closing of the letter, Paul's personal signature on all that has gone before: "See with what large letters I am writing to you with my own hand."

In all probability, Paul had dictated his letter to a trained scribe. Now he takes pen in hand to seal the deal, as it were. He begins by accusing his opponents of cowardice:

> It is those who want to make a good showing in the flesh who would force you to be circumcised, and only in order that they may not be persecuted for the cross of Christ. For even those who are circumcised do not themselves keep the law, but they desire to have you circumcised that they may boast in your flesh. (verses 12–13)

Three words jump out from these verses: flesh, boasting, and the Cross of Christ. We can only understand the force of Paul's rhetoric here by realizing how offensive, how shameful was crucifixion in the ancient world. Rome had devised this punishment—nailing men, often stripped naked, to a beam in a public place and leaving them to die and their flesh to be eaten by the birds—in order to humiliate its enemies and to horrify its subject peoples.

I think Paul is accusing his opponents of trying to avoid the scandal of Jesus' crucifixion by changing the subject—"Let's not talk about that unfortunate event, let's talk about the Law of Moses," which Law, as Paul has already pointed out states: "Cursed is everyone who is hanged on a tree" (Gal 3:13). For heaven's sake, let's not boast about the Cross, they are saying, let's boast about Jesus as the great rabbi and law-giver, even

Jesus the Messiah who fulfilled the Law and circumcision. Or let's boast about Jesus the social reformer or Jesus the Anglican.

Paul will have none of this. By his own large letters he shouts, as it were:

> But far be it from me to boast except in the cross of our Lord Jesus Christ, by which the world has been crucified to me, and I to the world. For neither circumcision counts for anything, nor uncircumcision, but a new creation. (verses 14–15)

Boasting in the Cross is a seeming contradiction. Imagine boasting about the hangman's noose, or the guillotine, or the electric chair. Think of the odd jewelry that would result! I said that boasting is what you stake your life on, our witness; that "stake" is ultimately the stake on which Jesus died. Another word for "boasting" is "bearing witness"; the Greek word is "martyr," and every justified believer is called to be both a saint and a martyr.

To be a Christian, Paul says, it matters not whether one is Jew or Greek, slave or free, male and female. To be a Christian is to hear the Gospel and believe, to die to sin in baptism and to rise up a new creation, an adopted son of God, and to take up one's cross and follow Jesus. To be a Christian is to boast, not in oneself but in the Cross. In the words of our hymn today:

> Forbid it, Lord, that I should boast,
> Save in the death of Christ my God:
> All the vain things that charm me most,
> I sacrifice them to his blood.

Paul's signing this letter, I think, is a world-historical moment. As God had called Saul on the road to Damascus, now God inspires Paul to write this letter as the apostle to the Gentiles. Most of Paul's apostolic ministry lay ahead—getting approval for his gospel by the Council of Jerusalem, further missionary journeys to Asia Minor and Greece, and a final imprisonment and death in Rome. Paul saw the rough road ahead when he says: "I bear on my body the marks of Jesus" (verse 17). But he also sees the formation and expansion of the worldwide Church from its Jewish roots to becoming "the household of faith" and "the Israel of God."

Now let me conclude this series. I titled it "What is the Gospel?" Since Christmas, we have been following the early life of the Lord Jesus and the early writing of Paul, Jesus' foremost apostle. Their lives and their teaching together form the Gospel. As the Church expanded in the first centuries, the canon of the New Testament came to be recognized in two basic sections: "the Gospel and the Apostle." In our services, we have readings from the epistles (letters) and from the gospels. I believe both these sections are required for the faith of the Church. The gospels narrate the life of Jesus, and preeminently his final week, as we have done today in our Passion reading. The Acts of the Apostles extends that narrative to show how the Gospel went out from Jerusalem to the ends of the earth, with Paul as the prime apostle to the Gentiles.

In Paul's letters, we find the full meaning of the Gospel expounded as it was and is received by the Church, which was first stated by Paul in Galatians when he says:

> I have been crucified with Christ. It is no longer I who live, but Christ who lives in me. And the life I now live in the flesh I live by faith in the Son of God, who loved me and gave himself for me (Gal 2:20).

So, my friends at Redeemer, I leave you with this greeting from the Apostle Paul: "The grace of our Lord Jesus Christ be with your spirit, brothers. Amen."

DOXOLOGY: RISEN INDEED!

Risen Indeed! The Testimony of the Empty Tomb

COLOSSIANS 3:1–4; LUKE 24:1–12

Alleluia! Christ is Risen!
The Lord is Risen Indeed! Alleluia!

"Welcome happy morning, age to age shall say!"* Last week on Palm Sunday, I concluded the sermon series on Galatians with St. Paul's words: "Far be it from me to boast except in the cross of our Lord Jesus Christ, by which the world has been crucified to me, and I to the world" (Gal 6:14). I suggested that Paul's idea of boasting is not bragging but *testifying* to that which he had seen and heard. Paul had not seen Christ crucified on Good Friday, but he had heard of it after his conversion from those who had. He had not seen the empty tomb on Easter Sunday, but he had met the risen Christ on the road to Damascus, when, as he put it, "God revealed his Son to me."

In the next three weeks, I shall commend three "Testimonies to the Resurrection," three "boasts" of the Easter season for us believers at Redeemer: the testimony of the empty tomb, the testimony of the apostles, and the testimony of the Lord's Supper.

When Anglicans speak of Easter, we mean not just a day but a *season*, running for fifty days from Easter Day to Pentecost. The season recalls the risen Jesus' repeated appearances to his disciples over forty days before he ascended into heaven and then his sending of the Holy Spirit, the Comforter, on the fiftieth day, which is what the word Pentecost means.

Today, Easter Day, commemorates the discovery of the empty tomb, which is the central clue in "God's whodunnit." It all begins with the

* The Redeemer congregation celebrated Easter Day at 8:30 a.m. The Presbyterians had kindly granted us this time, along with all their lovely Easter decorations.

women who had seen Jesus die on the Cross and had watched Joseph of Arimathea as he wrapped the body in a shroud and laid it in his personal and unused tomb. When the women returned on Sunday morning to anoint the body, they found the stone rolled away and the body gone. Suddenly, two angels appeared to them saying: "Why are you seeking the living among the dead. He is not here. He has risen!"

Mystery solved? Well not exactly. Questions remain. If he is not here, where has his body gone? What does "risen" mean? And most importantly, what does all this mean for Jesus' mission? It will take the whole fifty days to come to unravel these matters.

An initial clue comes as the angel continues: "Remember how he told you, while he was still in Galilee, that the Son of Man *must* be delivered into the hands of sinful men and be crucified and on the third day rise." And, the text continues, "they remembered his words." (Note that women, though not numbered with the Twelve, had accompanied Jesus' band of disciples throughout his ministry, as we see in *The Chosen*.)

By recalling Jesus' prediction of his own death and resurrection, the angels address the central objection to Jesus' resurrection, then and now. No one has been dead and buried and come back to life again. Ever. This is an ironclad law of science, history, and experience. Except, of course, when the Creator of science and the Lord of history proves otherwise. When Jesus said that the Son of Man *must* suffer, die, and rise again, he is not only overturning the natural law of life and death, he is establishing a new law of death and life: it is only by God's sending his Son as a sacrifice for sin that man can be redeemed and only by his rising again that man can receive eternal life with God.

Here is my question for us this Easter Day: what is our response, our testimony to the mystery of the empty tomb? Let's look at the responses of the first witnesses to help us along.

Let me suggest two kinds of response to Easter, a left-brain and a right-brain response. I'm sure you are aware of the concept that our brains are hemispheric and that the left hemisphere is the locus of logic—objectivity, analytical and critical thinking—whereas the right hemisphere is the locus of emotion—of subjectivity, appreciation of beauty, and responsiveness to others; and that people tend to be left-brain or right-brain dominant. The Myers-Briggs personality inventory, for instance, makes "thinking" and "feeling" a key indicator.

On Easter Sunday ten years ago, I preached a sermon at Uganda Christian University titled "The Logic of the Empty Tomb." I am not going to re-preach that sermon today—we do need to get out of here by 9:30!—but I'll summarize it by saying there are two strands of logic about the empty tomb that intertwine. The first strand has to do with the historical *fact* that the tomb was empty and that the women and Peter and John were reporting this fact about Easter morning.

The second strand of logic has to do with a sequence of implications that must—remember that word *must*—flow from this fact, what Josh McDowell has called "evidence that demands a verdict."

Since the tomb was empty, then Jesus of Nazareth, body and all, *is* not dead but alive. He *is* not returned to this life like Lazarus but alive eternally, having conquered sin and death on the Cross.

Since Christ *is* eternally alive, then he *is* alive today, April 17, 2022.

He *is* alive today, not as some cosmic survivor but as Lord of heaven and earth, which explains why the ascension is part of the Easter season.

Since he *is* Lord of all, then he is *our* Lord and *our* Judge, whether we know it or not.

Since he *is* our Lord and Judge, he has the exclusive claim to our love, faith and obedience.

Since he promised that "whoever believes in me shall have eternal life," then we can trust that our life *is not* futile and our death *is not* the end of it all.

And since he promised to prepare a place for us in heaven, then we know that we too *shall rise* in due time with transformed bodies in a new creation.

These strands of logic give me confidence in the truth of the Gospel. They also stir up in me a kind of excitement as when a research scientist cries out "Eureka"—"I have found the answer." Or better, "the answer has found me!" I am looking forward to the further unfolding of the mystery that began on Easter when I awake in the kingdom of God.

There is one more feature of logic: the evidence of the empty tomb demands not only a verdict but an *action*. For those who do not know Christ, that action is repentance and faith, as Peter stated on the Day of Pentecost: "Repent and be baptized every one of you in the name of Jesus Christ for the forgiveness of your sins, and you will receive the gift of the Holy Spirit" (Acts 2:38). For believers, Paul's logic goes like this: "If then you have been raised with Christ, seek the things that are above, where Christ is, seated at the right hand of God" (Col 3:1). Faith in the risen Christ requires dying to self and taking up the cross and following him—daily.

But the logic of Easter morning goes only so far, and the empty tomb itself is merely a cold rock cave—and, oh by the way, it's empty! (This is a fact which the Crusaders should have known as they slaughtered their way to the Holy Land.)

So let's consider the right-brain testimony to Easter morning which complements the stony fact of the empty tomb.

We begin with the responses of the women, the first witnesses. Why were they coming to the tomb? Surely it was out of devotion to the Jesus they had followed and loved. When they saw the stone rolled back and met the angel, their devotion was turned to shock and awe, as Matthew's gospel relates: "they departed quickly from the tomb with fear and great joy and ran to tell his disciples" (Matt 28:8). As they ran, Jesus himself appeared and greeted them, saying Shalom! When they heard his Shalom! their fear and joy were turned to worship, and they fell down at his feet.

Next there is the response of creation. The joy of Easter morning, at least in our part of the world, is accompanied by the return of spring. It is reflected in the ancient Easter hymn "Come ye faithful, raise the strain of triumphant gladness":

> Now the queen of seasons, bright
> with the day of splendour,
> With the royal feast of feasts,
> comes its joy to render;
> Comes to glad Jerusalem,
> who with true affection
> Welcomes in unwearied strains
> Jesus' resurrection.

Behind the superficialities of Easter egg hunts and chicks and bunnies and lilies lies the emotional truth of Easter morning: a new day has dawned for the world, and we are invited to join in it. The poet George Herbert expresses the transformation of the heart from Lent to the Easter season this way:

> How fresh, Oh Lord, how sweet and clean
> Are thy returns! even as the flowers in spring…

The late-past frosts tributes of pleasure bring.
Grief melts away
Like snow in May,
As if there were no such cold thing.

Finally there is the response of the apostles. On Easter morning the apostles were not so quick on the uptake. Cowering behind closed doors, their first response was to dismiss the women's report as a "wives' tale." Then two of them, Peter and John, were dispatched to the tomb, where they saw the folded grave-clothes inside. Peter saw but remained befuddled, but John saw and believed. Why the difference? Was John more logical than Peter? Perhaps, but I have another possibility. John first believed because he had first been loved. John the Beloved Disciple had laid his head on Jesus' chest at the Last Supper, and Jesus' words were ringing in memory: "Let not your hearts be troubled. Believe in God; believe also in me." He alone of the apostles had stood at the foot of the Cross and had seen Jesus die. Years later, John described his experience this way: "We love because he first loved us" (1 John 4:19). There is a spontaneity to God's love and our faith which surpasses mere logic, which penetrates our entire being. As John again put it famously: "The Word (*Logos*) became flesh and dwelt among us, and we beheld his glory."

The awesome joy of the women, the rebirth of creation and the believing love of John, these are the right-brain responses to the empty tomb.

I have been fortunate to be married to a woman of feeling and faith. We have celebrated more than fifty Easters together, and I have never ceased to marvel at how, despite the work of Easter dinner preparation, she enjoys the holiday, how she extends her cheer not only to family and guests at home but also via Easter cards to friends and extended family abroad. She has the gift of faith and of joy which is the testimony of Easter morning.

So with whatever complementary gifts we bring, Peggy and I extend our heartfelt greetings to our family here at Redeemer. May you with the Church of the ages go out with confident faith and overflowing joy proclaiming: *"Welcome happy morning! Christ is Risen! The Lord is Risen indeed! Alleluia."*

Risen Indeed! The Testimony of the Apostles

ACTS 5:12–33; EPHESIANS 4:1–16; JOHN 20:19–31

Alleluia! Christ is Risen!
The Lord is Risen Indeed! Alleluia!

This is the second sermon in a series on "Testimonies to the Resurrection." During the Epiphany season, I preached on "Jesus: The Early Years." In a sense, these three sermons are about "The Risen Jesus: The First Day." Today we are looking at Jesus' appearance to his disciples on the evening of Easter Day.

Our gospel reading today comes from John, and as often is the case, John has a unique perspective on the events of the Jesus story. John's gospel, like the other gospels, begins with the empty tomb, and also like them, it speaks of Jesus' first appearing to women who come to the tomb; but John focuses on one woman, Mary Magdalene, whom Jesus addresses by name: "Mary." Mary turns and recognizes him—"*Rabboni*, my dear Teacher"—and falls at his feet in worship. Jesus says to her, "Do not cling to me, for I have not yet ascended to the Father; but go to my brothers and say to them, 'I am ascending to my Father and your Father, to my God and your God'" (John 20:17).

John is describing here an Easter Day ascension, announced by Mary to the apostles. Later that day Jesus himself appears to the disciples, greets them and shows them his hands and his side. He is the same risen Lord, with the marks of the Cross but now clothed with all authority in heaven and earth. He breathes on them, saying: "Receive the Holy Spirit. If you forgive the sins of any, they are forgiven them; if you withhold forgiveness from any, it is withheld." Let's call this the Easter Evening Pentecost, or the *apostolic Pentecost*.

I do not think John is contradicting the horizontal timeline in Luke and Acts of the forty days from Easter to the Ascension and the fifty days from Easter to Pentecost. But he also knows that the vertical axis of salvation has been completed in one great arc: the lifting up of Jesus Christ on the Cross and his rising from the dead to the right hand of God. This ascension unlocks heaven and earth to the presence of the triune God, to "my Father and your Father," and to the Holy Spirit, about whom Jesus had told them at the Last Supper: "I tell you the truth: it is to your advantage that I go away, for if I do not go away, the Helper will not come to you. But if I go, I will send him to you" (John 16:7).

The Good News of Jesus' resurrection is first revealed to the women—to Mary Magdalene in particular—and then to the apostles. Later, he will appear to wider circles—more than five hundred at one time—and ten days after his final ascension into heaven, he will send the Holy Spirit to thousands who believe the Gospel on the day of Pentecost.

John's description of Jesus' appearance on Easter night makes clear that the Christian Gospel is an apostolic Gospel, and the Christian Church is an apostolic Church.

What do I mean by this?

First, Jesus appeared exclusively to the inner circle of his apostles. The apostles are God's chosen channel for communicating the Good News of Jesus to the world. Even though pagans had a religious awareness, sometimes crude and idolatrous, sometimes serious and philosophical, they were not God's chosen vehicle of self-disclosure. Even though the Jews had received the special revelation through the Old Testament Scriptures and constituted the "mother lode" of Christianity, they too were blinded to the Messiah when he came in the flesh. Paul put the matter this way:

> For since, in the wisdom of God, the world did not know God through wisdom, it pleased God through the folly of what we preach to save those who believe. For Jews demand signs and Greeks seek wisdom, but we preach Christ crucified, a stumbling block to Jews and folly to Gentiles, but to those who are called, both Jews and Greeks, Christ the power of God and the wisdom of God. (1 Cor 1:21–23)

The "we" who preach Christ are the apostles, among whom Paul is the latecomer but who, as we saw in Galatians, boasted in Christ crucified.

The fact that the apostles are God's chosen channel explains the emergence of the New Testament as God's Word, deriving from the apostles, who had seen the risen Lord. And through these apostolic Scriptures, the Church of all generations—and we here in Bellevue in 2022—has received the same Gospel as the first generation, "built on the foundation of the apostles and prophets, Christ Jesus being the cornerstone" (Eph 2:20).

Secondly, the apostles had been cowering behind closed doors on Easter morning, but later that day when Jesus appeared to them they were transformed into a band of brothers united by the Spirit and sent out on mission. This had been Jesus' goal from the beginning of his ministry, but it seemed to have foundered on Good Friday when Peter denied him and they all ran away. As is often the case, however, their betrayal became an opportunity for God to display his grace. The risen Jesus greeted them with his "Peace," breathed the Holy Spirit on them, and authorized them to build his Church. Jesus made clear that their "Great Commission" was part of his own mission, saying, "As the Father has sent me, so I am sending you," and this mission has been passed on to the Church down to our time.

Thirdly, the means of receiving the apostolic Gospel is faith and faith alone. John is explicit about his testimony, saying: "these things are written so that you [the readers] may believe that Jesus is the Christ, the Son of God, and that by believing you may have life in his name." The story of Thomas serves not only as an antidote to doubt, but even more as an assurance that through the testimony of the apostles we too have seen Jesus when we put our trust in him as our Lord and our God. The Holy Spirit emboldened the apostolic Church to witness to the Gospel even in the face of threats from the secular regime, as occurs in our reading from Acts today. Matters today have not changed, which is why we pray each week for the persecuted church, and in our secularized society today, we too are called to say in word and deed: "We must obey God and not men."

One final point to Jesus' two-stage appearance, first to the apostles and then to the wider community of believers: Jesus is establishing an ordered ministry. When he says: "As the Father has sent me, even so I am sending you," he says it to the apostles, who become the pillars of the Church. The apostles themselves "appointed elders in every church" (Acts 14:23), and later Paul deputized Timothy and Titus to continue his work. There are many variations in the precise shape of the apostolic ministry, including our Anglican threefold order of bishop, presbyter [priest] and deacon—but they are all "historic," in the sense that they have been passed on through the history of the Christian Church, and they are all "ordered" in the sense they look to the pattern of the first apostles.

Here is one expression of apostolic ministry, stated in the recent Jerusalem Declaration of global Anglicans:

> We recognise that God has called and gifted bishops, priests and deacons in historic succession to equip all the people of God for their ministry in the world. We uphold the classic Anglican Ordinal as an authoritative standard of clerical orders.

Of course, just as the entire Church is apostolic, so also the laity of the Church is part of the apostolic ministry. We Anglicans have what I'll called a *mixed polity*. The congregation elects the vestry, who serve as lay elders. Clergy are ordained by the bishop to their ministry and then called by a particular congregation and installed by the bishop. I thank God for leading Redeemer in calling the Rev. Ethan Carlson and look forward to his installation later in the year.

I thought I'd conclude by reading you some questions which the Prayer Book (pages 490–92) asks of its ordained clergy to ensure that they are committed to the apostolic Gospel and the apostolic Church.

> *Bishop*: Do you believe in your heart that you are truly called, according to the will of our Lord Jesus Christ, and according to the Canons of this Church, to the Order and ministry of the Priesthood?
> *Answer*: I do so believe.
>
> *Bishop*: Do you believe that the Holy Scriptures contain all things necessary for salvation through faith in Jesus Christ? And are you determined out of the Holy Scriptures to instruct the people committed to your charge, and to teach or maintain nothing as necessary to eternal salvation but that which may be concluded and proved by the Scriptures?
> *Answer*: I do so believe, and I am so determined, the Lord being my helper.
>
> *Bishop*: Will you then give your faithful diligence always so to

minister the doctrine, sacraments, and discipline of Christ, as the Lord has commanded and as this Church has received them, according to the Commandments of God, so that you may teach the people committed to your charge with all diligence to keep and observe them?
Answer: I will, the Lord being my helper.

Bishop: Will you be ready, with all faithful diligence, to banish and drive away from the Body of Christ all erroneous and strange doctrines contrary to God's Word; and to use both public and private admonitions and exhortations, to the weak as well as the strong within your charge, as need shall require and occasion shall be given?
Answer: I will, the Lord being my helper.

Bishop: Will you be diligent in prayer, and in the reading of Holy Scripture, and in such study as may further the knowledge of the same, laying aside all distractions of the world and the flesh?
Answer: I will, the Lord being my helper.

Bishop: Will you be diligent to frame and fashion your own life [and the life of your family], according to the doctrine of Christ, and to make yourself [and them, as much as you are able], a wholesome example and pattern to the flock of Christ?
Answer: I will, the Lord being my helper.

Bishop: Will you maintain and set forward, as much as you are able, quietness, peace, and love among all Christian people, and especially among those who are or shall be committed to your charge?
Answer: I will, the Lord being my helper.

Bishop: Will you reverently obey your Bishop and other chief Ministers who, according to the Canons of the Church, may have charge and authority over you, following with a glad mind and a good will their godly admonitions, and submitting yourself to their godly judgments?
Answer: I will, the Lord being my helper.

Bishop: Almighty God, our heavenly Father, who has given you a good will to do all these things, grant you also the strength and power to perform them, accomplishing in you the good work which he has begun, that you may be found perfect and without reproach on the last day; through Jesus Christ our Lord. Amen.

On May 22, I shall be formally bidding you farewell, and I am pleased that my old friend Bishop Minns can be present. It is also a significant date for me in that it is the golden anniversary of my ordination to the priesthood of the one holy, catholic and apostolic Church.

Risen Indeed! The Testimony of the Lord's Supper

ACTS 2:42–47; LUKE 24:13–49

Alleluia! Christ is Risen!
The Lord is Risen Indeed! Alleluia!

This is the third sermon in a series on "Testimonies to the Resurrection." Let's note that each of these testimonies is to Jesus but in distinct ways. The first testimony involves a fact of time and place: on Easter morning 30 AD the tomb where Jesus' body had been laid was empty. "He is not here" is a fact which requires an explanation. The second involves the band of disciples, whom he commissions to testify to his bodily resurrection. The third testimony, which we shall consider today, is to a meal.

There are several occasions in the Easter period, one recorded in John's gospel and two in Luke's, when Jesus appeared in connection with eating and drinking. The first occurrence, in our gospel lesson today, occurs on the afternoon of Easter Day when two disciples meet a mysterious stranger on the Road to Emmaus, a town just outside Jerusalem. After walking and talking with him about the events of the past three days, they invite him to dine with them, and the text says: "When he was at table with them, he took the bread and blessed and broke it and gave it to them. And their eyes were opened, and they recognized him. And he vanished from their sight."

The second occurrence follows on from the first, as the two disciples "rose that same hour and returned to Jerusalem" and told the Eleven "what had happened on the road, and how he was known to them in the breaking of the bread."

> As they were talking about these things, Jesus himself stood

> among them, and said to them, "Peace to you!" But they were startled and frightened and thought they saw a spirit. And he said to them, "Why are you troubled, and why do doubts arise in your hearts? See my hands and my feet, that it is I myself. Touch me, and see. For a spirit does not have flesh and bones as you see that I have." And when he had said this, he showed them his hands and his feet. And while they still disbelieved for joy and were marveling, he said to them, "Have you anything here to eat?" They gave him a piece of broiled fish, and he took it and ate before them.

This second night meeting is surely the same as the one we looked at last week in John's gospel where Jesus breathed on the apostles and commissioned them to testify to him.

Why did the risen Lord appear at a meal? It seems to me likely that Jesus chose to appear on both these occasions to remind the disciples of the Last Supper, where he had spoken of his body broken and his blood poured out as a sacrifice for many. This same Body, Jesus is showing them, has now conquered death and the grave and stands before them, forgiving their betrayal, bestowing the Spirit, and commanding them to build his Church. He was also instituting the remembrance of the Last Supper as the Sacrament of his death and resurrection and a foretaste of the final banquet in heaven.

For Anglicans, the Lord's Supper is one of the two Gospel sacraments commanded by Jesus. Anglicans may differ on how precisely Christ is present in the Sacrament, but I conclude that they all affirm that Christ is truly present in the Spirit through the elements of bread and wine and that we derive great benefits when we eat and drink with faith and thanksgiving.

This morning I intend to offer an "instructed Eucharist" by rehearsing the major elements of the Holy Communion service which we follow. Note if you will the *participation* of worshipers along with the *presence* of Christ in the Word and Sacrament through the Spirit.

[A brief summary of the Order of Service from the Book of Common Prayer 2019 followed.]

Dear Redeemer friends, on that first Easter evening, the disciples met the risen Lord in the breaking of bread. This evening we are invited to join them in enjoying the Lord's presence in Word and Sacrament—until we see him in his glorious Kingdom.

***

As I noted in my last podcast, I am planning to leave some space before your new rector arrives on July 1. I am formally stepping down today, but I shall continue to officiate at worship until May 22, when Bishop Minns will join us. For the remaining weeks in May and June I have arranged a schedule of supply clergy to preach. These clergy have had a role in Redeemer's walk and will give additional perspective and support.

Throughout this time until July 1, I shall be available for emergency pastoral care, and I shall also be meeting with Ethan when he arrives in the States to help him get oriented to his new call.

Please know that at all times Peggy and I will be holding you in our prayers and in our heart, as we have this past year.

> Now to him who is able to do far more abundantly than all that we ask or think, according to the power at work within us, to him be glory in the church and in Christ Jesus throughout all generations, forever and ever. Amen. (Eph 3:20–21)

Selected Pastor's Podcasts

Interim Pastor: Privilege and Responsibility

As of May 1, I have been named "interim pastor."

I think you understand "interim." I hope to be providing a bridge ministry here as Redeemer gets on its feet as an independent congregation and calls a new full-time priest. However, "interim" has to do with length of time, not the strength of authority. For this period, I am to you a full-strength pastor.

When I was in fifth grade—yes, friends, my wife Peggy was in the same class—our teacher Mrs. Burdette taught us the aphorism: "Privilege and responsibility go hand in hand." These words still apply, I think.

It is my privilege and responsibility to preach the Word of God at Redeemer. It is part of my larger vocation, which began when I was ordained almost a half century ago and the bishop handed me a Bible and said, "Take authority to preach the Word of God and to administer the Holy Sacraments. Do not neglect the trust committed to you as a priest of the Church of God."

This commission is directly referring to the words of St. Paul:

> For if I preach the gospel, that gives me no ground for boasting. For necessity is laid upon me. Woe to me if I do not preach the gospel! (1 Cor 9:16)
>
> O Timothy, guard the deposit entrusted to you. Avoid the irreverent babble and contradictions of what is falsely called "knowledge," for by professing it some have swerved from the faith. Grace be with you. (1 Tim 6:20)

Now a pastor has many responsibilities, from the mundane to the spiritual, from the public to the private and confidential. I have had something of a specialized vocation, as an educator and writer. But the one constant thing is that I am charged to preach the Word of God.

You will find that I have a standard "acclamation" when I preach. It goes like this: "May the words of my mouth and the meditations of our hearts be always acceptable in your sight, O Lord our Rock and our Redeemer."

This is a slight variation of Psalm 19, verse 14. I have always found Psalm 19 a wonderful summary of how God speaks to his people. First there is the "unspoken" testimony of creation:

> The heavens declare the glory of God, and the sky above proclaims his handiwork. Day to day pours out speech, and night to night reveals knowledge. There is no speech, nor are there words, whose voice is not heard. Their voice goes out through all the earth, and their words to the end of the world. (verses 1–4)

Next there is the spoken word of revelation in Scripture:

> The law of the LORD is perfect, reviving the soul; the testimony of the LORD is sure, making wise the simple; the precepts of the LORD are right, rejoicing the heart; the commandment of the LORD is pure, enlightening the eyes; the fear of the LORD is clean, enduring forever; the rules of the LORD are true, and righteous altogether. More to be desired are they than gold, even much fine gold; sweeter also than honey and drippings of the honeycomb. (verses 7–10)

Next, there is the application of God's Word to our lives, calling us to obedience:

> Moreover, by them is your servant warned; in keeping them there is great reward. Who can discern his errors? Declare me innocent from hidden faults. Keep back your servant also from presumptuous sins; let them not have dominion over me! Then I shall be blameless, and innocent of great transgression. (verses 11–13)

And finally, there is the prayer that God's Word would take root in our hearts:

> Let the words of my mouth and the meditation of my heart be acceptable in your sight, O LORD, my rock and my redeemer. (verse 14)

There is another prayer, this one a "collect" from the Book of Common Prayer, that says much the same thing:

> Blessed Lord, who has caused all Holy Scriptures to be written for our learning: Grant that we may so hear them, read, mark, learn, and inwardly digest them, that by patience and comfort of your Holy Word, we may embrace and ever hold fast the blessed hope of everlasting life, which you have given us in our Savior Jesus Christ. Amen.

Friends, as I begin my pastorate here, I hope I may live up to the privilege you and the Lord have given me to be responsible in "rightly handling the word of truth" (2 Tim 2:15).

On Canticles

This past week I was able to obtain free copies of the Book of Common Prayer for each family to use at home. I'd like to take some of my podcast time to introduce different features of the Prayer Book to you, whether you are a veteran or a new Anglican.

The Bible mentions several forms of praise singing. St. Paul urges his church to address each other singing psalms and hymns and spiritual songs (Col 3:16). The Book of Common Prayer includes two of these forms: psalms and hymns. The Prayer Book is chock-full of psalms. In fact, the entire book of Psalms is included on pages 267–467.

However, I want to look at the second form, the *canticle*. You can find many canticles as part of the Daily Prayer services, and a collection of them on pages 79–88. The canticles include some hymns from within the Bible, but also some famous hymns of the early church. They often are identified by their first lines (in Latin).

One of the most famous of these is called the *Te Deum Laudamus*, which translates as "We praise you, O God." You can find it in the Morning Prayer service on page 17.

The *Te Deum* is what I refer to as a creedal hymn. It includes most of the elements of the Apostles' Creed, the "basic believing" which we are surveying in the new sermon series.

It begins with the praise of God in heaven by the angels. It then turns to the praise of the human saints in light—apostles, prophets, and martyrs—and from there it includes the whole Church throughout the world, which we call the "communion of saints."

The object of this praise is the Holy Trinity: the Father of majesty unbounded, his true and only Son, and the Holy Spirit, advocate and guide.

The canticle now focuses in on Jesus Christ, the eternal Son of the Father. It recites the basic elements of his life according to the Creed: his virgin birth, his death on the Cross, his resurrection and ascension to God's right hand in glory, and his second coming to be our judge.

It concludes with an appeal by us, the Church, who are bought with the price of his own blood, to help us in our daily life and to preserve us for glory everlasting.

This great hymn can be said at home. It also has been set to music by numerous composers and can be sung by choirs and congregations.

Why don't you try it out!

Critical Lovers and Loving Critics

This morning I put out the flag on our porch, which I do on national holidays.* But before I did, I paused. Why? First, because showing the flag seems a provocative act at present, and second, because this year Independence Day falls on Sunday, the Lord's Day. But I went ahead and thought this coincidence in the secular and sacred calendars might be an opportunity to say why.

Let me take you back to 1968, long before most of you were born. My wife Peggy and I graduated from Cornell University on June 1, 1968. The commencement speaker was John W. Gardner. Gardner was Secretary of Health, Education, and Welfare and had helped implement much of President Lyndon Johnson's Great Society agenda. He went on to found Common Cause, an advocacy group for citizen participation in government, for which he was attacked from both the Right and the Left.

Gardner's speech at Cornell was widely reported at the time, particularly for his warning against "uncritical lovers and unloving critics" of America. Gardner imagined twenty-third-century historians looking back from two hundred years on this time:

> They pointed out that twentieth-century institutions were caught in savage crossfire between uncritical lovers and unloving critics. On the one side, those who loved their institutions tended to smother them in an embrace of death, loving their rigidities more than their promise, shielding them from life-giving criticism. On the other side, there arose a breed of critics without love, skilled in demolition but untutored in the arts by which human institutions

* The Fourth of July fell on a Sunday, and I preached this sermon at Redeemer Anglican Church that day. Like the podcasts, it is occasional in nature, so I have included it here rather than with the other sermons.

are nurtured and strengthened and made to flourish. Between the two, the institutions perished.

The twenty-third-century scholars understood that where human institutions were concerned, love without criticism brings stagnation, and criticism without love brings destruction. And they emphasized that the swifter the pace of change, the more lovingly men had to care for and criticize their institutions to keep them intact through the turbulent passages.

1968 was indeed a turbulent year. Vietnam protests had come to a head, with the burning of flags and draft cards, which led to the withdrawal of Lyndon Johnson from the presidential race on March 31. Five days later, on April 4, Martin Luther King Jr. was assassinated in Memphis, followed by destructive riots in many American cities, including Pittsburgh. Whole blocks in Washington, DC, came to look like a bombed-out war zone and remained so for years. On June 5, four days after Gardner's speech at Cornell, Robert Kennedy was assassinated. Kennedy was a frontrunner in the presidential race and considered a champion of human rights. In August, violent clashes of protesters and police broke out at the Democratic Convention in Chicago, which led in November to the election of Richard Nixon, who ran on a platform of law and order and patriotism.

In 1968, there was demonstrably a shortage of critical lovers and loving critics. I fear the same is true today. So let me add a small ounce of critical love for America on this Independence Day. I do so as a biblical Christian.

As Moses prepares to send the people of Israel into the Promised Land, he puts the moment in this perspective: "When the Most High gave to the nations their inheritance, when he divided mankind, he fixed the borders of the peoples according to the number of the sons of God. But the Lord's portion is his people, Jacob his allotted heritage" (Deut 32:8). God's people have a dual loyalty: to their land and to their God. The land of Canaan comes with a promise and a warning: settle down in the land of milk and honey, but do not forget God, or you will lose it.

When one thinks of our native land, the first thing that comes to mind is its *beauty*. Take a popular national hymn like this one, with a paraphrase added by Ray Charles:

Oh beautiful, for spacious skies
For amber waves of grain
For purple mountain majesties
Above the fruited plain…

But now wait a minute, I'm talking about
America, sweet America
You know, God done shed his grace on thee
He crowned thy good, yes he did, in brotherhood
From sea to shining sea.

To my mind, one of the great loving critics of our day is Ken Burns, who has produced films about Americans and American culture, from Mark Twain to the Wright brothers, from baseball and Jackie Robinson to jazz and Louis Armstrong. Most recently, Peggy and I watched a Ken Burns film, *The National Parks: America's Best Idea*. What an awesome inheritance of natural and human beauty and resources we have access to as Americans!

Secondly, nations have a history. The entire book of Deuteronomy and the historical books that follow it recount Israel's past with a warning about its future. It is not an idyllic past: the entire generation that left Egypt had rebelled and was consigned to forty years of wandering in the desert. Nor did the nation have an idyllic ending: destruction of Jerusalem and its temple and exile to Babylon. Nevertheless, the people of Israel owned this history as their history, accepting God's judgment along with his mercy.

Likewise, we loving critics must own our history with the good and the bad. One of our great celebratory historians is David McCullough, a Pittsburgher for whom a bridge over the Allegheny River was recently named. McCullough, like Ken Burns, has celebrated in readable prose many historical figures and events from John Adams to the Johnstown Flood, from Harry S. Truman to the Brooklyn Bridge. There is much we can take pride in as Americans this July Fourth.

But, we must also confess, there are dark, damning clouds overhanging our country. One of them is the scourge of abortion on demand. Conceived in the sixties, legalized in 1973, abortion violates the most basic human right and instinct. "Can a woman forget her nursing child," Isaiah asks, "that she should have no compassion on the son of her womb?" (Isa 49:15)

I will not pursue this matter further except to quote the author of the Declaration of Independence, who said: "I tremble for my country when I reflect that God is just, that his justice cannot sleep forever." And to note that this evil has called forth many acts of compassion and generosity.

There is another dark cloud which hovers over our national identity and destiny: the legacy of slavery and racism, which was sparked anew by the death of George Floyd last year and led to upheavals like those in 1968, which will follow us long after the coronavirus pandemic has faded in memory. During the lockdown, I turned back to history for perspective. I was taken by Frederick Douglass's address "What to the Slave is the Fourth of July?" Written in 1852, not long after his escape and emancipation from slavery, Douglass begins: "The Fourth of July is the birthday of your National Independence and of your political freedom." But, he goes on, "the rich inheritance of justice, liberty, prosperity and independence, bequeathed by your fathers, is *yours*, not *mine*. *You* may rejoice, *I* must mourn."

> Standing with God and the crushed and bleeding slave on this occasion, I will, in the name of humanity which is outraged, in the name of liberty which is fettered, in the name of the Constitution and the Bible, which are disregarded and trampled upon, dare to call in question and denounce, with all the emphasis I can command, everything that serves to perpetuate slavery—the great sin and shame of America!

That, I would say, is about as critical as one can be, addressing an assembly of white abolitionists. He proceeds to knock down one by one the slaveholders' attempts to "slander" the Constitution, which he says is "a Glorious Liberty Document." He ends on a note of hope: "I do not despair of this country. There are forces in operation, which must inevitably work the downfall of slavery"—forces which ten years later led to the Civil War and hundreds of thousands of white and black soldiers who died for the cause of freedom.

Slavery died, racism did not, in both the South and the North. It took another great man to move the country forward a century later. I was privileged to attend the March on Washington in August 1963 and hear Martin Luther King Jr.'s "I Have a Dream" speech at the Lincoln Memorial. If you have not heard it, let me urge you to find and listen to an audio version online. King begins with an indictment of white America:

> Five-score years ago a great American, in whose symbolic shadow we stand today signed the Emancipation Proclamation...But one hundred years later, the Negro is still not free; one hundred years later, the life of the Negro is still sadly crippled by the manacles of segregation and the chains of discrimination.

He proceeds with a litany of present injustices and warns in the words of the prophet Amos: "we will not be satisfied until justice rolls down like waters and righteousness like a mighty stream."

But like Frederick Douglass, King ends on a note of hope:

> I still have a dream. It is a dream deeply rooted in the American dream. It is a dream that one day this nation will rise up and live out the true meaning of its creed—we hold these truths to be self-evident, that all men are created equal.

In his peroration, King summons the deepest chords of our national memory and love of country, recalling the patriotic hymn "My country, 'tis of Thee, sweet land of liberty, of thee I sing; Land where my fathers died, land of the pilgrims' pride, from every mountainside, let freedom ring":

> So let freedom ring from the mighty mountains of New York. Let freedom ring from the heightening Alleghenies of Pennsylvania. Let freedom ring from the snow-capped Rockies of Colorado. Let freedom ring from the curvaceous slopes of California. But not only that. Let freedom ring from Stone Mountain in Georgia. Let freedom ring from Lookout Mountain in Tennessee. Let freedom ring from every hill and molehill of Mississippi, from every mountainside, let freedom ring.
>
> And when we allow freedom to ring, when we let it ring from every village and hamlet, from every state and city, we will be able to speed up that day when all of God's children—black men and white men, Jews and Gentiles, Catholics and Protestants—will be able to join hands and to sing in the words of the old Negro spiritual, "Free at last, free at last, thank God Almighty, we are free at last."

Redeemer folks, we are a tiny molehill in the American landscape. Some say our country is moving backward, some say forward. But whatever your judgment, I would appeal to you to hold out hope for our deeply flawed nation. As Christians, let us speak the truth in love with our neighbors. As citizens, let us be critical lovers and loving critics.

That's why I put out my flag today—with a trembling hand.

The General Thanksgiving

And let the peace of Christ rule in your hearts, to which indeed you were called in one body. And be thankful. (Col 3:15)

One of the themes that pervades the Book of Common Prayer is thanksgiving. The entire service of Holy Communion is also called "Eucharist," the Greek word for thanksgiving. There is also a section of the Occasional Prayers for thanksgivings (pages 680–83) that you can use on various occasions.

The best-known thanksgiving prayer is called "The General Thanksgiving," which concludes Morning and Evening Prayer (pages 25–26 and 51–52). Let me read it in full and then show how biblical it is.

> Almighty God, Father of all mercies, we your unworthy servants give you humble thanks for all your goodness and loving-kindness to us and to all whom you have made. We bless you for our creation, preservation, and all the blessings of this life; but above all for your immeasurable love in the redemption of the world by our Lord Jesus Christ; for the means of grace, and for the hope of glory. And, we pray, give us such an awareness of your mercies, that with truly thankful hearts we may show forth your praise, not only with our lips, but in our lives, by giving up ourselves to your service, and by walking before you in holiness and righteousness all our days; through Jesus Christ our Lord, to whom, with you and the Holy Spirit, be honor and glory throughout all ages. Amen.

Almighty God, Father of all mercies,

> Blessed be the God and Father of our Lord Jesus Christ, the Father of mercies and God of all comfort… (2 Cor 1:3)

we your unworthy servants give you humble thanks for all your goodness and loving-kindness to us and to all whom you have made.

> So you also, when you have done all that you were commanded, say, "We are unworthy servants; we have only done what was our duty." (Luke 17:10)

We bless you for our creation, preservation, and all the blessings of this life;

> The LORD will keep you from all evil; he will keep your life. The LORD will keep your going out and your coming in from this time forth and forevermore. (Psalm 121:7–8)

but above all for your immeasurable love in the redemption of the world by our Lord Jesus Christ; for the means of grace, and for the hope of glory.

> O Israel, hope in the LORD! For with the LORD there is steadfast love, and with him is plentiful redemption. (Psalm 130:7)

> Through him we have also obtained access by faith into this grace in which we stand, and we rejoice in hope of the glory of God. (Rom 5:2)

And, we pray, give us such an awareness of your mercies, that with truly thankful hearts we may show forth your praise, not only with our lips, but in our lives, by giving up ourselves to your service, and by walking before you in holiness and righteousness all our days;

> But be doers of the word, and not hearers only, deceiving yourselves. (James 1:22)

> that we, being delivered from the hand of our enemies, might serve him without fear, in holiness and righteousness before him all our days. (Luke 1:74–75, the Song of Zechariah)

through Jesus Christ our Lord, to whom, with you and the Holy Spirit, be honor and glory throughout all ages. Amen.

> to the only wise God be glory forevermore through Jesus Christ! Amen. (Rom 16:27)

I have found it valuable over the years to memorize a few of the great prayers of the Prayer Book. The General Thanksgiving is one I love in particular. I commend it to you.

AUGUST 5, 2021

On Vaccines and Mask Mandates

In lieu of a weekly podcast for this week, I wish to send this message.

One month ago, we at Redeemer began to relax our Covid-19 protocols, stating: 1) that vaccinated members, clergy and laity, should feel free to worship outdoors or indoors without masks; 2) that any member may choose to wear a mask at any time; and 3) that members not fully vaccinated should note the Centers for Disease Control guidance that "if you are not fully vaccinated and aged 2 or older, you should wear a mask in indoor public places" (June 29).

Over the past weeks, there has been increasing public concern about coronavirus transmission, even among the vaccinated, leading the CDC (July 30) to advise that "given the spread of the highly transmissible Delta variant, local decision-makers should assess the following factors to inform the need for layered prevention strategies across a range of settings." As of August 2, Allegheny County's level of Covid-19 was raised from "moderate" to "substantial," and the Pennsylvania Department of Health "recommends"—not mandates—that everyone, vaccinated or not, wear a mask indoors.

My role as a pastor is to bring some biblical and spiritual perspective to this question. So let's begin with St. Paul's advice on obedience to the authorities. He says: "Let every person be subject to the governing authorities. For there is no authority except from God, and those that exist have been instituted by God" (Rom 13:1). While we know there are occasions where Christians must "obey God rather than men" (Acts 5:29), and while our democracy makes room for freedom of speech and association and for civil disobedience, nevertheless, as I see it, Paul's general rule stands. So, if the proper governmental authority (in this case the Governor of the Commonwealth or the national or diocesan heads of the Anglican Church in North America) were to *mandate* wearing masks in certain settings, I would comply and urge members to comply as well. Otherwise, a church and its members will need to exercise good judgment in its policies and practices. At this point, I do not think an across-the-board requirement to wear masks indoors or outdoors is warranted.

The second biblical case has to do with Christian conscience. In Corinth, Paul advised his church concerning the matter of eating meat from the market that may have been offered to pagan gods. He states that personally he feels free to eat such meat because "we know that an idol has no real existence and that there is no God but one" (1 Cor 8:4). At the same time, he recognizes that some members don't share his confidence, and so he advises, "take care that this right of yours does not somehow become a stumbling block to the brother for whom Christ died" (cf. 1 Cor 8:8–13). Paul goes on to say, perhaps a bit rhetorically, "if food makes my brother stumble, I will never eat meat, lest I make my brother stumble."

Taking this biblical example to heart, let me make this statement as your pastor:

First, I would urge all members of Redeemer to get vaccinated, unless you have a specific medical reason not to do so. My own judgment is that the current vaccines have proven safe and highly effective in reducing hospitalizations and deaths and, somewhat less so, in preventing transmission of the virus. If as a matter of prudence or of conscience you choose to remain unvaccinated, I would urge you to be sensitive to the increased risk that you may be infected and transmit it to others.

Secondly, while I myself am vaccinated and feel confident to minister unmasked, I am prepared to return to wearing a mask, outdoors or indoors, during Holy Communion if any member of the church would feel more secure in my doing so. Please let me know in this case. Otherwise, I shall continue to follow our revised practice.

We as a church and as a nation have been through a difficult time over the past eighteen months. The situation has improved dramatically with the arrival of vaccines, but the crisis is not yet over. Let's try to finish well, obedient to God and his Word.

Sonrise for Redeemer

Dear Redeemer Saints,

I am sending this from Atlantic Beach in North Carolina, where Peggy and I have taken a week's holiday. Every morning Peggy goes out to the little gazebo near our condo in order to see the sun rise. Each day is different. Today (Wednesday) sunrise was accompanied by a rainbow. These little glimpses of God's glory and covenant love remind me of the hymn which begins like this:

> When morning gilds the sky,
> our hearts awaking cry:
> May Jesus Christ be praised!
> In all our work and prayer
> we ask his loving care:
> May Jesus Christ be praised!

Let me take this time to thank all of you who helped to make last Sunday's service glorious. I'd like to call it "Sonrise for Redeemer." Not to say that there has not been much prayer and work done here over the past five years. But I believe Redeemer may now be on a path toward a new stage of maturity.

We had close to full attendance on Sunday, and even Matt and Madelyn, who were confirmed virtually, gave their Amen from cyberspace. Bishop Martyn Minns once again was thrilled to be with us for all the ceremonies: Blaine's baptism, the confirmation of ten and reception of six members into the church, and the standing reaffirmation of our baptism and faith in Jesus by nearly the whole congregation.

The Psalmist says the rising sun "comes out like a bridegroom leaving his chamber, and, like a strong man, runs its course with joy" (Psalm 19:14). Let me now encourage you all not to flag and fall back but to continue to come together for worship and, as Bishop Minns urged us, to seek to "add to our numbers" day by day.

This week I have asked Dan Omar, our seminary apprentice, to preach and give his testimony to the Lord. We shall have time after the service for individuals to testify and give thanks, so please come with that thought in mind. Bobby Brown will be officiating at the service. (Let me add here a special prayer request. Pastor Greg Miller, who was scheduled to be with us, has fallen ill with Covid and is in the hospital as I write. Please pray for his full recovery.)

I am looking forward to being back with you on October 3. We'll be changing the tone and topic of the sermons from teaching about "Basic Believing" to following the Bible in worshiping God in psalms and hymns and spiritual songs.

May this day be to each one of you a "Sonrise" in your hearts and together in the life of our church. I conclude with Charles Wesley's "Morning Hymn":

> Christ, whose glory fills the skies
> Christ, the true, the only Light,
> Sun of Righteousness, arise,
> Triumph o'er the shades of night;
> Dayspring from on high, be near,
> Daystar, in my heart appear.

Making Melody in My Heart

Fifty years ago I began my ministry in a large suburban church outside Washington, DC. I was a twenty-five-year-old right out of seminary, having read Karl Barth's *Dogmatics* (well, a couple volumes anyway) and written a master's thesis on "the knowledge of good and evil in Genesis 2–3."

As part of my job description—one that I was pretty sure only the Lord Jesus could fulfill—I was expected to make thirty-five parish calls a week, be present at all services (four on Sunday), and—surprise, surprise—run the youth group. In addition, I found out I was also supposed to lead the children's chapel on Sunday morning with about 100 kids aged 6–12.

I was an only child and at that point had no children of my own. What was I to do? Help! Well, here is what I did: I bought a guitar and taught myself three chords—that's what you need to fudge your way through most songs—and then began trolling for children's songs. Fortunately, there were a lot of songbooks out there. So as you may have noticed, I have a pretty big voice, and I would shut the kids up long enough to give a brief Bible story and then get them up and singing "This Little Light of Mine," "The Wise Man Built His House Upon the Rock," "Father Abraham Had Many Sons," "God Said to Noah, 'Build Me an Arky, Arky.'" You get the idea.

When it comes to musical taste, personally I prefer Haydn's *The Creation* and Handel's *Messiah*. But truth be told, some of these children's songs still circulate in my head, and I find myself humming them as I prepare the garden for winter.

One song that I learned later on—I think it was in Uganda—had the chorus "making melody in my heart," accompanied by some funny bodily contortions: *thumbs in, elbows out, head tilt, knees knock, tongue out, turn around,* and, finally, *fall down*. I'm getting pretty creaky to do the contortions now, but I still can recall the melody in my heart. You can find multiple versions of this on YouTube. Maybe we'll try this one out next Sunday.

As I mentioned in a previous sermon, I'm a bit concerned that much contemporary music, secular and sacred, is unsingable, unhummable, and unwhistleable. Whether it is children's songs, gospel choruses, or black spirituals, I wish to commend you parents and others to get your guitars or ukuleles and make some melodies in your heart for your kids and for yourself.

Blended Worship

I am speaking today about "blended worship," which was slated as the last topic of our sermon series on "Biblical Praise: Psalms and Hymns and Spiritual Songs." I have decided to condense that final session into this podcast in order to allow time this coming Sunday, October 24, to discuss the rector search, which was launched this week.

"Blended worship" is a term that is used today to describe a congregation's use of a variety of worship and musical styles. I have suggested that this variety can be found in the early Christian church as well, as is indicated in Paul's exhortation: "Let the word of Christ dwell in you richly, teaching and admonishing one another in all wisdom, singing psalms and hymns and spiritual songs, with thankfulness in your hearts to God" (Col 3:16).

In the first sermon of the series, I noted that the collection of Old Testament psalms, called the Psalter, is the foundational hymnbook of the Church, which is why it occupies two hundred pages of the Book of Common Prayer and is found in almost every service. There was a time in the Protestant Reformation when *only* the psalms were sung in church. However, gradually psalm paraphrases like "A Mighty Fortress" and "My Shepherd Shall Supply My Need" came in as hymns. English hymnody became one of the richest sources of church music, with authors ancient and modern like Isaac Watts ("When I Survey the Wondrous Cross") and Charles Wesley ("Hark! The Herald Angels Sing"), John Mason Neale (translator of many Latin hymns such as "All Glory, Laud, and Honor"), Graham Kendrick ("Shine, Jesus, Shine"), and Keith and Kristyn Getty ("In Christ Alone").

Finally, I noted that the New Testament includes "spiritual songs," some of which may have been choruses in tongues, but others which were short exclamations and acclamations to the glory of God, such as "Hallelujah (Praise the Lord)," "Jesus is Lord," and "Amen (So Be It)." Also, just as Jesus said "let the children come to me," many Christian writers have written children's carols like Martin Luther's "Away in a Manger" and Sunday School favorites like "Jesus Loves Me." Some are intended to be playful, as in "This Little Light of Mine."

It is my hope that Redeemer will embrace all the riches of biblical and Christian worship and music. It is my hope that we can strengthen our music teams—grateful though we are to Melissa and those who have been leading worship here. It is my hope that our congregation can participate in singing out together, "making melody in our hearts" and "making a joyful noise unto the Lord," with thankfulness for all he has done for us.

Do Churches Have a Personal Identity?

This past weekend I was the guest preacher at Truro Anglican Church in Fairfax, Virginia, where I began my ministry fifty years ago. I preached at the early service in the lovely colonial building, then outdoors to the congregation on the lawn (brrr, it was chilly), and finally at the 11:15 service in the main church. You can see that service on YouTube. Finally, Peggy and I spoke at a luncheon in the "undercroft," a.k.a. basement, of the church. I titled my talk "Truro Church: A Half Century of Witness."

I met some of the old-timers from my day, including two or three of my confirmands, who were now middle-aged (one is a local politician). But, not surprisingly, most of the church membership was new to me and I to them. So that raises a question: does a church have an identity that transcends its individual members and clergy?

I want to give a qualified *yes* to that notion. In our day, we recognize a corporation as having a legal identity that goes beyond any particular CEO and board of directors. We also recognize a person's right of inheritance in an "estate" that can be passed on to another. Likewise, I think, the New Testament recognizes the Church as the Body of Christ, as a divine institution that endures through time.

In chapters 2 and 3 of the Revelation to John, the exalted Jesus addresses the "angels" of the seven churches in Asia Minor (eastern Turkey today) about fifty years after they had been founded by St. Paul and others. The mother church was in Ephesus, the largest city in the eastern Roman Empire. Jesus says these words of prophecy:

> To the angel of the church in Ephesus write: "The words of him who holds the seven stars in his right hand, who walks among the seven golden lampstands.'I know your works, your toil and your patient endurance, and how you cannot bear with those who are

> evil, but have tested those who call themselves apostles and are not, and found them to be false. I know you are enduring patiently and bearing up for my name's sake, and you have not grown weary. But I have this against you, that you have abandoned the love you had at first. Remember therefore from where you have fallen; repent, and do the works you did at first. If not, I will come to you and remove your lampstand from its place, unless you repent.'" (2:1–5)

As I read it, the church at Ephesus has an identity (a "star"), an angelic guardian, and a physical place or lampstand. It has a history of faithful witness and suffering. However, it has lost its first love, and the Lord warns that if it does not repent and return to its first love, that identity can be lost.

Now it strikes me that a church, like a person, grows up from infancy to maturity with a certain identity. A church like Truro had a long history and was prepared for the spiritual renewal which came in the 1970s and which continues to the present, although lately its mettle has been tested.

What about Redeemer Church here in Bellevue? It does seem to me that Redeemer has inherited some spiritual DNA from its mother church St. Stephen's and from its founding pastor. It is now toddling into the next stage as a mission fellowship in the Anglican Diocese of Pittsburgh.* It will be the privilege and challenge for a new rector to guide Redeemer into adolescence and even to full maturity if he stays long enough. It will also be the challenge of the people here to pray for and work with the new rector to establish a church that will long endure.

* The annual convention of the diocese approved Redeemer as a mission fellowship on November 6, 2021, the same week as this podcast.

How to Read a Budget

My theme for this month's sermon series is "Managing God's Economy." This podcast—"How to Read a Budget"—is a sidebar to the series.

Let me begin by confessing I have never figured out how to read a balance sheet. I simply don't get how something can be an asset and a liability at the same time. Also, I find it somewhat miraculous that balance sheets always balance out to the last penny.

However, I have been pretty good over the years at reading budget sheets. So here are some tips as we look at the three-year projected budget for Redeemer Anglican Church, which was circulated for congregation members in hard copy form only.

First, budgets are made up of hard numbers. Annual budget projections begin with "actuals" from the previous year or years. For 2021, we have actuals from St. Stephen's for the first half of the year and from our own accounts for the second half. Budget projections for future years are "softer" than actuals and increasingly so as they stretch into the future. The current budget is conservative in its growth calculations, but it is open to revision as the Lord provides the increase. Nevertheless it projects a modest deficit at the end of the third quarter in 2024. This should be a blinking yellow light as we move ahead, even if it is three years down the pike. We're not the US Government!

Secondly, the key elements of an operating budget are *income* and *expense*. I call this the "daily bread" of an organization. Most charities run very close to the line and have little cushion for budget deficits. A few wealthy churches may have an endowment, but most live hand-to-mouth. I suppose we can think of the payment from St. Stephens as a one-time start-up grant, but after that, we are on our own.

Thirdly, when reading a budget, focus on the big-ticket items and don't get entangled in the petty details. This is where a condensed budget like the one before you is helpful. On the income side, virtually everything depends on member offerings, rising slowly year by year. The lion's share of expenses entails personnel expenses (full-time salary/benefits for the rector and part-time for an administrative assistant). Let me note in passing that most non-profit organizations that serve people are personnel-heavy.

Having made these calculations, there is a final critical element: God's provision. "God's work done in God's way will never lack God's supply," the great missionary Hudson Taylor taught. Clearly the current budget is lopsided on the personnel side, but this short-term investment in a full-time pastor is a tactical decision with a much wider strategic vision for Redeemer. We are looking for a leader who is seeking the Kingdom returns of thirtyfold, sixtyfold, a hundredfold (Matt 13:23).

Next week I'll be talking about "Reading a Strategic Plan."

NOVEMBER 18, 2021

How to Read a Strategic Plan

As we near the end of the year and we also begin interviewing rector candidates, the vestry has approved a projected budget through 2024 and a strategic plan outline. The budgets have been circulated to members in hard copy only; the strategic plan outline is now available on the website and Facebook page.

Last week I spoke about "How to Read a Budget." Today I am turning to "How to Read a Strategic Plan." Before I get going, let me say that I am not a credentialed strategic planner nor is Redeemer's plan a full-fledged strategic plan, which often extends to many pages in length. But what I do think our outline does is to give someone a bird's eye view of who we are and where we hope to go. And after all, that is what *strategy* is all about. *Tactics* have to do with how we get there.

So let's start at the top. First, there is the name: Redeemer Anglican Church. The name tells us that we are Christian (since Christ is the only Redeemer of the world). Second, we are part of the Anglican tradition, joining millions of Anglicans worldwide. Third, we are a congregation of the one, holy, catholic, and apostolic Church. We began as a church plant, but as of this year we have become legally independent and recognized as a mission fellowship of the Anglican Diocese of Pittsburgh. A mission fellowship is a young church seeking to become "self-governing, self-supporting, and self-propagating." We aim to reach the first level of this goal within five years, aided by a permanent pastor.

The vision statement of Redeemer was developed during Seth Zimmerman's tenure. It reads: "We aspire to overflow with the redeeming love of Christ where we live, work, and play." Like the church's name, the vision statement encapsulates the ethos and hopes of the church. The strategic plan notes four characteristics of this vision: aspiration, abundance, Christ-centered discipleship, and local focus. While these characteristics may be true of most churches in theory, the measure of our success will be the extent to which we can be true to them and carry them out.

The objectives that follow are general in scope: to grow in numbers; to deepen members' personal faith; to learn more of the Anglican way of being church; to support families and singles, i.e., "all sorts and conditions" of people; to establish a church home (God's household—1 Tim 3:15); and to be good stewards of what God has given us. Each of these objectives is fleshed out briefly by some bullet points, what me might call "action items."

One way to check out the adequacy of this outline is to ask: "Is this a balanced plan? Is there something important left out?" You may feel free to contact me or the vestry members if you do have criticisms or proposals.

Clearly an incoming rector will have a large influence on how this outline is developed. But we hope that it will give him some "hand-holds" as he gets to know the church and works with the vestry and congregation toward the next stage in our young church's life.

Have a blessed week and a joyous upcoming Thanksgiving.

Come, Ye Thankful People, Come

This being Thanksgiving week, I thought I would send you a few thoughts on this celebration, which in many ways is the least secularized and most sacrificial of our holidays, with people enduring major travel time and traffic jams in order to be together for a meal.

The theme of thanksgiving is central to the Christian gospel, as we remember God's great gift to us in Jesus Christ. St. Paul urges us to "give thanks in all circumstances; for this is the will of God in Christ Jesus for you" (1 Thess 5:18). It is central to our celebration of the Eucharist: "Almighty and ever-living God, we thank you for feeding us, in these holy mysteries, with the spiritual food of the most precious Body and Blood of your Son our Savior Jesus Christ."

I thought I'd call to your attention a section of occasional prayers in the Book of Common Prayer (pages 641–90), which includes thanksgivings for various occasions. I find this one (#117 on page 681) especially appropriate for Thanksgiving Day.

> Accept, O Lord, our thanks and praise for all that you have done for us. We thank you for the splendor of the whole creation, for the beauty of this world, for the wonder of life, and for the mystery of love. We thank you for the blessing of family and friends, and for the loving care which surrounds us on every side. We thank you for setting us at tasks that demand our best efforts, and for leading us to accomplishments that satisfy and delight us. We thank you also for those disappointments and failures that lead us to acknowledge our dependence on you alone. Above all, we thank you for your Son Jesus Christ; for the truth of his Word and the example of his life; for his steadfast obedience, by which he overcame temptation; for his dying, through which he conquered

death; and for his rising to life again, in which we are raised to the life of your kingdom. Grant us the gift of your Spirit, that we may know Christ and make him known; and through him, at all times and in all places, may give thanks to you in all things. Amen.

I'd also remind you that Thanksgiving Day is a national holiday with a significant history. President Abraham Lincoln authorized it in 1863, two years into the bloody Civil War, with two more horrific years to come. The year 1863 had begun with the Emancipation Proclamation, declaring freedom of the slave population in the South; at mid-year came the decisive Battle of Gettysburg, which was the turning point of the war, followed on November 19 by Lincoln's famous Gettysburg Address. On September 29, Lincoln was sent a letter from Sarah Josepha Hale, editor of the prominent *Godey's Lady's Book* magazine, requesting that he establish a single date for a national Thanksgiving holiday. Five days later, he did so in a proclamation setting the fourth Thursday in November to be a recurring holiday. Speaking of the awesome events of the year, it says:

> No human counsel hath devised nor hath any mortal hand worked out these great things. They are the gracious gifts of the Most High God, who, while dealing with us in anger for our sins, hath nevertheless remembered mercy. It has seemed to me fit and proper that they should be solemnly, reverently and gratefully acknowledged as with one heart and one voice by the whole American People… And I recommend to them that…they do also, with humble penitence for our national perverseness and disobedience, commend to His tender care all those who have become widows, orphans, mourners or sufferers in the lamentable civil strife in which we are unavoidably engaged, and fervently implore the interposition of the Almighty Hand to heal the wounds of the nation and to restore it as soon as may be consistent with the Divine purposes to the full enjoyment of peace, harmony, tranquillity and Union.

Lincoln repeated many of these sentiments in his Second Inaugural Address, given days before the end of the war and his assassination.

So, Redeemer friends, as you gather together to ask the Lord's blessing this Thursday, I wish to remind you and our neighbors and fellow countrymen of all the mercies we have received.

Tidings of Comfort and Joy

Last Sunday (December 19) we had our parish Christmas service, a "Service of Lessons and Carols."

In my greetings that day I commented briefly on the tradition behind this service, which, like the Book of Common Prayer, is a distinctive Anglican contribution to Christian worship. Many other churches now use this service as well, including the thousands of Anglican churches around the globe.

While this Anglican tradition of Lessons and Carols goes back to about 1870, it achieved its classic form in the annual service at King's College Chapel in Cambridge, England. This service is broadcast live by the BBC around the world on Christmas Eve at 3 p.m. GMT, and you can hear it at 10 a.m. this year on WQED radio. The service has also been recorded on video for many years. In 1994, when we were in Cambridge on sabbatical leave, my wife Peggy and daughter Abby queued up in the cold to get into the live service.

The idea of a collection of lessons goes all the way back to biblical times. The people of God made a point of making collections of their sacred writings: hence we have the Law, the Prophets, and the psalms in the Old Testament, the gospels and epistles in the New. The early Christians compiled and memorized collections of Old Testament "testimonies" to the coming of Christ.

I mentioned in my greetings last Sunday the famous *Messiah* oratorio by George Frederick Handel. It is nothing more than an extended Lessons and Carols service, beginning with Old Testament prophecies of the coming Messiah and ending with his triumphant enthronement in heaven. (We often think of *Messiah* as a Christmas piece, but the Hallelujah chorus is actually Easter praise to the risen Christ.)

This brings me back to our humble service last week. I say "humble" service because we do not have university dons as readers and trained singers to perform it. But I'd like to think our congregation might be similar to the Christians whom Paul addressed when he said:

> For consider your calling, brothers: not many of you were wise according to worldly standards, not many were powerful, not many were of noble birth. But God chose what is foolish in the world to shame the wise; God chose what is weak in the world to shame the strong; God chose what is low and despised in the world, even things that are not, to bring to nothing things that are, so that no human being might boast in the presence of God. (1 Cor 1:26–29)

Brothers and sisters at Redeemer, take a few minutes and go back and look at our livestream from last Sunday. This is God's Church celebrating the greatest event the world has ever seen: the coming of God himself into our midst as a babe in Bethlehem.

The message of Christmas is indeed "tidings of comfort and joy." Have a blessed Christmas! Hope to see you next Sunday if you are in town. We'll be thinking about three great witnesses to the Messiah.

Changing Calendars

I suspect that many of you like me are using these last days of 2021 tidying up your files and accounts and, finally, changing old calendars to new. So I thought I'd say a bit about the church calendar, which begins on page 687 of the Prayer Book.

Sometimes Anglicanism is called the *via media* or "middle way" between Catholics and Protestants. In this case the description fits. Catholics have tended to accumulate a welter of special "holy days" dedicated to saints in heaven who would pray for souls in purgatory. Many Protestant Reformers reacted to this practice by abolishing holy days altogether.

Anglicans fall in between. To begin with, we do not pray *to* the saints. We do, however, celebrate several "principal feast days." Four of these days are tied to the lunar (Passover) calendar—Easter, Ascension Day, the Day of Pentecost, and Trinity Sunday—and they jump around in our secular calendar from year to year. Three other principal feasts have fixed dates: Christmas (December 25), Epiphany (January 6) and All Saints' Day (November 1).

A second level of feasts, called red-letter days, remember and honor key figures in the New Testament—John the Baptist, the notable apostles and evangelists, and Michael and All Angels—and key moments in Jesus' life and the life of the Church. There are thirty-two of these days spread across the year, and you can find them listed in the left-hand column of the calendar beginning on page 691. While we do not usually celebrate these days corporately, each of these days has a separate collect (page 624ff.) and lessons (page 730ff.), which you can use privately. There is even a third level of "optional commemorations" that remind us of the many heroes of the faith that have gone before.

So let's just look at the calendar for January. January 1 is not "New Year's Day" but "The Circumcision and Holy Name of our Lord Jesus Christ." (I'll be preaching on this topic on Sunday.) This may sound like something of a downer to start the year off, but it reminds us that the Christ-child was like us in every way except sin, being circumcised, named, and then at his coming of age presented at the temple. (See the red-letter day for February 2; no, campers, it's not Groundhog Day!)

No one is commanded to observe these days in the church calendar, but many people find using them enriches their prayer and immerses them in the great story of the Bible, the coming into the world of our Lord and Savior. In any case, I wish you all a very Happy New Year in 2022.

Naming and Numbering God's People

I think it is fair to say that there are two kinds of texts in the Bible that most readers stumble upon—and then move on. There are the genealogies, the lists of "begats" beginning in the book of Genesis and popping up again in the books of Chronicles and Ezra and in Matthew and Luke; and then there are the rosters, the numbering texts, found particularly in—surprise, surprise—the book of Numbers and again in the book of Revelation.

These are tough reading, let's be honest. But ask yourself: what if these names were part of *your* family genealogy, or if you were a general in the army preparing your regiments and divisions for battle? Wouldn't you want to have an accurate account of name, rank, and serial number? Names and numbers alone do not make a family or win a battle, but they have a role to play.

For this reason, I have been working up a set of record books for Redeemer Anglican Church. I received a spreadsheet from Seth Zimmerman when I became interim rector. We went over the names on it, and based on that I have been trying to make contact with many of you. A second thing happened last September 19, when Bishop Minns baptized, confirmed, received, and asked for a renewal of baptismal vows. "An Anglican congregation is born!" I commented afterward. Many of you received signed certificates from the diocese to that effect.

Now I am completing three documents that I hope to pass on to the new rector when he is called. The first is a register of church membership and rites; the second is a register of church services; the third is a member directory with photographs, contact info, and brief bios of Redeemer folk. All of these documents will begin on July 1, 2021, when Redeemer officially became independent, but we are also keeping a Friends of Redeemer list of many who helped launch Redeemer over the past six years.

Clearly the names and numbers in the Bible are hardly the whole story. Many of these names and numbers were not faithful to God and denied their birthright. Many of the numbers are hyperbolic, reminding us that God's elect people are of his calling, not ours. Still, names and numbers are important. Anglican Article 19 defines the "visible church" as "the congregation of faithful men [and women] in which the pure Word of God is preached and the sacraments duly administered." There is of course an invisible Church known to God alone, and nowadays there is a virtual church, kept in Redeemer's Elexio database. But it's good to have names and numbers in pen and ink, just in case some enemy destroys the iCloud with one fell pulse.

Radical Hospitality

I want to begin with a shout-out to the Redeemer community who hosted Ethan and Natasha Carlson last weekend. I could mention individuals by name—and I will mention Matt and Madelyn, who opened their home to the Carlsons—but it was the entire church that came out to meet them in different venues. The highlight of the weekend, as I see it, was the worship service on Sunday. The core membership of the church turned out, along with other friends of Redeemer. It was wonderful to sit down at table after the service, to talk, to laugh, to enjoy what Africans call "swallowship," and above all to share the Lord's Supper together, the fellowship meal where Jesus is host. For this weekend, I hear him saying, "Well done!"

Table fellowship is a fundamental part of Christian community. It begins in the home with the family, but it extends outward to friends, neighbors, and strangers. It begins with the hard work of preparing a meal, setting a table, seating people (with phones switched off!), and promoting pleasant conversation. The spirit of table fellowship is giving thanks. (I suppose that is why the Thanksgiving Day meal is so iconic.)

Years ago, Peggy and I adopted a simple grace before meals. It goes like this:

> Come, Lord Jesus, be our guest. Make what you have given us blest. Thank you for the gift of food in a hungry world.

Here is another grace we have used in our home:

> Give us grateful hearts, our Father, for all your mercies, and make us ever mindful of the needs of others, through Jesus Christ our Lord.

There are several other graces in the Prayer Book (see pages 78 and 671).

These graces assume that the good things we enjoy at supper are not ours by right but by gift and that in receiving them we also have a responsibility to share with others who are not so fortunate. For this reason, many Christians give of their time on major holidays or in bitter weather to serve at soup kitchens and contribute generously in crises of famine and to refugees.

Meals where Jesus is host are inherently evangelistic, especially at the Church's banquet. Jesus said to his Church: "Behold, I stand at the door and knock. If anyone hears my voice and opens the door, I will come in to him and eat with him, and he with me" (Rev 3:20). Some people have the gift of evangelism, and everyone should be prepared to share their testimony with others. But I also think in this age where so many people are lonely and suspicious of big-time preachers, radical hospitality at the local table may be a primary way by which we can introduce people to Jesus.

As Redeemer looks forward to the next step in its "adolescence," let's take seriously the words of the Bible: "Do not neglect to show hospitality to strangers, for thereby some have entertained angels unawares" (Heb 13:2). Let us practice radical hospitality not just on special occasions like last weekend, but daily as we break our daily bread.

FEBRUARY 9, 2022

I Believe in Satan

I believe in Satan. I am saying this provocatively. I am not a Satanist. I do not believe in Satan the way I believe in God or in Jesus or in the Apostles' Creed. But I believe Satan really exists, just as I believe Joe Biden really exists or I believe the Internet really exists, or yes, in the way I believe that God really exists.

But many people today do not believe that Satan exists. Even many Christians think Satan is an optional or outdated appendage to the faith—"a guy in red tights," they say. Some even feel it is morally objectionable to think there is some external being or power that tempts and deceives people and seeks to destroy them.

Christians who say they do not believe there is a Satan have a problem, because Jesus believed there is.

> "I saw Satan fall like lightning from heaven." (Luke 10:18)

> "Simon, Simon, behold, Satan demanded to have you, that he might sift you like wheat, but I have prayed for you that your faith may not fail. And when you have turned again, strengthen your brothers." (Luke 22:31–32)

> "Depart from me, you cursed, into the eternal fire prepared for the devil and his angels." (Matt 25:41)

> "Lead us not into temptation, but deliver us from the evil one." (Matt 6:13)

Jesus not only taught about Satan but he was tempted by the Devil in person after his baptism. (That will be the subject of my sermon next week.) And the rest of the New Testament is full of references to Satan, the "dragon, that ancient serpent who wages war against the people of God" (Rev 12:9; 13:7).

Here is a quick profile of Satan:

He is an angel created by God in the beginning, who along with other angels rebelled against God for no reason other than pride and was cast down to hell, where he will spend eternity. Although created with an angelic body—Lucifer the light-bearer they called him—he and his companions have been degraded into bodiless demons who can possess others, e.g., the snake in the Garden, the Gadarene pigs, and vulnerable people.

Satan is a liar and deceiver (that's what the word *diabolos* or Devil means) who tempted Adam and Eve into sin and continues to use our fallen desires of flesh and spirit to tempt and destroy men and women.

He is called the "prince of this world" (John 12:31) because he also corrupted the God-given authorities. These so-called principalities and powers, while they continue to serve God's purposes in this age, are fallen and fallible and in times of crisis exalt themselves in place of God.

He is the source of false religion, i.e., idolatry, which leads whole nations astray. A modern form of idolatry is ideology, which enslaves contemporary "elites" just as much as ancient superstitions (and contemporary conspiracy theories) delude the ignorant.

Satan's aim in our day is to make people doubt that God exists. Ironically, he does this by making people doubt there is a spirit world at all and into thinking we do not have an immortal soul but are merely complex, disposable computers. Ultimately, Satan tempts people to doubt that God is a loving God and leads them to loneliness, despair, and suicide.

So, yes, friends, I believe that Satan really exists, just as I believe Jesus of Nazareth really existed and lives today. But my belief in Jesus goes far beyond the fact of his existence. My belief is *trust* in Jesus and in Jesus' death on the Cross for my salvation, and that makes all the difference.

Thanks be to God who gives us the victory through our Lord Jesus Christ!

Men and Women of the Word

As I have worked through the texts of Jesus' early years and early ministry, I have been struck by how often he is a man of the Word. Even in his infancy, the gospels make clear, his life was "in fulfillment of the Scriptures." Clearly Jesus studied and, yes, memorized the Scriptures—which of course in his day was the Old Testament—and he understood them as God's "living and active word." Answering Satan's temptations in the wilderness, three times Jesus rebukes him saying, "it is written..." Supremely, the evangelist John calls Jesus "the Word made flesh," the summing up of God's words in the Bible from Alpha to Omega.

The early Christians were remarkable in their devotion to the Old Testament Scriptures and to the emerging apostolic gospels and writings. They did not have printing presses or iPhones to read from, but they managed to know the Bible and to test whether "the faith once for all delivered to the saints" was in accordance with the Bible.

With this in mind, I am proposing preaching through the letter to the Galatians this Lent. Having considered the Lord Jesus during the Epiphany season, I hope to turn to St. Paul and expound the six chapters of Galatians during the six weeks of Lent, under the title "What is the Gospel?: St. Paul to the Galatians." Paul is often referred to as *the* Apostle, and his letters to the Romans and Galatians are the supreme expression of his gospel. Martin Luther once said of Galatians, "it is my epistle, to which I am betrothed. It is my Katie von Bora [his wife]." During my years at Trinity Seminary, I regularly taught a semester-long course on Galatians in Greek. This time I'll stick to English.

I want to urge you Redeemer folk to read and study along with me. We are going to make available to you a booklet free of charge with the text of the letter and room for notes. I would also suggest that groups might want to consider using the study guide *Reading Galatians with John Stott*, available from various booksellers.

Jesus was a man of the Spirit, and we too are to be born again and full of the Spirit. He was also a man of the Word. My hope is that this Lent we may draw close to him and his Gospel and strengthen our discipleship as men and women of the Word.

My Most Memorable Wedding

The subject of the last of my sermons in this series on Jesus is the Wedding at Cana. Following the service, we'll also be showing the Wedding at Cana scene from the television series *The Chosen*, which I think brings the text to life.

One thing that jumps out from the text of John chapter 2, and the television scene, is the exuberant and, yes, wine-soused community gathering at a Jewish wedding. Many Jewish wedding celebrations went on for a week. We found the same spirit at work in African weddings during our years in Uganda.

Our house in Uganda was a stone's throw from the Anglican cathedral. On Saturdays, weddings would run back-to-back all afternoon, each ending with the music of "Here Comes the Bride"! The attendees would then proceed to a reception that lasted the rest of the day, with food and drink (no alcohol for Anglicans), singing, and many speeches.

One problem with marriage in Uganda has to do with expense. It begins with an elaborate engagement ceremony, where the two families are "introduced" to one another. The wedding follows later, much later, or maybe not at all. Often we would be approached by couples with a budget that far exceeded their annual income. This double financial whammy often causes such a problem that an engaged couple begins to live together as they fundraise. This arrangement is called a "customary marriage."

So this brings me to my most memorable wedding. In 2005, our university administration had sent a notice to our staff that as a Christian institution, we expected staff to be properly married in church. For those members who were in customary relationships, we offered to prepare them for marriage and to provide them with a joint wedding service and reception in the vice chancellor's compound (that is, in our garden). As it turned out, eighteen couples signed up. Most of them came from the lower-paid workers on campus, like security guards and dining hall workers.

On the appointed day, the couples processed into the worship hall, the brides all gloved and dressed in white, the grooms looking "smart" in black tuxes. In several cases, their children (!) served as flower girls and ring-bearers. One bride was so pregnant she couldn't stand for the vows. And three couples were late coming (shades of Jesus' parables). As each tardy couple arrived, we halted the service so they could march in. The last couple was so late, we had to repeat the vows for them separately. Afterward, everyone came to our garden in a spirit of solemnity and gaiety.

Interestingly, the dean of the Mukono cathedral had attended the event. A couple years later, when he became a bishop, he began offering mass weddings in his diocese.

Somewhat in jest, I used to say to American visitors: Don't send us containers full of used T-shirts. Send us your second-hand wedding dresses. They will be freshened up and become a treasure to some couple here.

I am attaching a photo of the *bagole* (newlyweds) as we welcomed them to the reception in our garden.

Postscript: One serious correction. This was not my most memorable wedding. That one occurred on August 12, 1967!

Reading Galatians for All Its Worth

During Lent, we at Redeemer will be reading one book of the Bible: Paul's letter to the Galatians.

One of the great recoveries of the Protestant Reformation was the belief that all Christians, from priests to ordinary "ploughboys," can and should read the Bible. The English Reformation included new translations of the Bible plus a Prayer Book that is full of biblical readings.

But it's not always easy knowing how to get into a Bible passage. One way to start is to ask three questions: *What does it say? What does it mean? And what does it mean for me?* So let me take our text from Galatians chapter 1 and apply these questions.

What does it say?

The chapter in your Lenten booklet is one continuous text. Read it over several times and see if you can mark out several paragraphs by theme. To get you started, I would suggest something like this:

- verses 1–5: Introduction
- verses 6–10: Appeal to the Galatians
- verses 11–23: Story of Paul's call

Surprise, surprise: preachers often give three-point sermons, but you can divide it up differently.

Then you can also look up matters of fact online or in a study Bible, e.g., where is Galatia?, and a few key words, e.g., *apostle* and *gospel.*

What does it mean?

Paul was a skilled writer and intended something when he wrote the letter, both for its original recipients and more widely for the universal Church (through God's inspiration). How does he do this? See if you can paraphrase his argument in several sentences. For instance:

> Paul establishes his authority as an apostle to address the Galatians. He rebukes them for abandoning the Gospel. He claims that there is only one truth of the Gospel and warns that anyone who does not believe it should be excluded from the church. He then begins to tell how God revealed the Gospel to him.

What does it mean for me?

This question is a matter of *implication* and *application*. Here you turn to your own experience, but you should keep checking back to see if what you are coming up with is connected to the text.

For instance, you could ask yourself:

- Am I really Gospel-centered in my daily life? If not, how important is this? What can I do to focus more on the Gospel?
- Have I ever been in a church where the Gospel was not preached? Why do I think this? How does Redeemer measure up in this regard?

I'm sure many of you have taken classes in Scripture before or been in Bible study groups. But these are just tips for us as a congregation seeking to know Paul better, and in doing so to know the Gospel of Jesus Christ better.

There is no single "right answer" to understanding a biblical text. So enjoy yourself even as you seek to read Galatians for all its worth.

Have a blessed Lenten season.

The Great Litany: Full-Strength Christian Prayer

This week you get a twofer of podcasts, as I want to explain the unusual format of the service for next Sunday, March 6. It's called "Litany and Sermon."

Many Anglicans have come to expect Holy Communion as the principal service every week (see the Prayer Book, page 104 for this instruction). This was not always the case. For much of Anglican history Morning Prayer and sermon was normal. Now I am fine with the current practice, but I don't think it needs to become "the law of the Medes and the Persians."

There is another resource in the Prayer Book which should claim our attention, especially in a penitential season like Lent. It is called "The Great Litany and Decalogue" (pages 91–101). While it is possible to use both this and Holy Communion at the same time, it is not necessary.

Let me say a word first about the Decalogue ("Ten Words or Commandments"). At our normal Communion service, the pastor begins with a "summary of the law," Jesus' two Great Commandments to love God and neighbor, followed by the so-called *Kyrie eleison*, "Lord, have mercy upon us." The Prayer Book also offers an expanded version, which states each of the Ten Commandments, followed by our response, "Lord have mercy upon us, and incline our hearts to keep this law." It is helpful for us at times to drill down into the specifics of God's holy will and ask God's help to keep all his ways. (Read Psalm 119 as an extended meditation on this.)

Similarly the Great Litany (a "litany" is a sequence of prayers with a common format) is all-encompassing in its scope. It begins with a series of prayers for forgiveness: "Spare us, good Lord," and "Good Lord, deliver us." It then proceeds to a series of prayers for "all sorts and conditions of men," with the petition "we beseech you to hear us, good Lord." The word "beseech" is somewhat archaic, but I don't think there is a good synonym in English; it means "to humbly request," or, simply, "to beg." Next, look through the different *kinds* (the original Prayer Book says "sorts and conditions") of people in this list. It is really quite a remarkable catalogue, I think, and different from praying for scattered individuals, as we often do. The Great Litany ends by appealing to Christ, the Lamb of God, who is our ground of confidence that "what we have asked faithfully according to your will, we may obtain effectually."

The Great Litany is full-strength Christian prayer. On occasion, I have chanted the Great Litany while moving up and down the aisles of the church, with the congregation joining in the refrain. It is a great example of the church "lifting up holy hands to God, without anger or quarreling." Please come on Sunday with this same spirit as we begin to observe a "holy Lent."

St. Paul's Allegory of Sarah and Hagar (Galatians 4:21–31)

Given the time crunch with the annual meeting next Sunday, I cannot cover the last part of Galatians chapter 4, so I thought I'd make a few comments here about verses 21-31, which may seem strange to the average reader.

One of the wonderful gifts of C.S. Lewis was his ability to adopt a variety of kinds of writing: apologetic (*Mere Christianity*), fiction (*Screwtape Letters*), a science fiction trilogy, children's stories (Narnia), letters, literary criticism, and allegory (*The Discarded Image*). The Bible also brings together many kinds or genres of writing, e.g., narrative, law, psalms, prophecies, proverbs, gospels, letters, and an apocalyptic allegory (the book of Revelation).

In Galatians chapter 4:21–31, Paul introduces an allegory based on the story of Sarah and Hagar in Genesis 16 and 21. In the Genesis story itself, the characters of Abraham and Sarah are problematic. In chapter 16, Sarah is barren and urges Abraham to beget a son with his serving-girl, Hagar. Hagar bears a son, Ishmael, much to Sarah's chagrin. Later in chapter 21, when the elderly Sarah has borne a son, Isaac, according to God's promise, the rivalry reemerges. Sarah demands of Abraham: "Cast out this slave woman with her son, for the son of this slave woman shall not be heir with my son Isaac" (verse 10). Reluctantly, Abraham sends Hagar and Ishmael away to fend for themselves in the wilderness.

Paul's allegory zeroes in on Abraham's two sons, Ishmael and Isaac, as types of those who live according to the Law and those who live by faith in God's promise. The first son is described by the terms "slave" and "the flesh," the second son by the terms "free" and "the Spirit." Paul then links the two sons with two locations—the first with the physical locations of Mt. Sinai in Arabia and "the present Jerusalem"; and the second with the supernatural "Jerusalem that is above." The allegory serves to illustrate Paul's overall point that seeking to be justified by the works of the Law and receiving the Gospel by faith are incompatible, the one aiming to control the sinful flesh, the other liberating the spirit for eternal life.

The allegory reminds me of John's gospel where Jesus shocks Nicodemus, saying, "Truly, truly, I say to you, unless one is born of water and the Spirit, he cannot enter the kingdom of God. That which is born of the flesh is flesh, and that which is born of the Spirit is spirit" (John 3:5). And later he says to the Samaritan woman: "Woman, believe me, the hour is coming when neither on this mountain nor in Jerusalem will you worship the Father…The hour is coming, and is now here, when the true worshipers will worship the Father in spirit and truth, for the Father is seeking such people to worship him" (John 4:21).

Paul concludes the allegory with Sarah's harsh demand, "Cast out the slave woman." It is possible that Paul was calling on the Galatians to expel the false teachers, the Judaizers. But I think that may be taking him too literally. The "slave woman" in the allegory is a *deceptive mindset* that says you can have both Law and faith equally yoked as the basis of your life. No, Paul is saying, one has got to go. Choose the free woman and her son!

On Sunday I'll have more to say as to why Paul takes this stern attitude when I talk about "Not Slaves but Sons"—our identity in Christ by faith alone.

Christ's Presence in the Lord's Supper

Next Sunday I am preaching on "Risen Indeed! The Testimony of the Lord's Supper." At that time I want to focus on the *shape* of the Communion service—why we do what we do?—rather than on the meaning of Holy Communion as a sacrament. So I am giving a brief summary of this latter matter here.

The incarnate Jesus was present at the Last Supper; the risen Jesus was present at the two meals on Easter night (Luke 24:30, 42). The Church ever since has recognized the connection between these meals and the "breaking of bread" as a sacrament of the Gospel (Article 25).

The question of how Christ is present in the Lord's Supper (also known as Holy Communion or Eucharist) is a delicate matter among Christians. Let me address this issue by looking at the two-sentence "words of administration" which the priest may use with the bread and the wine (see the Prayer Book, page 120):

> The Body of our Lord Jesus Christ, which was given for you, preserve your body and soul to everlasting life. Take and eat this in remembrance that Christ died for you, and feed on him in your heart by faith, with thanksgiving.
>
> The Blood of our Lord Jesus Christ, which was shed for you, preserve your body and soul to everlasting life. Drink this in remembrance that Christ's Blood was shed for you, and be thankful.

The first sentence of each of these words of administration emphasizes God's grace in the Person and saving work of Jesus Christ for us. The second sentence emphasizes our response in receiving this sacramental grace with heartfelt thanksgiving. The word *remembrance* as it is used here goes beyond mere reminiscence to *participation* in Christ, as St. Paul puts it: "The cup of blessing that we bless, is it not a participation in the blood of Christ? The bread that we break, is it not a participation in the body of Christ?" (1 Cor 10:16)

Anglicans historically have rejected memorialism, i.e. "mere reminiscence," by calling the Sacrament an "effectual sign of grace," through which God works invisibly within us. They have also rejected transubstantiation—the view that the bread and wine, while appearing the same, undergo a "substantial" change of nature to become Christ's literal Body and Blood. This view, we say, is unbiblical (cf. John 6:63) and may lead to venerating the gift rather than the Giver.

The classic Anglican view is that "the Body of Christ is given, taken, and eaten in the Supper only after a heavenly and spiritual manner." This view, which is shared by Reformed Protestants, can be called *spiritual presence*. Some Anglicans, along with Lutherans, speak of the *real presence* of Christ in the Communion, without resorting to physicalist rationalizations like transubstantiation.

While I do not intend to write off the differences between these two views, I do not think they are utterly incompatible and church-dividing. That's why I would prefer to say that Christ is *truly present* when we lift up our hearts with thanksgiving to him and partake of the bread and wine of the Sacrament, as was the case on the first Easter when "their eyes were opened and they recognized him."

***

As a final note, let me say farewell to those who have been following these podcasts over the past year (yes, fifty-two of them!). I have considered them a kind of "table talk" on various topics and hope they may have been of benefit to Redeemer during this important transition period.

The grace of Christ be with you all!

References

Page 3—Cf. Kevin J. Vanhoozer and Owen Strachan, *The Pastor as a Public Theologian: Reclaiming a Lost Vision* (Grand Rapids: Baker, 2015).

Page 22—Maurice Lamm, "Acceptance of the Yoke of the Commandments," My Jewish Learning, https://www.myjewishlearning.com/article/acceptance-of-the-yoke-of-the-commandments/

Page 32—Dane Ortlund, *Gentle and Lowly: The Heart of Christ for Sinners and Sufferers* (Wheaton, IL: Crossway, 2020), page 18.

Page 41—Jay Pathak and Dave Runyon, *The Art of Neighboring: Building Genuine Relationships Outside Your Door* (Grand Rapids: Baker, 2012).

Page 64—Thomas A. Smail, *The Forgotten Father* (Eugene, OR: Wipf & Stock, 1980).

Page 68—Nabeel Qureshi, *No God but One: A Former Muslim Investigates the Evidence for Islam and Christianity* (Grand Rapids: Zondervan, 2016), page 62.

Page 71—Stephen F. Noll, *Angels of Light, Powers of Darkness: Thinking Biblically About Angels, Satan and Principalities* (Eugene, OR: Wipf & Stock, 1998).

Page 87—Iris DeMent, "Let the Mystery Be" from *Infamous Angel* (1992).

Page 92—C.S. Lewis, *The Last Battle* (The Chronicles of Narnia, Book 7; New York: HarperCollins, 1956).

Page 106—Dietrich Bonhoeffer, "Wedding Sermon from a Prison Cell" in *Letters and Papers from Prison* (New York: Scribner, 1972).

Page 112—John Updike, "Seven Stanzas at Easter" (1960).

Page 113—Keith Getty and Stuart Townend, "In Christ Alone" (2001).

Page 133ff.—Barbara Robinson, *The Best Christmas Pageant Ever* (New York: Harper & Row, 1972).

Page 140–41—Adam Grant, *Think Again: The Power of Knowing What You Don't Know* (New York: Penguin Books, 2023).

Page 145–46—Melissa McKinney, "The DNA of God" (2021). Used with permission.

Page 173—Cf. Stephen Noll, *Marriage According to the Book of Common Prayer* (Newport Beach, CA: Anglican House, 2021), Part Three: Stages of Marriage.

Pages 174, 215—George Herbert, "The Agony" and "The Flower." In *George Herbert: The Country Parson, the Temple*, ed. by John N. Wall, Jr. (Classics of Western Spirituality; New York: Paulist Press, 1981).

Page 180ff.—Martin Luther, *Lectures on Galatians* [1535] from *Luther's Works*, vols. 25–26 (St. Louis: Concordia, 1963–64), 35, 38.

Page 183—Heinz Cassirer, *Grace and Law: St. Paul, Kant, and the Hebrew Prophets* (Grand Rapids: Eerdmans, 1988).

Page 213—Josh McDowell, *Evidence That Demands a Verdict: Historical Evidences for the Christian Faith* (1975).

Page 231–32—Cf. John W. Gardner, *On Leadership* (rev. ed. New York: Free Press, 1993).

Page 234–35—Frederick Douglass, "What to the Slave is the Fourth of July?" (1852) in *Frederick Douglass: Speeches and Writings* ed. by David W. Blight (New York: Library of America, 2022).

Lections Index

CATECHETICAL CYCLE

INCARNATIONAL CYCLE

John 21:20–25
Acts 8:54–60
1 Corinthians 10:1–14
Ephesians 3:1–13
Philippians 2:5–11
Hebrews 2:14–18

EVANGELICAL CYCLE

Galatians 1
Galatians 2
Galatians 3
Galatians 4
Galatians 5
Galatians 6

DOXOLOGY: RISEN INDEED!

Luke 24:1–12
Luke 24:13–49
John 20:19–31
Acts 5:12–33
Acts 2:42–47
Ephesians 4:1–16
Colossians 3:1–4

About the Author

THE REV. DR. STEPHEN NOLL

Sephen Noll was born in 1946 and raised in Arlington, Virginia, where he met his wife-to-be in grade school. After his conversion and baptism in the Episcopal Church in 1966, he was ordained in the Episcopal Church as deacon (1971) and priest (1972). He served five years in parish ministry at Truro Church in Fairfax, Virginia, before going into academic teaching. He has been a priest in the Anglican Diocese of Pittsburgh since 1979.

Dr. Noll received a BA degree from Cornell University (Phi Beta Kappa), an MDiv from Church Divinity School of the Pacific, and a PhD from the University of Manchester (UK). He served as Professor of Biblical Studies and Academic Dean at Trinity School for Ministry, now Trinity Anglican Seminary, from 1979 to 2000 and is now professor emeritus there. He has been awarded the Doctor of Divinity degree from Trinity and from Nashotah House Theological Seminary.

Dr. Noll was appointed the first vice chancellor (president) of Uganda Christian University in October 1999. He and his wife, Peggy, served as missionaries with Global Teams (formerly Episcopal World Mission), arriving in Uganda in September 2000. He retired after two terms in 2010. Since its founding in 1997, Uganda Christian University has grown from 120 theological students to 12,000, taking courses in many fields including business, engineering, law, and nursing; recently it graduated its first class of doctors and dentists.

Dr. Noll is the founder and a current board member of Uganda Christian University Partners, a US-based support society for the university. Over the last twenty years, UCU Partners has sponsored hundreds of students with scholarships, facilitated the "Uganda Studies Program," bringing more than five hundred American college students for a semester abroad, and has raised $6 million for capital projects at the university.

Dr. Noll has been committed to the importance of parish ministry, serving on several occasions as interim rector. He has been active in Anglican church affairs as a founding board member of CMJ USA and the American Anglican Council. He has served as chairman of the ACNA Task Force on Marriage, the Family and the Single Life and is a current member of the provincial Executive Committee.

Dr. Noll has been active in global Anglicanism, serving as a member of the statement group at the first three GAFCON assemblies, and he addressed the GAFCON IV assembly in Kigali, Rwanda, in 2023. From 2015–2020, he was convener of the GAFCON Task Force on Women in the Episcopate.

Dr. Noll's most recent "interim" assignment was as interim CEO of Anglican House Publishers in 2023–2024.

Stephen Noll has been married to his wife Peggy for fifty-seven years. They have five grown children and seven grandchildren. The Nolls have lived in the same house in Sewickley, Pennsylvania, for forty-five years.

Printed in Great Britain
by Amazon

49651865R00165